one
for
sorrow,
two
for joy

To Niav and Ronan, Saava and Brian, and their seven lively children, Luke, Sive, Aobha, Felim, Caoimhe, Cara and Sadhbh.

But especially to Trudi, for her support and patience throughout the whole process.

John Killeen

Growing up in
1950s Ireland

one
for
sorrow,
two
for joy

MOON RIVER BOOKS

First published in 2020 by
Moon River Books
Portlaoise
County Laois
Ireland

Paperback	ISBN: 978 1 78846 151 1
Amazon paperback edition	ISBN: 978 1 78846 154 2
eBook – mobi format	ISBN: 978 1 78846 152 8
eBook – ePub format	ISBN: 978 1 78846 153 5

Produced by Kazoo Independent Publishing Services
222 Beech Park, Lucan, Co. Dublin
www.kazoopublishing.com

Kazoo Independent Publishing Services is not the publisher of this work. All rights and responsibilities pertaining to this work remain with Moon River Books.

Kazoo offers independent authors a full range of publishing services. For further details visit www.kazoopublishing.com

Cover design by Andrew Brown
Printed in the EU

Contents

First Lessons

~

1949

Our town, Athlone, was not walled in for nothing. Strategically straddling the River Shannon, every invader, from the Normans to King Billy, had had a go at it. The result was two fortified towns, one on the west, or Connaught, side, the other on the east, or Leinster, side.

In June 1691 King Billy's Dutch army, under Ginkel, launched a ferocious attack across the bridge that joined the two sides of the town. King James's Jacobite army held out, thanks largely to the heroism of Dragoon Sergeant Custume, who, under fire, dismantled the bridge so recently repaired by the Dutch.

But it was all in vain when the Dutch forded the river south of the bridge and chased the Jacobites twenty miles west, to the Hill of Aughrim, where Jacobite general the Marquis de St Ruth had his head blown off as he charged the grim Dutch gunners.

Thus began a lingering defeat that echoed through

the centuries, until Catholic bells once more rang out across the Shannon.

The descendants of King Billy's lot, in the meantime, with the new Protestant work ethic coursing through their veins, established the town's prosperity on the Leinster side.

I spent the first ten years of my life on the Connaught side. It seems to me now that life there began with my first haircut in Jimmy the Barber's, on Connaught Street, in 1949.

'Usually, now,' said Jimmy the Barber, 'you have to go to hospital to have an operation like this.' He looked dead serious. He had me trussed up like a chicken, in a white sheet, on the high barber's chair.

'Ah, will you leave him alone, Jimmy!' said Peggy Hannon. 'He's only four years old.'

I liked Peggy. She was a big, soft country girl who worked for us.

'I'm going to be five next week,' I told Jimmy.

'Five!' echoed Jimmy. 'Sure I thought this man must be six or seven,' he told Peggy. 'He's such a big lad!'

The sheet was wrapped tightly around my neck. In the mirror I saw a boy with a mop of black, unruly curls. I wondered what it would feel like and what my head would look like without them.

'Oh, it's a shame!' wailed Peggy. She sat on the bench in front so she could see me and I could see her. She had tears in her eyes.

'Will we try one?' said Jimmy to the mirror, taking hold of one of my curls.

I saw my image in the mirror nodding uncertainly in assent.

'Snip!' exclaimed Jimmy as he made the cut. The long curl floated to the lino below like a whisper.

'Snip!' he said again and a second one fell to the floor.

'Oh, I can't bear to look!' Peggy hid her face in her hankie.

There was an old farmer on the side bench, filling his pipe. 'Sure, 'tis only like shearing a sheep!' he said helpfully.

'Or like plucking a chicken,' murmured Mickey from the opposite bench. He was my age and he was Jimmy's son. He was engrossed in the *Beano* that he was going to swap with me after my operation.

'Listen, Mickey, will you go like a good man and get a brush to sweep up the curls,' said his father.

'Oh, no!' protested Peggy. 'I want to take them home with me.'

The bell above the door pinged. Mrs Brady from across the street breezed in, with a boy of about my age. 'Hello, Peggy. Jimmy, how are you?' she said.

'Howya, ma'am? Is this the latest Brady champion?' said the old farmer.

'This is Tommy, and he'll be starting school on Monday with these two lads.' She nodded at Mickey and myself. Mrs Brady was a large, kindly woman.

The latest Brady champion was big and well fed. He had a mop of reddish brown curls and a few unevenly distributed freckles. He stared at me and I stared at him. Mickey had a quick little stare before immersing himself again in his comic.

The chat went back and forth. Jimmy undid the sheet and dusted off my neck with a little brush. The farmer stood up, ready to sit in the chair. I realised the operation was over.

'Oh, isn't he a different boy without his curls!' said Mrs Brady.

'He's a great little man now to have his operation without making a sound,' said the farmer.

'Thanks, Jimmy,' said Peggy. 'Goodbye, Tommy. Goodbye, Mickey.'

'We'll see you on Monday, Peggy,' said Mrs Brady.

'Right so!'

We left to a chorus of goodbyes.

Jimmy the Barber's was only down the street from us. Peggy held my hand tightly the whole way to our door. In the other hand she clutched the brown-paper bag with my curls in it. She kept glancing at my head and sniffing. It definitely felt cooler up there.

The following Monday morning, we stood in the shade outside our house.

'What are we waiting for, Peggy?'

'We're waiting for Tommy Brady and Mickey Maher. We're all walking down to school together.'

Across the street, a cat slept peacefully on the sunlit windowsill of Dr Nolan's house. Way above the quiet, empty street, crows fidgeted noisily on the crumbling chimney of Brady's bar. Six or seven doors up, someone was opening the doors of Heffernan's hardware store. Galvanised buckets clanged as they were tied to the horizontal bar that protected the shop window.

Suddenly, a gaggle of voices echoed down the narrow gorge of the street. Like a rushing mountain torrent, a group of country girls on bikes bore down on us and then whooshed past. They were raucous and carefree as starlings, calling to each other at the top of their voices. Then they were gone, echoing all the way down O'Connell Street, fading gradually as they zoomed down Chapel Street hill.

'Who are all the girls, Peggy?'

'They're the big girls, going down to the convent secondary school.'

'Where's my new school?'

'It's where we went on Friday to meet your teacher, the nun, you remember?'

Peggy was waving. Mrs Maher, with Mickey in tow, waved back. Big girls in uniform were already walking down the street behind them. Mrs Brady appeared in her doorway, with Tommy pulling away from her. She crossed the street and we all blended with the swelling river of chattering children that flowed down Chapel Street hill towards St Peter's, as the three schools run by the Sisters of Mercy were called.

Down at the convent, Sister Margaret Mary didn't say a thing about my new haircut. She was small and round like a rosy-cheeked robin and she spoke in Irish half the time. She told me I could be first up on the rocking horse.

'An maith leat an capall luascáin?' Do you like the rocking horse?

I nodded dumbly.

'*Well, suas leat, a Sheáinin!*' Well, up you get, Seánie!

So I mounted, aided by Peggy. The horse had buck teeth and a permanent grin. Tommy watched me with a sly look, as I rocked self-consciously back and forth.

Sister Margaret Mary was already turning her attention on Mickey. '*Anois, tusa, a Mhicheálin!*' Now, you, Mickey! she said to him, with so much gesticulation that anyone without even a word of Irish would have understood.

'*Go raibh maith agat, a Shiúir*' Thank you, Sister, said Mickey, 'but I don't want to.'

'You don't want to!' Clearly she had never encountered this response before. '*Cen fá?*' Why? she shrieked.

'Because,' said Mickey coyly, 'I want to ride a real horse.'

'When you grow up, you mean?'

Mickey shook his head very slowly but did not reply. Everyone on our street knew that his father, Jimmy the Barber, had been a very promising jockey in his youth. Mickey was proud of his father's reputation. All he ever wanted to be was a jockey.

We charged out the door at breaktime, snorting and neighing like horses. We galloped around under the shadow of the high curtain stone wall, down to where the huge wrought-iron gates stopped us going into the nuns' walk and gardens. There we wheeled around, hooves thundering across the gravel up by the tall, green hedge. We snorted and whinnied, came to a halt and surveyed the vast arena we had traversed.

One for Sorrow, Two for Joy

'We can be a Roman chariot!' exclaimed Tommy. 'You and you can be the horses and I'll be the driver.'

'I'm not a horse,' snorted Mickey. 'I'll drive.'

'No, I'm the driver!' shouted Tommy and he pushed Mickey in the chest.

Faster than we could follow, Mickey shot a real punch into Tommy's stomach. Then Tommy was sitting on the gravel, a surprised look on his face. The glasses with the black patch that he was supposed to wear were lying on the ground.

'Now look what you done!' he shouted. But he made no attempt to fight back.

Sister Margaret Mary came out ringing a big brass hand-bell and we all traipsed back into class.

Mickey, who was no scholar, sat beside me and copied what I did. Tommy was in the seat across the aisle, close enough to watch everything I did.

Little, round Sister Margaret Mary had quick, quick movements that made the long ropes of beads rattle as she walked up and down the aisles, watching us working. Her starched wimple and her veil rubbed drily together with the bird-like movements of her head. I was labouring away, painstakingly copying the letters of the alphabet chalked up on the blackboard, in our first endeavours with pen, ink and headline copybooks. The clacking beads, familiar dry rustling and the clean nun smell behind me warned me that my labours were under scrutiny. A gentle hand on my back gave pause to my efforts. Suddenly my headline copybook was whisked from under my nose and held aloft for all the class to see.

'Well, children,' Sister Margaret Mary said to all the surprised and interested faces, 'hasn't Seán done the most beautiful *a*?'

She pronounced it *ah*.

She stood on her toes and held it even further aloft, turning the copybook slowly to the left and right so that all could have a chance to see. I felt my chest expanding to its full capacity, feeling lightheaded with the sudden unexpected fame and exposure to universal approval. Then I caught Tommy's sly, knowing grin and was brought down to earth. The copybook landed on my desk again and she moved on. I glanced over disparagingly at the untidy mess Tommy had made of his letter *a*. So I bent to improve on my perfect letter *a*.

Minutes later, a very un-nun-like shriek behind me startled me and everyone else.

'Oh, what have you done to your beautiful *a*!' Sister Margaret Mary cried. Her hand was up to her mouth, aghast at the monstrous thing on the page before her. I had transformed my beautiful *a*, in my effort to improve on perfect. My beauty had become a beast. The copybook was held aloft again, but now to looks of horror from some and indifference from most. Tommy's deepening grin was the most unbearable thing of all.

A few weeks later, I woke to the sound of Johnny Madden's pony and trap rumbling over the cobbles below my room, in the archway that led into our yard. As usual he was singing 'O What a Beautiful Morning', cheerful and offkey. I jumped out of bed, just in time to see the kitchen window thrown wide open and one of the girls, Bridie, stick her head out, a big enamel jug already in her hand. I was down the stairs and out the door in a flash. Johnny had just pulled up at the window.

'Here's the milk and honey man!' called Bridie over her shoulder, teasing him, and another head appeared beside hers. It was Peggy.

'Just arrived from the land of milk and honey,' said Johnny, poker-faced, as he lifted the lid off one of the big churns.

'Honeyed words as usual,' quipped Peggy, teasing him. I could see she liked Johnny.

'Extend your milk-white arm, my lovely milkmaid,' he said to Bridie.

'And you'll fill my vessel to overflowing, will you?' she shot back, holding out the jug.

'I will, I will,' he said and he started to ladle in the milk until the jug was full.

'Johnny,' I said, 'can I walk the pony around the yard?'

The banter halted and all the laughing faces turned towards me. Suddenly I felt shy and exposed.

'Well, of course you can, darling, can't he, Johnny?' said Peggy and she gave me a huge smile.

I could see that Johnny couldn't refuse her.

'You can, of course,' said Johnny. 'Once or twice around the yard and there's no need to pull her. Just walk and she'll follow.'

I gripped the pony's reins near her mouth and gave a little tug. She paid as little attention as if I had been a fly. She remained as immobile as a rock. Then Johnny made a sound with his lips and immediately she started walking with me.

'So that's how you get the girls running after you, is it?' teased Bridie.

'Oh, there's more to it than that!'

The two girls laughed.

The sun sloped shadows into the enclosed yard and birdsong echoed against the walls. I stopped to watch a bee alight on a wallflower and quickly received a nudge from the pony's nose, as if to say, 'Move on!'

Johnny and the girls were watching this, their faces full of laughter.

'Oh, soon she'll be telling you what to do!' Johnny called out to me. 'Like all women!' he added, throwing a significant look on the girls.

They laughed again, Bridie throwing her head back as she did so.

I liked the pony's smell. The harness had an acrid tang like my grandfather's pipe. I had hardly completed one round of the yard before Mickey came running in through the archway, his mother walking in behind him. She was dark, petite and neat.

'Johnny, Johnny, let me sit up on her! Go on, please!' he shouted.

'Oh, go on, Johnny, let him,' said Bridie. 'Sure, they'll be going to school in a minute.'

'Go twice around the yard, now,' Johnny said, bending down to grab Mickey under the armpits. He swung him high then settled him neatly on the pony's back behind the collar, which Mickey gripped immediately without being told. 'Then I must be off.'

Mickey called, 'Hup, hup, hup!' bouncing as if to speed up the pony, but the pony continued at its own pace as if there was nothing on its back.

As I walked her calmly around, I was surprised to see that Johnny and the two girls were now gazing seriously at Mickey's mother. She was far from smiley, as she usually was, and the women were always smiley with Johnny. As I passed, I heard Mrs Maher saying what a good summer it had been for the farmers, and the others were nodding silently in agreement. But it was as if they were really talking about something else. I couldn't understand it at all.

'Was this ever a riding pony, Johnny?' called Mickey.

'That pony,' said Johnny, 'carried old Mrs Webb to the hunt for God knows how many years.'

'Is there a saddle, Johnny, is there?' Mickey was bouncing on the pony with excitement.

'There's a saddle, all right. It's above in the hayloft in our yard.'

'Johnny, can we ride the pony in your yard? Can we, can we?'

'Well,' said Johnny slowly, gazing at Mrs Maher. 'You'd have to ask your father about that, wouldn't he, ma'am?'

'He would indeed,' she replied drily. 'Come on now, Mickey, or the pair of you will be late for school.'

She lifted Mickey down and walked slowly towards our gate.

Johnny and the two girls silently watched.

'Right, mister,' Peggy whispered to me with a smile, 'let's get your schoolbag and follow them down.'

About a week before this, Mrs Maher had said, smiling, as we were all walking down to the school, 'I hear you got engaged, Peggy.'

'What's engaged?' I asked.

'It means that Peggy is going to get married.'

'Will you still be taking me to school, Peggy?' I asked anxiously.

The two women laughed.

'She will for the moment anyway,' said Mrs Maher gaily.

The two women exchanged a look. They chatted on but I was thinking deeply.

'Peggy, what does *getting married* mean?'

The two women laughed again.

'She's going to marry Johnny Madden, aren't you, Peggy?'

'Mickey! Mind your manners now.'

'Oh, it's all right, ma'am. Sure, they have to know.'

The women chatted on. Peggy was carrying a blue bag like a pillowcase and she held it by the strings.

'What's the blue bag for, Peggy?' I asked.

'That's for the laundry!' piped up Mickey.

'It is indeed,' said Peggy, suddenly looking serious. 'Your mother asked me to leave it in.'

At the school, Mickey's mother took him straight into Sister Margaret Mary's class. Right beside the school, the entrance to the laundry was through a large archway with MAGDALENE LAUNDRY painted in blue and white across it. We could see an expanse of gravelled yard beyond. Peggy hesitated.

'Peggy, what are we waiting for?'

'God, I hate going into that place,' she said.

'C'mon, Peggy, we'll be late!'

She gripped my hand and we went in together.

To the right was a long, grey, two-storey building, with a low, open door. We went through.

'Mind the step,' said Peggy, gripping my hand more tightly. I almost missed it in the gloom inside.

Behind a wooden counter, a grim nun with steel-rimmed glasses was bent in concentration over a ledger, her pen poised. She glanced up briefly but otherwise completely ignored us. Peggy hesitated. I looked at her but she put a warning finger to her lips. In the silence, the clock high on the wall behind the nun counted out the time with its pensive pendulum. The nun's hand shot forward and, with the precision of a kingfisher, dipped the nib of her pen into the inkwell. We watched and listened in fascination as the nib scratched across the ledger.

'Yes?' she rasped. The steel-rimmed glasses glinted under the light bulb.

'Laundry for Mrs Killeen up Connaught Street, Sister,' said Peggy demurely.

'Put it over there.' With the slightest movement of her head she indicated a huge, open wickerwork hamper.

Peggy silently put the bag in the hamper and turned to go.

'Mrs Killeen, you say?'

'Yes, Sister.'

She nodded severely, wrote something in the ledger and without looking up barked, 'Thank you.'

It was a dismissal. We headed for the door.

'Lily Dunne!' shrieked a voice behind us.

A young woman, pushing a trolley across the yard, stopped dead in her tracks. She stared fearfully at the nun behind us. She looked no older than some of the big girls who went to our school. She had lank, unkempt hair and a downcast, beaten demeanour. I thought she looked like some kind of slave.

Peggy stared at her, aghast.

'Thank you!' repeated the nun icily.

Peggy walked swiftly, with her head down, almost dragging me.

'Come here,' I heard the nun say in a low, menacing tone.

I looked back. The girl, or young woman, had dropped her head and was walking meekly towards the nun like a lamb to the slaughter.

'Peggy, why—'

'No more questions, now, sweetheart. We're already late.'

In the weeks that followed, it seemed to me that everything went on just as before and yet everything was different. The first thing I noticed was that when Johnny came into the yard to deliver the milk, there was no banter, only serious silence. I came out to watch, as usual, but something stopped me from asking to walk the pony.

In the kitchen, too, the girls were quiet and my mother seemed to be keeping an eye on them. Peggy was often tearful, as was Bridie. I was used to chatting to Peggy, so one morning I said, 'Peggy, when are you going to marry Johnny?'

To my astonishment, Peggy burst into tears and rushed from the kitchen. Bridie looked upset. My mother came in at that moment, glanced at Bridie and said to me, 'You come with me now, John-John, and I'll take you down to school.'

We were halfway down O'Connell Street before I said, 'Mammy, why was Peggy crying?'

It was unusual for her to take me to school. Normally she would be opening the shop.

She sighed. 'Oh, it's a long story. And it's not easy to explain.'

'I only asked her when she was going to marry Johnny.'

I counted several steps before she spoke.

'She won't be getting married, after all.'

'Why?'

'No more questions now, *a grá*. I'll explain it all some time.'

Something else became clear that week. Bridie was leaving.

'Why is Bridie leaving, Peggy?'

The whole world was changing and it made me feel anxious.

Peggy became tearful again. She had always answered my questions. She stood up very straight, gazing into the distance. There were two big tears in her eyes.

'She's leaving because she's going to have a baby.'

'But only married mammies have babies.'

Peggy sobbed but said nothing.

Sister Margaret Mary suddenly fell seriously ill and we got a new teacher. She was cross and I didn't like her at all. Now I had problems that made me forget all about Bridie and I was upset anyway, because Peggy went away somewhere for several weeks. I was allowed to spend a lot more time up in Mickey Maher's house.

One Saturday, we were sitting beside the stove at the back of the barbershop, looking at comics. The wind hummed in the chimney. Logs crackled and hissed. The stove ticked with heat and gave off its cast-iron smell. Every time the door opened, the smells of oils and powder got blown around.

All that busy afternoon, the *slap slap slap* of the open razor on the strop was background noise to the chatter as Jimmy shaved the farmers and shopkeepers. Above it all, from a high shelf near the ceiling, the wireless poured out frenetic racing commentary. Nobody seemed to notice that Jimmy was answering like a machine. His thoughts were clearly elsewhere. An old farmer had just climbed into the chair. Jimmy hadn't said a word. His hands snipped busily at the farmer's hair as if they were someone else's hands.

'Is that Ascot or Cheltenham, Jimmy?'

Jimmy was facing me. His eyes were black and his face was pale. He seemed to be all coiled up and ready to spring, like our cat at a mousehole. 'It's the big race – Cheltenham,' he snapped.

The farmer gave him a long look in the mirror, licked his lips and said nothing.

I nearly laughed. Jimmy reminded me of the clown we had seen at the circus when I was four. Peggy had pointed out that the clown had put on a policeman's helmet to pretend he was someone else. We had laughed because we could see that he was still a clown. Jimmy, with his slight build and bow legs, looked like someone poorly disguised as a barber. Combs, scissors and brushes bulged from the top pocket of his white coat. Every so often he paused to stare at his image in the mirror, as if to check on something.

Without warning, Jimmy threw down the scissors and comb and headed for the door, peeling off his white coat. He dumped it on the floor and the door slammed after him.

The farmer got down off the chair, calmly packed his pipe and said, 'Tell him I'll come back another time.'

'Where's he gone?' I asked.

'Across to the betting shop,' said Mickey quietly.

Mickey's mother came out from the kitchen. She walked past us without a word and stood staring out the barbershop window, arms akimbo. She turned and said, 'I think it's time for you to go home for your tea now, John-John.'

I knew it wasn't time and it made me sad. Something

else had changed. We were only a few doors down, but Mickey walked me home.

When Peggy came back, she seemed to be her old self again. That night, she read me a story in bed. It was about a fox that played a trick on a crow. I had no questions and Peggy took this to mean I was almost asleep. She lifted the blanket gently up across my shoulders and tip-toed out.

I was wide awake, though. I crept out of bed and gazed at the frosty sky. A little star seemed to be tumbling across the heavens and breaking up. Every thought was silenced by the wonderful mystery of it. But the other mysteries, the ones adults kept secret from me, made me feel locked out and sad. I wondered if I would ever understand them.

Peggy was the one consistent thing in my world. She never married and stayed with us until we all grew up and went away.

Elbow Grease

1950

How was I to know, when I was only six years old, that blacksmiths were supposed to be muscular giants? Tommy Brady said they always were. Mickey Maher said they weren't, because brothers Johnjo and Micko Devlin were dinky little men, no bigger than jockeys. And they had their forge down a lane at the end of our street, six or seven doors beyond Jimmy the Barber's.

On wet days, when the older gang members went to our hideout, we would go to the forge, especially if a horse was being shod. We usually stood just inside, well back from the horse's hind legs, eyes adjusting to the semi-darkness. It was a huge cavern of a barn, accessed through a stone archway. To the left, just inside, a rusting mountain of discarded horseshoes posed a permanent threat of landslide. A single bare light bulb swung uselessly in the gloom far above. Its movement was regulated by the currents of warm air that billowed upwards from the furnace in the middle of the floor below. It was suffocating everywhere except close to the doorway.

Being young boys, we always had plenty of questions.

'Johnjo, why do horses have to be shod?'

'Why do you go to the barber's, to get shaved?'

'But you put shoes on horses, Johnjo!'

'Of course I do. I'm an equestrian shoemaker!'

'But why do you pare his hooves first?'

'First, we manicure the horse's hooves then we fit a nice new pair of shoes.'

'Why do you paint varnish on the hoof?'

'Why does a woman paint her nails?'

And so it went on.

Dinny Hoctor, the butcher's son, when he wasn't out on his messenger bike was nearly always to be found in the forge. Johnjo let him operate the bellows, because it was one way to keep him out of harm's way, seeing as he was a bit 'simple'. Dinny looked just right for the part. He pumped the bellows, staring into the hungry inferno. The fixed, obsessed expression gave him a gargoyle's face on which the reflected flames flickered.

Of course we all wanted a turn at the bellows, but Dinny could never be persuaded. Tommy would always insist, and the result was that Johnjo or his brother often ran us out of the place.

'Scat!' Johnjo had yelled at us once. 'Get t'hell! No, not you! You come back!' he shouted, pointing at me with his hammer.

'Me?' I said, wondering what I had done.

'You stand and hold this horse's head.'

I stared up at the huge horse, and the horse blinked down at me, not unkindly.

'But I don't know if I could hold—'

'Course you can!' shouted Johnjo, exactly the way his brother would.

The brothers were as alike as two nails in a horseshoe. What differentiated them was their functions. Johnjo shod the horses and Micko mended hasps for barn doors, hames for horses or broken ploughshares. He could make you anything you wanted, so long as it was in iron.

They both wore ankle-length divided leather aprons and brown braces to hold up their trousers. They wore matching, greasy, peaked caps that never came off, even when beads of sweat stood out on their brows. They were bow-legged, had quick darting movements, and shouted even if you were right beside them. No one seemed to know what age they were.

When one of them stood at the anvil, holding a piece of red-hot iron with a pair of long tongs in his left hand, delivering clanging hammer blows with the right, there was only one way to tell them apart. If the tongs held a red-hot horseshoe, it was Johnjo. If it was anything else, it was Micko.

'What'll I do?'

'Just take a hold of him by the halter, close up to the head collar, like this, and . . . what's your name?'

'John.'

'John! What kind of a name is that? You're Seán, and because you're only a little *gossin*, we'll call you Seánie. And who's yer fader?'

I told him my father's name.

'Ah, sure I know him well. And you're in that house down the street, just across from Brady's?'

'Yes.'

'Now, Seánie,' he said confidentially, suddenly dropping his voice as if he didn't want the horse to hear, and leaning back against the huge beast as he might against a wall. 'This fella is just a big baby, between you and me. Now, you know how to be quiet around horses. Just hold him and talk to him, right?'

'Hould up there, ya big eejit!' he suddenly shouted as the horse shifted its weight to accommodate Johnjo's leaning.

The huge beast tossed its head in surprise, but obeyed. I had noticed that Johnjo could say or do what he liked with horses and they didn't seem to mind.

I tentatively reached up and gripped the halter, high as I could. The horse gazed down at me calmly with its huge liquid eyes and I could see that it was in fact quite placid. He was looking at me with curiosity though.

'What will I say to him, Johnjo?' I called out.

Johnjo was now at the horse's rear end, with a great hairy hoof hoisted onto and between his knees, busily extracting nails from a shoe.

'Ah, just tell him anything you like. Any oul' shite will do. Just tell him what you did at school today or what you had for dinner. He won't mind.'

I started telling the horse what we had done in history that day, and he did seem interested.

'What does it mean, Johnjo, when he puts his ears

forward?' I shouted, just as loudly as Johnjo.

'It means he's interested in what you're telling him!' he shouted back. He was paring and filing the hoof by now.

I started telling the horse about my problem with maths. He wasn't so sure about that and kept putting one ear forward and one back. I shouted down to Johnjo, asking him what that meant.

'Ah, you're confusing the poor oul' divil. Sure what would a horse know about addition and subtraction? And I'll tell you something else. Don't mention that oul' bollix of a teacher again. He must be some awful gobshite, and hearing about him will only upset the horse.'

'How will I know when he's upset?'

'He'll put the ears back and show his teeth!'

'What'll I do if he does that?'

'Drop that halter and run for your feckin' life,' he shouted calmly.

Suddenly, a cloud of acrid smoke rose from behind the horse and seemed to hover above Johnjo's head. He didn't seem to notice, as he was busy nailing on the horse's shoe.

'What's that, Johnjo?'

'Oh, that's just the final fitting for her new high-heel shoes, so she can go dancing tonight.'

I wasn't in the best physical position to check this out, but by holding the halter high above my head and ducking down, I was able to establish that the horse was indeed a mare.

'Johnjo,' I shouted, 'I didn't know this was a mare.'

'Ah, sure a horse is just a feckin' horse, male or female.'

The mare threw her head up in indignation so suddenly that I nearly lost my grip.

As if on cue, a huge farmer came squelching in through the archway in his boots and gaiters, and the mare let out a little whinny of recognition, or something.

'Y'see that, Mikey,' Johnjo shouted, 'she's missing you already. What's that weather doin' out there?'

'Ah, 'tis a miserable oul' hoor of a day, so it is. Howya, darling,' Mikey shouted to the mare, giving her a big, affectionate slap and rub on the neck. She whinnied again with pleasure.

'I told you that you two should get married,' said Johnjo to Mikey, nodding towards the mare.

'I hear you're sniffing around a nice young filly yourself, down this very street! But tell us, what's the damage?'

'For a nice set of dancing shoes, Mikey, I'm only charging you two-and-six.'

'Two and . . . are you out of your tiny mind? I'm not buying her back from you, you know. It's only a set of feckin' shoes.'

'All right, Mikey, all right! I don't want you to get started on your life story or the current economic situation. Give us two shillings and take her home.'

'Jaysus, I'd want a share in the forge for that! I'll give you one-and-six, and not a penny more.'

'Jayz, Mikey, you're a real hardship! Listen, for oul'

time's sake, one-and-six it is, but' – he pointed the hammer meaningfully at the big man's chest – 'I want two pints of porter from you, down in Maguire's tonight!'

'Done!' shouted Mikey, and spat in the palm of his hand. Johnjo reciprocated and the two palms smacked loudly together in the gloom, to seal the bargain.

When man and mare had gone, Johnjo collapsed onto the anvil, still clutching his hammer.

'How much is it to shoe a horse, Johnjo?' I asked.

'It depends,' said Johnjo, fetching a big sigh, 'on whether he's friend or foe, big farmer or small, cute hoor or honest man.'

'What's a cute—'

'Listen now, Seánie, I want you to do a message for me—'

'Down to Brady's shop, I'll bet,' said his brother Micko, wandering in.

'That's right,' said Johnjo. 'This man,' he said, throwing a nod in my direction, 'lives just across the street and he's best buddies with the young Brady lad, what's-his-name?'

'Tommy,' I said.

'And hasn't he a big sister works in the shop?' said Micko.

'That's Moira,' I said. 'She's studying to be a teacher.'

'Is she, now? And what sort of a lassie is she at all?'

'Oh, she's fierce nice.'

'See that, now! And how old would that lassie be, I wonder?' Micko wondered aloud.

'Oh, she's fairly old, I'd say. She must be twenty-five or twenty-six.'

This clearly astonished both brothers. They gaped at each other.

'That old?' exclaimed Johnjo.

'Jaysus,' said Micko, 'she'll soon be collecting the pinshin. Shouldn't you,' he said to his brother, 'be looking further afield for a younger model?'

'You're only jealous, that's what you are,' shouted Johnjo. 'Now, Seánie, you're to go down to Brady's shop now and get me a tin of elbow grease.'

'Elbow grease? What's—'

'Never mind what it is. Ask Moira. She'll know what it is. If the mother is in the shop, just ask her if young Tommy is home. Have you got that?'

'I have. Will I need money?'

'You'll only need to have your wits about you.'

'Hello, John-John,' Moira greeted me cheerfully as soon as I entered the shop.

She always made me feel shy but I explained as exactly as I could Johnjo's request, to which she listened impassively.

'Elbow grease?' she mused, a speculative index finger drumming on her cheek. She had the same calm, kindly expression her mother had and she was very, very pretty. 'Well now, John-John,' she said at last, 'I have just the thing for Johnjo!' She rummaged under the counter and produced a sticky label. She wrote something rapidly on it, stuck it across the front of a small green-and-gold tin and slapped it down triumphantly on the counter before me. 'There,' she said. 'That should do it.'

I stared at the object in front of me. It looked suspiciously like a tin of Tate & Lyle's Golden Syrup. I looked dubiously up at Moira, but she was all reassuring smiles.

'Now, John-John,' she said, dropping her voice and suddenly looking serious, 'there's something I need to tell you in confidence.' She looked quickly in the direction of the bar, out of sight behind a screen, and bent down towards me across the counter. My senses swam as her perfume hovered around me. I would have believed anything she said at that moment.

'You see,' she told me, 'Johnjo has a bit of a problem that he's embarrassed about. Have you noticed he never takes that cap off his head?'

I nodded dumbly.

'Well, the reason is, he's as bald as an egg, and this' – she indicated the tin on the counter between us – 'is a special ointment old Mrs Broderick made up that makes hair grow back again.'

She paused to examine my face. I felt suffocated by her proximity and there was no way I was going to question anything. Seeing that, she resumed in a matter-of-fact tone.

'Now,' she said, lifting the tin and examining her own writing, 'Johnjo must apply this ointment to the top of his head twice a day: when he gets up in the morning and especially last thing at night, before he goes to bed. Have you got that?'

I nodded dumbly.

'And,' she added dramatically, 'on no account must

he get this stuff on his lips or tongue. For exterior application only, all right?'

I nodded, grabbed the ointment and fled.

Both brothers stopped what they were doing as soon as I entered. They gave me no chance to explain what was in the tin because they wanted to know, word for word, what I had said to her and what she had said to me.

Faithfully as I could, I recounted the dialogue and proceeded to explain her express instructions concerning the application of the contents of the tin firmly gripped in my hand.

They both listened to me with as much interest and respect as they might accord the parish priest in the pulpit, only occasionally glancing at each other, mouths open or jaws dropped at each stage of my account.

Then Johnjo leaped from his sitting position on the anvil, threw the hammer he was holding into the gloom and let out a wild whoop of laughter.

The two brothers laughed, they howled, they whooped. Johnjo whipped off his famous greasy peaked cap, threw it on the ground and danced a rapid little jig on it.

Moira was right. He was bald as an egg, with tiny tufts of hair above his ears.

I watched the spectacle in open-mouthed astonishment.

Finally, Micko sobered sufficiently to grab the tin from my hand and insisted that his brother sit patiently on the anvil while he gently applied a little of the 'ointment' to the top of his head.

I genuinely thought they were crazy. What came out of the tin was clearly Tate & Lyle Golden Syrup, same as we had at home.

Suddenly, Micko was staring in amazement at the backs of his hands.

'Look!' he shouted ecstatically 'Look! It's working already!'

Johnjo and I rushed over. The backs of his proffered hands were covered in long coarse black hair!

'It's a miracle!' he shouted, crossing his arms over his chest and gazing heavenwards.

I wasn't at all convinced at this stage. I knew they were clowning, because Johnjo had exactly the same long coarse hair on the backs of his hands.

'Gawd!' said Johnjo suddenly, looking dumbfounded and dazed. He sat down weakly on the anvil.

'What's the matter?' Micko enquired.

'I have this strange feeling on the top of my head. Something is happening!'

Of course, Micko and I were obliged to examine the top of his head. In the dim light from the bare bulb overhead, I could discern two or three longish hairs standing up in isolation on the crown of his head.

Johnjo's eyes had grown enormous in wonderment.

'It's working! It's working!' he shouted.

But I had had enough of it by then. As I left to go home to my tea, I heard the hoots and yells continue behind me.

*

Whatever aspirations Johnjo the blacksmith entertained, things in fact took their course as they were meant to. This began when our local vet, Frank Martin, took a new man into his growing practice. The new man certainly caused a stir when he played his first game for the town rugby club. The fact that he was tall, good-looking and drove a low-slung Riley sports car rapidly elevated him to the position of the town's most eligible bachelor. From the start, however, there was no competition, because he had eyes only for Moira Brady.

They got married about a year later in St. Peter's. It was a perfect June day. Moira looked stunning as she appeared at the top of the church steps on the arm of her new husband. She stood waving happily amidst the storm of confetti and the waves of cheers and clapping.

Tommy, her little brother, looked suitably angelic in his all-white suit. Nevertheless, his demeanour suggested that this was just another great day out. And there was something speculative about the expression on his face, as if he were already calculating the cash to be made from tipsy uncles and fond old aunties and grannies. He caught my eye, winked and grinned, focused on the business of the day.

Bride and groom descended the steps, waving like royalty to the waiting maroon saloon, where driver Tommy Lenehan smilingly held the door for them.

Doors slammed in quick succession and the cavalcade moved majestically down Grace Road for the brief trip to Watergate Pier. From there they would board the first of the flotilla of houseboats that would take them and their guests up the river to the Hodson Bay Hotel for the reception.

Suddenly, there was a tremendous grating, screeching sound, as if the bottom had dropped out of the leading vehicle. The whole cavalcade ground to a halt. Tommy Lenehan jumped out and, forgetful of his good suit, got down on his hands and knees to stare under the car. Slowly his head came up and we saw him gazing in bewilderment towards the rear. Mystified, he got up and walked around to the back of the car. By this time, the entire congregation was standing around. Bride and bridegroom had also got out and were gazing down, as mystified as everyone else.

'God, look!' yelled Tommy, pointing down. Then he too was down on his knees, dragging some large object from among the traditional boots and tin cans attached to the back bumper.

'What is it?' demanded the bridegroom.

'It's a huge, huge horseshoe!' yelled Tommy, pulling at it strenuously, but it would not move.

'There's a chain holding it!' I shouted. It was a perfect, new horseshoe, eight or nine times the size of the biggest horseshoe I had ever seen.

'What's that attached to it?' Moira asked, frowning.

Tommy tugged it free of the boots and cans, holding it up for all to see. At the toe of the horseshoe, melded into the metal, was a large iron heart with a jagged split that almost rent it asunder. A suitably outsize horseshoe nail was deeply embedded in the left side and a little trickle, forever hardened in iron, flowed from it.

'Who in God's name?'

'I know who done it!' yelled Tommy.

'Shush!' said his mother firmly but quietly behind him. Mrs Brady was tall and elegant in her wedding outfit, but there was no mistaking the iron grip her fingers had on young Tommy's shoulder. I could see that he was wincing. In any case, he kept quiet.

Moira was staring at the object. Then she started laughing. She laughed and laughed until the tears came, and then she was crying. I couldn't understand it at all. How could someone laugh and cry at the same time? I felt that I would never understand grown-ups, especially the female of the species.

Blessed Amongst Women

~

1951

The noise in the archway that led into our yard was deafening.

'Eight, nine, ten, red-light!' shouted Steffi Nolan, spinning round.

It was almost all girls – my sister's friends – and Peggy had shooed us out of the kitchen, having fed us cakes and tea.

'Aren't ye blessed amongst women, now,' Mrs Halligan, the washer-woman, had said to Tommy and me and she roared with laughter. Mrs Halligan came every Monday. She would stand at the sink, a cigarette dangling from her upper lip. She was a huge, jolly woman, her head always swathed in a polka-dot scarf and her great body wrapped in a faded, blue, wrap-around coverall. Soap-suds covered her arms, and her raw-meat hands pounded clothes against the washing-board.

We went out to the yard.

'Will we join in?' said Tommy. Darkness was closing in and the October sky released the occasional little warning drop. The dim electric light came on in the archway.

'Okay,' I said reluctantly.

'Tommy and John-John, you'll have to stand at the back,' my sister Mari called.

'No, they'll have to wait until we finish this one!' called Steffi Nolan.

I knew they were all older, but what I disliked most about girls was that they were so bossy.

'No, we're going back in the *kitchen*,' I shouted angrily and made for the door, Tommy following.

I complained to Peggy and Mrs Halligan turned from the sink.

'Well, now, me young *gossin*,' she said in her gravelly man's voice, 'you've learned an important lesson early in life: women *are* bossy, and make no mistake about it!' Again she exploded in laughter. Mrs Halligan seemed to look for anything that would make her laugh.

'And,' I continued, 'that Steffi is the worst. She's always pulling out of me. Look what she's done to my *geansaí*,' I said, showing Peggy how the back of my jumper had been stretched out of shape.

Mrs Halligan roared with laughter. 'Well, now, *there's* a woman in love! What do you think, Peggy?'

Peggy smiled. She seemed to enjoy Mrs Halligan. Peggy went to the door and called, 'Now girls, time to go home for your tea!'

'We're just finishing this game, Peggy,' my sister Mari called.

'Then can we play just one more game, Peggy? Please, please!' called Steffi.

'Play one more game,' said Peggy, 'and put John-John and Tommy up at the front so they have some chance of winning.'

We watched as they finished the game and then Steffi came marching up to me.

'You come with me, John-John,' she said, taking me by the shoulders, 'and I'll put you up front.'

She was doing it again! I shrugged her off testily and made my own way to the front. She was taller than me and had brownish-red hair and glasses. She even had something on her teeth!

'What about me?' Tommy asked.

'Tommy, you go in the second row, behind John-John.'

'I don't want to go in the second row. Peggy said the front row.'

'You're to go in the second row!'

'I will *not!*' He stepped into the front row beside me, pushing one of the girls aside.

'You're to go back!' Steffi insisted.

'You can't make me!'

'And don't push me!' cried the girl who had been pushed, pushing Tommy even harder. Tommy pushed her violently so that she fell and started snivelling.

'Hey, what are you doing?' I shouted at him and pushed him so hard he staggered against the wall.

He came at me, running, aimed a clumsy punch and missed. I punched him hard in the ribs and he fell. He immediately scooped up a stone and threw it. It caught me on the side of the head. I was shocked when I reached up and found blood on my hand. But Steffi was rushing at him like a tigress and grabbed him by the hair. She pulled so hard that he yelled in pain, crouching almost to the ground. But he forced himself up and slapped Steffi hard across the face. Steffi stood still a minute, shocked and pale. Something seemed to go off inside my head and I threw myself at Tommy, punching furiously. We were rolling on the ground when I realised that everything had gone quiet. My father stood over us. He must have come out of the bar. He pointed at Tommy and with the quietest voice said, 'You go on home now.'

Tommy got up and left. My father just looked at the girls and they started quietly moving towards the gate. Peggy had come out and was standing, holding me by the shoulder. My father was looking at the cut on my head.

'I'll take him in and clean him up,' said Peggy. My father nodded and went back to the bar.

Mrs Halligan made way for Peggy so that she could clean my wound at the sink.

'Fightin' over a woman,' she chortled 'just like my own two lads would!'

Mrs Halligan's 'boys', well in their thirties, were Connaught Street's famous layabouts. They made no secret of their low opinion of work. Somehow, in spite of this, they seemed to spend most of their time in Maguire's pub. Tommy had told me all that because they weren't allowed into Brady's bar. No one could say a bad word about Mrs Halligan's boys, unless they wished to discuss the matter with Mrs Halligan. Apparently, no one did.

'Ow, Peggy,' I protested, but it didn't really hurt much. She was dabbing the cut with a soft cloth, soaked in warm water and carbolic soap.

'Nearly finished,' she murmured.

'Ah, sure he'll be better before he's married,' said Mrs Halligan. She had hoisted one great hip onto the table and was puffing away.

The kitchen door flew open and a breathless Steffi came in. She stood watching what Peggy was doing. 'Daddy uses Dettol for cuts like that,' she said.

Peggy paused to look at her. We all knew Steffi's daddy was a doctor.

'We have a bottle in the press over there,' said Peggy in a cool voice. 'Would you get it for me, please?'

Steffi had it over in a thrice.

'Now, John-John,' said Peggy 'this will hurt a little bit. Are you going to be brave?'

I nodded, screwing up my eyes in anticipation. She applied the cloth and it really stung. I sucked my breath in sharply through my teeth but made no other sound. Peggy started cutting gauze and a strip of Elastoplast.

'Can I help you do that, Peggy?' said Steffi.

'Thank you, Steffi,' said Peggy in her cool voice, continuing what she was doing. 'I think we can manage.'

She applied the last piece of sticking plaster with a little flourish and said quietly, 'Now, I think it's time for you to go home for your tea, isn't it, Steffi?'

The two girls, one nine years old, the other in her twenties, looked at each other. It seemed to me that something passed between them. Steffi glanced at me and left without a word. There was silence for a moment in the kitchen.

Mrs Halligan hauled her bulk off the table and said, 'Well, Peggy, *a grá*, I'm off, and I'll see you next week.' She paused at the door and reached into her apron pocket. She produced three large coins, each showing a hen with her chicks. 'And here's three medals for this brave young warrior.' I took the coins in surprise and out she went with her gravelly man's laugh.

She breezed back in immediately, clutching something aloft in her fingers.

'Well, look what I found in the bottom of the same pocket!' It was a tiny silver coin with a rabbit on it. She pressed it into the palm of my hand, closed my fingers on it and left, with another big laugh.

'Peggy, she gave me sixpence!' I cried, staring at the four coins on my palm.

Peggy was smiling. She glanced up at the clock on the wall. 'We need to get your sister home for tea. She's up at McGee's.' She was looking at me, thinking something.

'Oh, can I go for her, Peggy, can I?'

Peggy smiled. I had money and McGee's meant sweets.

*

Peggy watched me crossing over. Halfway down the street, the window of McGee's shop blazed like a cheerful beacon in the gathering gloom.

To enter McGee's shop of a dark winter's night was to enter a haven of warmth, filled with noise, laughter and the aroma emanating from the glass jars on the shelves behind the counter. These contained bull-eyes, Peggy's leg, curling black snakes of liquorice and every variety of toffee and chocolates. It was where the older girls hung out. Peggy took me in there one evening after a concert when the oldest girls had met there before going on to the Thursday night dance. As soon as we entered, the noise struck us like a wave. The place was jammed with girls. Some were standing, some sitting coquettishly up on the counter, some sitting on the bench along the wall. The aroma of perfume and powder was overpowering. All were talking at once, all smoking, all laughing, some teasing. The atmosphere was electric.

'Hello, Peggy,' called Mags McGee from behind the counter. Mags seemed to be enjoying the whole thing. Apart from myself, there wasn't a male of the species in the place.

The ping of the bell above the door always drew the attention of these laughing faces to anyone who entered. I found this terrifying, to have this gaggle of girls suddenly turn their collective attention on me. And there was no Peggy with me this time. I stood frozen in horror, clutching my four coins.

'What can I get you, John-John?' called Mags, coming to my rescue.

I went over to the counter and pointed upwards.

'The liquorice, is it?'

I nodded.

'There's your little brother, Mari!' a girl shouted to my older sister.

Mari was too busy coughing, having tried a puff of one of the bigger girl's cigarettes.

'Is it teatime?' she gasped in my direction.

'It is, and you're to come home now, Peggy says.'

'Oh, isn't he only gorgeous!' called one of the big girls. 'Oh, I could eat him!'

'Hey, look! There's Steffi's little boyfriend, John-John!'

There was general laughter and attention focused on me. I was horrified. I caught a glimpse of Steffi at the back. She hung her head, silently grave, and faced away from me.

'Come here to me, now, John-John, and give us a kiss,' called my sister's friend Marcie Coleman.

I almost died of fright and was ready to bolt. Marcie Coleman was gorgeous.

'Ah, come on now, girls! Leave him alone. Now here's your sister,' said Mags.

I was silently fuming on the way back to our house.

'What's the matter?' said Peggy, when my sister had gone upstairs.

'I *hate* girls!' I shouted. 'I hate them, I hate them!'

My mother came in quietly, glanced at me and directed a frowning enquiry at Peggy.

'It's all right, ma'am. John-John has just been finding

out a bit about what girls can be like.'

They exchanged a look. There may have been a hint of amusement in it, but I felt that they understood.

After the Christmas holidays, Steffi stopped wearing her glasses. I couldn't help but notice what a difference it made. She and her older sister came out their front door each morning the same time as we did. They went left down Connaught Street to their school, and we went right to ours. Steffi never waved or said anything. But she had a way of looking sideways at me with a kind of slow, sliding look. Without her glasses, her eyes were large and I knew they were a deep brown. They glowed with a warm light that seemed to come from deep within.

'She's looking at me again,' murmured my older brother one morning, with his self-satisfied grin.

I was astonished. He really believed it. 'She's not looking at you!' I said.

'Who do you think she's looking at?' he sneered.

I wanted to punch him hard as I could in the head. Who did he think he was anyway?

The Faithful Departed

~

1951

Our town kept its secrets well. This had always locked me out of the lives of people important to me. When Molly Shine died, I asked Peggy to tell me that particular secret.

'I *will* tell you, and that's a promise, but not when you're seven years old!'

It was three years later when she kept her promise. It was the evening after the terrible fight with my brother. I was in a particularly emotional state. That's when she told me Molly's story, which began in Staunton's Store.

Staunton's General Hardware Store was at the bottom of our hill. I was sent down there once, when I was seven years old, to get some brass cup hooks of a certain size. That would have been in 1951.

As soon as you went into Staunton's, bells clanged and pinged above whichever of the half-glazed double doors you happened to open.

Any prospective client therefore immediately

became the centre of attention, but not necessarily of interest, and certainly did not galvanise any of the shop boys into any action that could be construed as an offer of service, much less politeness.

Eventually, one of the boys, Tom Stack, wandered up to where I waited patiently, my head just above the parapet of the high wooden counter. He leaned heavily on the counter; his yellow, nicotine-stained fingers splayed out to support him, and glared down balefully.

'Yes?' he snapped.

'I want four brass hooks, size four.'

'Number four!' he shouted contemptuously.

'Yes,' I said.

'Don't have any!' he said, without any visible attempt to go and look.

'What are you talking about?' barked a female voice I knew very well. That galvanised him, all right.

'Tom Stack,' she bawled at him, 'your brains, if you have any, are in the arse of your trousers! Will you move yourself, you *amadán*, and look in that drawer right behind you!' Then she turned to me. 'He won't be a minute, darling!' she purred with a great big smile.

I stood stupefied. This was the famous, irrepressible Molly Shine.

She was hardly five feet tall, stocky to the point of muscularity. Made up with lipstick and powder like a grotesque doll, she was Staunton's renowned cashier, accountant and floor manager. I couldn't believe that this was the slim, pretty, champion amateur dancer my mother said she had been.

I had often seen her as she sat up in a tiny kind of crow's nest office high above the back of Staunton's Store, queen of all she surveyed. Woe betide the shop boy who didn't immediately put any payment received into one of the wooden cups that were suspended above the counter. The cups had then to be screwed up into a device above. A lavatory-type handle on a chain was pulled, and the cup zinged along the wires aloft to Molly's office. Swiftly, the correct change and receipt came zinging back, and the customer departed. On busy days, wooden cups zinged back and forth above the heads of customers and staff alike. Nobody in Staunton's General Hardware Store paid much attention when Molly developed a deep hacking cough. After all, it had happened frequently before and she had smoked heavily all her life.

The hacking cough had gone on all one morning up in the crow's nest. Just before lunchtime the shop boys, always aware of her movements, saw her come slowly down the stairs. When she collapsed in a heap at the bottom, they were rendered immobile with shock before someone had the sense to call an ambulance.

Molly was taken to hospital and she never left it. She had terminal cancer.

My mother took me once to the hospital to see Molly. It was a vast, bleak Victorian relic, out on the edge of town. Regular trains thundered past on the railway bridge that spanned the road outside. I could watch them from the third-floor window of Molly's room as they disappeared, their thunder fast fading, towards distant Dublin or Galway.

Molly talked to my mother in quiet, gentle tones, in stark contrast to the stentorian tones employed over a lifetime with the shop boys in Staunton's. She also addressed her as Babs, which meant she was an old friend.

'Hello darling!' she croaked when she saw me. It was a chilling sound, but I felt the warmth of her greeting.

They chatted in desultory fashion for a while. I watched doctors and nurses and patients pass below, three floors down. Leaves stirred uneasily at the foot of a huge chestnut tree. They lay still momentarily before the harsh December wind moved them on again.

Their voices dropped at one point behind me, putting me on full alert. They paused as I turned around. She and my mother fixed their eyes on me. I understood.

'I'm just going down the corridor a bit,' I said. 'Is that all right?'

'Remember the number of the room, darling,' Molly called hoarsely as I left, 'and the floor!'

'I will.'

As we were leaving, we met Molly's nephew in the corridor. He had just qualified as a solicitor. He and my mother exchanged the usual pleasantries and enquiries. I noticed the coolness in my mother's manner. There was a definite pause. My mother stood gazing silently at him a moment.

'You know, Michael, what Molly has done for you and your brothers and sisters—'

'Oh, I know, I know . . .'

Michael and his siblings, all adopted, were brought

up in a seriously dysfunctional family situation. Their alcoholic father kept his government job only because of a political friend of the family. Molly had paid for their schooling and put Michael through college. This was long before student grants were introduced.

'What I wanted to say, Michael,' my mother continued quietly, 'is that it's a shame Molly should end up in a public hospital ward. She won't last long. I think you and the others should think about getting her into a nursing home.'

It was very interesting to watch Michael's face. All kinds of things were going on there, some kind of struggle. It was clear that Molly had managed the family much as she had the staff in Staunton's Store.

As it happened, she died before she could be moved to the nursing home. Molly had accumulated more than enough to secure a long retirement. She left everything to Michael and his siblings.

The evening before the funeral, Molly lay in an open coffin in the centre of the large square room in Lenehan's Funeral Home. Lights were dim, candles burned discreetly at strategic points and the air was heavy with the scent of flowers. Upright wooden chairs lined all four walls.

Molly's nephew Michael and his siblings sat together just inside the door as the first mourners began to arrive. Townspeople, acquaintances, old customers of Staunton's, drifted in quietly and respectfully. Most gazed in briefly at the tiny figure in the coffin, blessed themselves and sat down.

Some women paused at the open coffin, shedding a tear or two. Old friends even touched her face. My mother was the first to bend in gently to kiss her, after which she resumed her seat beside me. Some would go over to Michael and the others, bend over them, shake hands with loud whispered condolences, and take their leave. Others seated themselves quietly, mouthing silent prayers or fingering Rosary beads, gazing sadly at the open coffin. Throughout it all, Michael and the others solemnly played their expected role, anxiously watching every development.

A natural segregation had already taken place among the mourners. The Staunton employees, mostly country lads, came in silently one by one. They looked awkward and unfamiliar in their Sunday suits. Newly shaved, with hair slicked down, they gladly joined their fellow workers along the far wall.

They hardly moved, only occasionally exchanging solemn whispers. At a signal, they all stood up and ambled shyly up to Michael's group. They repeated the bending, the whispered condolences and the hand-shaking with each and every member of the family before respectfully resuming their seats. Michael, clearly uncomfortable in his role as mourner, and stiff in his new suit, was gracious to these country lads.

Later in the evening, Michael's friends and acquaintances began drifting in, subtly changing the atmosphere. These were the young inheritors of long-established businesses in the town, or the scions of generations of the professional class.

Political correctness demanded of them a certain concession to wearing black, to talking in whispers, to gazing into the coffin and blessing themselves, but the manner of doing it was markedly different from that of the Staunton employees.

Having performed their duty, they paid no more attention whatsoever to Molly in her coffin. The silent Staunton workers watched them uncomprehendingly from the opposite wall.

These well-heeled friends of Michael's were discreetly jovial, exuding something that looked more like celebration. Molly, notwithstanding her tremendous contribution to the lives of Michael and his siblings, had always been seen by them as a serious social impediment for Michael. At least, that's what I heard my mother say to my Aunt Eva, her sister, that morning.

Suddenly the room went silent. Significant noises indicated that the hearse had arrived outside.

As if on cue, Tommy Lenehan, dark-suited in his role as funeral director, entered slowly and solemnly, looking neither to left nor right.

He paused before the open coffin, gazed in, blessed himself and waited. The old priest shuffled up behind and performed the closing ceremony, with timeless prayers and holy water. Tommy nodded to his assistant, and silently they lifted the coffin lid into position. All their movements were deliberate and respectful, and a silent audience watched their every move. The coffin was wheeled out and everyone started to move.

They crowded in the doorway as the rain came down

and Tommy Lenehan, hatless, continued to carefully place the many wreaths on top of and around the coffin.

Finally, the cortege moved off in a downpour.

Besides the hearse, Tommy also had a long saloon, with deep leather seats and burgundy paintwork, a superior taxi much favoured for weddings.

But people didn't die or get married every day of the week, so Tommy also ran a typical combination pub-grocery, which was an especially good place to go on days when there were funerals, because there was a snug where older women could sip their sherry and talk in hushed tones about the day's events. No doubt plenty was said about Molly on the day of her funeral.

Tommy's pub was in fact an old Bianconi Inn, which in my time had become the usual pub-grocery combination. It was at the top of our hill, just around the corner on O'Connell Street.

A few days after the funeral – I think it was Christmas Eve – I watched my mother filling an old shoebox with odds and ends. She was in the kind of solemn mood that invited no questions. She gazed at the box when the lid had been put on. Thoughtfully she began to wrap it in Christmas gift-paper and secured it with a blue and pink ribbon, tied in a bow. I was to take it up to Tommy Lenehan's and give it to him myself.

Right inside the doors of Tommy's place were two massive pillars. To the right, three regal steps led up to an arched double door.

Just inside the doors to the left was the snug, with its high ornamental wooden screen. Tommy would typically be stationed behind the high marble-topped counter beyond it, clad in the usual brown cotton shop coat.

Rising high in serried ranks behind him were shelves of large, dusty cylindrical tins, labelled COCOA, DEMERARA SUGAR, and loose-leaf teas of every denomination. There were stacked cartons of every brand of cigarette, including the favourites of the day: Sweet Afton, Woodbine and Players Please. There were tins and boxes of plug and loose tobacco. There were open tins of biscuits in a glass-fronted display unit that bore the legend JACOBS.

On the counter top was a big manual slicer with a circular blade, beside it a great breaded cooked ham. I was to get a pound of it before presenting Tommy with the shoebox.

Behind the partition, the men were already beginning to sing in the bar.

Tommy came into the grocery part when he heard the bell pinging above the door. He could only have been in his late forties then but he looked sixty. He exuded a kind of quiet sadness.

'Now, what can I get you?' he enquired.

I told him, and he started thoughtfully setting up the slicer, carefully and deliberately slicing the cooked ham and placing each slice on the waiting square of greaseproof paper. He glanced once or twice at the beribboned parcel under my arm but said nothing.

As he carefully folded the ham and the greaseproof paper into a brown-paper bag, I said, 'Tommy, my mother said I was to give this to you.'

He paused a moment, glanced at the parcel and finished what he was doing. He handed the brown-paper bag down over the counter and I handed the parcel up to him.

That was the last time I saw him.

'Did you know what was in that parcel?' I asked Peggy.

'Your mother told me that it was old photographs and letters from Molly Shine.'

'Why?'

'Because,' she said, 'they had a child together when they were young.'

She paused. She gazed steadily at me and I gazed back.

'You mean they weren't married?'

'That's right, they weren't.'

I needed to think about that. 'What sort of problem would that have been?'

'Do you remember, when you were starting school, we went one morning into the Magdalene Laundry?'

'I remember the frightened young girl and that awful nun!'

Peggy just nodded, gazing at me.

Then I understood. 'What happened to the child?'

'He was adopted.'

There was a pause, full of things unsaid.

'Would I know him?'

Something like mischief gleamed for a moment in her eyes.

'You should. He was Molly's nephew, Michael!'

'Michael, the solicitor: her nephew? You mean her son?'

'Yes, I mean her son.'

'Did Tommy Lenehan know that Michael was his son?'

'Yes, he knew.'

'And said nothing all those years?'

'How could he?'

'Did Michael ever find out that Molly was his mother?'

'No, he never did.'

'Did he know that Tommy was his father?'

'No, he never knew.'

'Why did Molly and Tommy keep silent about it?'

'Now John-John, think! To protect their son!'

'Why did Molly just take over Michael's family?'

'What could Molly's sister do, with a drunken husband and no money to feed and clothe the children?'

'And she had no children of her own?'

'No. All adopted, including Michael.'

I thought of Michael, that ambitious young solicitor. I thought of Molly's life, and Tommy's life. I found Peggy gazing at me. She was nodding gently, her expression somewhere between sad and ironic. She knew I had understood.

Rumour Had It

1952

'Peggy, are ghosts real?' I dumped my schoolbag on the table and collapsed in a chair.

'I thought *you* were a ghost, mister, you're so late.'

'I mean, isn't the banshee supposed to wail at night before someone dies?'

'It's not the banshee you need to worry about,' said Mrs Halligan, turning round from the sink, 'it's the pooka you need to watch out for. He's the lad on two legs that has fur all over and horse's ears!' She roared with laughter and went back to thumping her washing-board.

'Anyway,' said Peggy, smiling, 'I don't think we're going to hear the banshee on Connaught Street. So that's why you were late home! You were talking to Tommy about ghosts?'

'No, we went up to Battery Hill. But it was too dark to go inside. And we heard *rats*!'

'Now they're the lads you really need to look out for,'

said Mrs Halligan, 'never mind the pooka.'

'What took the two of you up to Battery Hill anyway?' said Peggy.

'Oh, Mr Finneran was telling us all about its history.' I started telling Peggy what he had said.

Our headmaster, Mr Finneran, said that what happened in Athlone, back in 1803, would surely have made Napoleon smile. A town he'd never heard of, on an island he rarely spoke of, was expecting an imminent attack by him. Rumours, you see, had run wild at the sight of French ships off Killalla. So, day and night, swarms of soldiers moved mountains of earth and tons of stone to make eight gigantic anthills west of our town. The resulting eight batteries, gun emplacements pointed north-westwards, stood stark against the sky from Gallows Hill out to Fort Hill.

The attack, of course, never happened. Over time, good limestone blocks mysteriously disappeared and rain washed the sandy soil, leaving broken, lumpy hills. Gallows Hill was the only battery to survive, but we called it Battery Hill. It towered above our school, the Dean Kelly Memorial School, built in 1860. We could see it above us from our classroom window.

The stone mantelpiece above the open fire that heated our classroom was a miniature museum. It held shell casings, uniform buttons and a couple of cannon balls. These were some of the relics of military activity dug up over the years in the surrounding hills.

That morning, I was walking to school with my older

brother when Tommy Brady came running up behind, out of breath. 'Hey, what's your hurry?' he gasped. He hitched his schoolbag higher and looked behind him. 'Come on!' he called.

Mickey was walking along at his own calm pace. He rarely got excited. It was the end of a golden, warm September, summer holidays long forgotten.

'Hey, I want to tell you something,' murmured Tommy. We slowed our pace, letting my brother walk ahead.

The Battery Bridge was at the end of Connaught Street. We crossed its hump, close conspirators. The canal, way down below it, was a sluggish sliver. Water-hens darted through it. We turned right, heads together, and through the gate. Tommy was waiting for the right moment to speak. I watched faceless sheep move in a dream across close-cropped, waving hills. My brother had caught up with his teammate, Flanagan, and the two heads swivelled back and forth, talking football.

'Listen,' said Tommy. 'You know there's a full moon tonight?'

'So?'

'Do you want to become a member of the Connaught Street gang?'

'I thought I was a member!'

'Don't listen to him!' said Mickey, catching up.

'The gang,' said Tommy significantly, 'goes on the haunted trail tonight.'

'The Banshee T-t-rail!' mocked Mickey, in a high moaning voice.

'Listen,' said Tommy to me confidentially, 'we'll do the test together.'

'What test?'

'To show you're not scared of ghosties, banshees, bogeymen or graveyards,' said Mickey.

'What do we have to do?' I asked, trying to sound brave.

'Just be outside our house at nine tonight.'

'I'm not supposed to be out at that time.'

'Just say you'll be over in my house. I'll say I'm over in yours.'

We walked and thought. I watched the bulk of Battery Hill emerging, inching up the skyline with each step up the dusty road. We topped the hill at the dean's house, all brick and stone and ivy.

I had to speak: 'Right; I'll be outside your house at nine.'

We both looked at Mickey. He grinned. 'I'll be there,' he said.

Our school was coming closer, more brick and stone, the yard echoing calls and bouncing balls. A whistle shrilled and the hubbub died; time to line up. We started to run.

'Peggy, can I go over to Tommy's house after tea?'

'I suppose he has all his toy soldiers lined up, ready to defend Athlone?'

'No, I'm defending the town. He's attacking with the blue soldiers because they're the French.'

I felt an awful fibber, telling Peggy a story like that.

And Mrs Brady would be out for the evening.

'All right, you can stay until bedtime. Then I'll come over to collect you.'

I felt worse when I heard that. I knew we wouldn't be there when Peggy called over. We would be miles away, following the railway line out past Battery Hill.

The harvest moon hung high in the sky. And corncrakes *did* call after dark, never mind what Tommy claimed.

From the hill above, we watched the steam train whoosh under the first bridge, then the second with a double echo, in the little valley below. Then we were slithering down the steep stony hill and onto the tracks.

'Put your hand on the rails,' said Tommy, in a loud, hoarse whisper, 'like this.'

The tracks still trembled from the passing train. A rumble echoed back down the line. We scanned the gloom, listening intently. Gang members at the other bridge stopped shifting in the shadows. The night was velvet, smelling of mown hay.

The steam train chugged, distant and faint, wagons rattling from side to side. Cattle bawled, the steam whistle shrilled, both sounds snatched by the wind.

'Hear anything?' Tommy demanded.

'That's a corncrake we just heard,' I whispered back. 'I thought you said they didn't call at night.'

'Shush!' he said fiercely. We listened hard. A curlew faintly called from Clonown bog.

'That was a friggin' curlew you heard. It's—'

Suddenly, the night was torn in two by a piercing

scream that froze my neck and head. Something was moving onto the tracks, strangely silvered by moonlight. Horror held my breath. Could it be the gatekeeper's little daughter, crushed to screaming pulp that nineteenth-century moonlit night? We waited for her long-dead mother to scream again. The shadowed creature turned, fully catching the moonlight, a large, bedraggled dog-like creature dragging something behind – a phantom dog, slavering poison from his chops?

'It's a bleddy oul' fox!' yelled Tommy, standing up. He grabbed a stone and threw it at her. She was big, and she was limping, all skin and bones, probably starving. She screamed her horrible scream again and disappeared into the night.

Gravel crunched and shadows bobbed against the sky. One of the shadows materialised from the gloom as Dekkie Brady, Tommy's older brother and the gang leader.

'Right, Tommy, you know where to go. Take John-John round the course.'

'Okay,' said Tommy, nodding obediently. To me he said, 'Let's go!'

Off we went at a trot, across two rolling hills and onto the whitened Battery Road. No questions had been asked. We leaned, gasping, on the parapet of Battery Bridge. Nothing stirred on Connaught Street. Faint amber light lit McNeil's pub and a dog barked in the distance.

A hall door opened at Mannion's grocery, throwing out a shaft of light. Women's voices tumbled after it. Ria

Mannion stood framed in her doorway.

'So, that's settled now, isn't it, Mags?' she cried, in her gruff man's voice.

'That's grand, Ria. Listen, I'll see you tomorrow,' said Mags McGee. The door slammed on the quiet street and the high heels went click-clacking down the footpath, growing fainter.

'Why are we stopping?' I wheezed.

'First test is here!' said Tommy.

'Where?'

'Over the other side.'

We crossed over to the other parapet and gazed down the sheer drop to the canal below. The steep bank rose to a parallel road that led out to the flood-lands of Clonown.

'There's nothing down there,' I said.

'Look,' said Tommy, pointing down.

I stared down at the grey-white shapes that I thought were rocks. Then one of them moved. 'Gawd!' I gasped.

Tommy laughed and slapped me on the back. 'It's only Ned Delaney's old donkey and his two mangy goats!'

'Is that all that's here?'

'Listen; the fella that built this bridge and the canal down there built tunnels into the walls below, to make stables for the horses that pulled the barges.'

The 'fella' in question, Mr Finneran had told us, was Thomas Omer, the engineer who had built the bridge and the town canal back before anyone had heard of Napoleon.

'Right, let's go,' said Tommy. We ducked under the barbed wire and began to descend the steep slope.

'What are we looking for?' I called, in a loud whisper. We both stopped.

'One of the bargemen,' he whispered back, 'fell asleep in the stable one night and his cigarette set fire to the hay.'

'Where?' I asked.

'Down there,' he said, pointing down at a large stone archway at the base of the bridge. 'That's the stable.'

'So, what happened?'

'The bargeman and the two horses that were chained inside got burned alive.'

'So?'

'Every night there's a full moon you can hear the horses screaming, pulling at the chains trying to escape.'

We slithered down the last of the slope onto the flat part and cautiously approached the tunnel. We hunkered down, completely still, listening for every sound. The donkey snorted once, frightening us, and the goats made munching sounds with the dry grass.

Suddenly, a high, screaming, whinnying sound rent the velvet night and chains clashed and rattled. There were loud thumping sounds as of hooves on hardened earth.

We were scrambling, gasping, clawing grass up the steep incline and ducking under the wire before we collapsed, our breath choking us, on the road above. We got to our feet and ran, wordless, until we stood, gasping on familiar Connaught Street. A car purred quietly up from the Pearse Street end, the lights dipping down into the deep dark of Magazine Road.

Something was bothering me. We were walking past Jimmy the Barber's when it struck. 'Hey!' I said. That brought us to a halt.

'What?'

'Big old draught horses that pulled barges wouldn't need to be chained up at night.'

'Whadaya mean?' Tommy was examining me closely. 'You weren't scared, were you?' His eyes were the giveaway. He started to grin.

'So,' I said, 'the whole thing was fixed. Was that your brother rattling the chains?'

'What if it was? It's still a test.' He was changing tack, preparing to convince me that black was white. But Mickey and someone else were walking up the street towards us.

'Shite! It's Dinny Hoctor. He shouldn't even be *out* tonight!'

Every gang member knew that Dinny Hoctor, the butcher's son, was, to say the least, *simple* and nights of a full moon he had to be kept indoors.

'Hey,' said Tommy to Mickey, '*he* can't come with us!'

'You can't stop me,' boomed Dinny in his strange, deep, man's voice, the words all strung out. Besides, he was a head taller than Tommy and he had big, raw, bony knuckles.

'Let's go,' snorted Tommy, as if he was still in charge. We went quickly past my house. I could hear the men murmuring in the bar. Dull yellow lights showed from behind the blinds in Brady's bar across the street. I had no idea of the time but guessed it must be nearly ten o'clock.

We went down the steep incline of McFarlane's Lane, onto the raised towpath along the canal. The jagged tooth of the old lock-house ruin rose before us in the gloom. On our left was the high curtain stone wall of Staunton's estate. Beech trees, leaning over, whispered at us in the breeze. I shivered in anticipation of the screams of the murdered lock-keeper's wife as he pursued her up the winding stone stair that ended in the narrow chimney-turret thrust up towards the moon.

Something white moved or fluttered at the top of the naked winding stair, halting us in our tracks.

'Jeez!' said Mickey in a whistle through his teeth. I tried to tell myself the whole thing was a fix. Nothing happened. We stood transfixed. Something splashed in the water below that made us jump. I was beginning to relax when a horrible, unearthly, blood-curdling scream came from somewhere, freezing my whole neck and shoulders. I was completely disoriented, realising that the scream had come, not from up front, but from behind us.

I turned in horror to see Dinny Hoctor making savage chopping movements with his hands, his face a horrendous, livid mask.

We ran. We ran like hell, up McFarlane's Lane towards the lights above in Connaught Street. Dinny trailed erratically behind us, stopping to throw back his head and let out the strangest howling, mooing sounds that echoed all along the walls that lined the lane.

'I'm going home!' I told myself again and again, but I knew the test wasn't over. Momentum carried us along Connaught Street. We turned left, down Pearse Street hill. My mother's shop was all closed up but I could see the lights on in the bakery behind. I knew she would be staying late because a wedding cake had to be ready by the next day. Bells boomed from St Peter's, below in the square. St Mary's too rang out, more faintly, from across the river. Ten o'clock!

The courthouse was pale all over. The moon played hide-and-seek, winking in every window as we trotted past. Halfway down the hill, we veered left into the lane at the Munster & Leinster Bank. Shadow filled the narrow canyon between the houses. Our footsteps echoed off the windowless walls.

Down at the end, the ancient walls of the Protestant graveyard were bathed in light. A humpbacked hill rose high above them, stabbed with crooked crosses. A cage of solid iron crowned the crest.

A gate creaked and we froze. Huge yews heaved in the breeze. The night was warm but a shiver went down my back.

'Let's go in the gate,' said Tommy in a loud, hoarse whisper.

'What are we supposed to be doing?' Mickey demanded.

'Wait and see!'

We moved as one shadow towards the wrought-iron gate. The screech of hinges made us jump. We froze again.

'Okay,' whispered Tommy, 'let's—'

A sudden sound, like falling gravel, turned us to stone. My ears felt as big as trumpets and they homed in on something behind the crosses. It was a soft, dry sound, like someone shifting sand. A shadow moved. Then two more shadows. They were squat and shapeless, close to the ground. Something rose and fell from one of the shapes, with piston-like movements. The shapes rose up and became three men standing close together. Tall hats like chimney pots stood stark against the sky. Shaded faces were grey mottled masks in the moonlight. They were pulling something up out of the ground with ropes!

'Run!' yelled Tommy, and we raced back up the lane, right up Pearse Street hill and onto Connaught Street.

We stood panting for some time outside Jimmy the Barber's. Tommy was unusually silent.

'Was that your brother and the gang?' I asked.

He shook his head, looking puzzled.

'What next?' Mickey asked.

I tried not to think about what awaited me back home.

'Battery Hill,' said Tommy. There was something flat in his voice.

Twin lines edged the rising ridge, ancient scars of the sunken road that led up to Battery Hill. Grazing sheep were blobs of white, inching across the moonlight. The death's head rock face of the battery watched with empty eyes as we climbed up towards it.

'Jeez,' wheezed Tommy, as we topped the ridge. 'Let's have a break.'

'Gawd!' I gasped and we threw ourselves down on

the grass. I gazed back down the way we had come. 'Hey, where have Mickey and Dinny gone?'

'Weren't they right behind us?'

'They *were*, but they've just disappeared.'

We scanned the countryside below; not a sign of them.

'Ah, well,' said Tommy, meaning *just as well they're gone*. We wheezed and gasped for a bit.

'Right,' said Tommy, assuming his leadership role, 'let's push on.' He was on his feet.

'In a minute,' I said lazily, unwilling to always let him lead. But I had seen something. Down at the bottom of the little valley on the other side of the ridge, our stone school was squat and empty, part of the stony landscape. Standing way above it, on the opposite rim of the bowl-like valley, a perfect rounded hill had two sheep inching across its top. A perfect little stone entrance, that I knew was made with three great blocks of limestone, looked remarkably like a keyhole from where I lay.

'What do you see?' demanded Tommy.

'Nothing,' I fibbed. I thought I had seen a slight movement near the doorway. I guessed it was where the older gang members were holing up. There was a great big stone-lined room inside, slanting deep down into the earth. Rats and rubbish and the dark had always kept us hovering just inside the doorway, ready to run.

We were inside the sunken road now, heading up the hill. Right at the top, the double walls were still intact, rising above us to ten feet or more. We heard the thumping, regular muffled sounds of running feet.

'Quick! In here,' said Tommy. A niche had been built into the wall, probably a gun emplacement. The runners stopped, very near, just behind a jutting corner. The roadway was all sharp angles. Defensive little walls jutted out. They were built, Mr Finneran had told us, so that the soldiers could shoot from behind them if the enemy got in the road. They were so close that I could hear their wheezing breath. We held ours, listening too.

We heard them murmuring, then footsteps softly swishing through the grass. They paused, right beside us, looking the other way. Tommy nudged me hard in the ribs. We sprang out like wolves and grabbed our victims.

'Oh, Jaysus!' screamed Mickey when I grabbed him.

'Let go!' boomed Dinny, chopping down hard on Tommy's arms. Dinny let out one of his horrible howling sounds. My hair seemed to stand up straight.

'Shush, for God's sake!' said Tommy.

'Listen,' said Mickey, 'the rest of the gang are already inside the hill.'

'Doing what?' said Tommy.

'Telling ghost stories, that's what.'

Without another word, we headed across the valley. We knelt silently near the door, listening to the muffled voice of the storyteller. There was a faint glow behind the sacking that covered the doorway. We burst in, startling them.

'Hey!' said Dekkie. 'Where did you come out of?'

They sat in a circle, on rocks embedded in the earthen floor. Candles were stuck down on an oil drum in the centre, flickering shadows onto the walls behind them. Dripping stone had formed teeth on the ceiling.

'Shush!' called Dekkie. Everyone went still, listening. There were faint scuffling sounds, then heavy breathing at the doorway. A hand moved the sacking aside.

'Right,' said Sergeant Kelly, 'thought you might be in here.' He stood, massive, inside the doorway, a bicycle lamp in his hand. He switched it off. He called back over his shoulder: 'They're in here, Tom!'

Garda Tom Dowling came in, blinking owlishly.

We were escorted down the hillside in the moonlight. Not a word was spoken. We knew we were in deep trouble. Down Connaught Street we trudged, the two gardaí flanking us like outriders as they walked their bikes, the lamps lighting the way. Down the middle of the street we went. Not a car came by. Early stragglers coming up from the cinema stared at us but didn't utter a word.

The first stop was at Jimmy the Barber's, and we watched Mickey go in. Next was mine. The wicket gate had been left open and I heard men murmuring in the bar. My mother stood in the lighted hallway, her face as cold as stone.

'You come here now,' she said, her voice low and tight with anger. She was reaching up for something on the back of the door. She quickly twirled me round and I received three ferocious whacks on the backs of my legs. The pain seared right up through my body, but I was trying to see where Peggy was.

'Up to bed you get!' my mother said, pointing towards the stairs.

Peggy was looking into the sink, fiddling with something, as if unaware of what was going on.

I felt mortified more than anything, because Peggy had seen me being beaten. I longed to go to her, to tell her how sorry I was for telling fibs.

I couldn't sleep at all. The stinging in my legs didn't matter and soon died down. The pain I felt was where my heart was supposed to be. I felt pain because of Peggy. She hadn't even looked at me. I was sure I had got her into trouble. She was supposed to know where I was at all times. I wished with all my heart that Peggy was my mother. I felt that my mother was like the catechism we had at school. She stood for rules that had to be obeyed. If they were broken, you got punished. It was the same with my father. The catechism said to honour thy father and mother. I didn't really know what it meant. I knew I couldn't make myself love them, if that's what it meant. Maybe that was a mortal sin? I got really worried at that. If you got knocked down in the street in a state of mortal sin, you would go straight to hell. I thought of the awfulness of burning down there forever. I wondered how God could be so cruel. What in God's name was He thinking?

I realised I was sweating. I threw off the blankets. The first thing I had to do was get to confession as soon as possible. And I was going to be very careful crossing the street. Venial sins were nothing. A few minutes in the confession box, three Hail Marys and your soul was washed clean again. The thought of mortal sins, though, made me toss and turn.

I was amazed to discover that Peggy was shaking me out of a deep sleep.

'Time for school, sleepyhead!' She smiled. She was just the same as ever!

At breakfast, I didn't know what to say. Peggy bustled around the kitchen, exactly her same old self. There was no mention of the night before. I anxiously watched her every move. Suddenly I got down off my chair. Peggy was standing at the sink. I stood a moment then took hold of her apron at the hip. She turned, smiling down at me.

'Peggy,' I said, 'I'm really, really sorry!'

She gazed at me a moment. Then she turned and gave me a long hard hug. I felt my chest almost bursting with joy. I swore never, never again to tell fibs to Peggy. I never did.

Sins of Omission

~

1952

The Halligan house was on a sandy hill, way above Clonown bog. Early morning sun was burning off the mist. Turf banks rose high above the flatness, like moist chocolate cakes roughly sliced with a *slane*. A curlew called across the distance. The door was open long before we got to the house because of the barking sheepdog. Mrs Halligan gave us the warmest welcome. Her two sons were just finishing breakfast. Neither spoke for a while, concentrating on the business in hand.

'You know why I was christened Daniel?' enquired Danny Halligan.

We shook our heads. We knew he was going to tell us anyway.

'I was called after Daniel O'Connell, The Liberator. You know why?'

We responded silently, as before.

'It was because I was to be liberated from the slavery of work, free forever from all sweat and toil.' Danny looked serious and sincere.

Mrs Halligan bent down to us as she passed.

'Don't pay any attention to these lads at all,' she advised us, but she was amused.

Tommy grinned uneasily and squirmed in his chair. I didn't know what to think either.

'As for Larry,' continued Danny, nodding at his brother in the other chair, 'he had an even more interesting christening.'

'I was called after Lawrence of Arabia,' said Larry seriously, slurping the last of his tea.

I nearly burst out laughing. The vision of Larry aboard a camel clashed violently with the picture of Larry, with his battered hat and droopy eyes, on his ancient, rusty bike.

'What's the joke?' said Tommy to me out of the corner of his mouth.

'Fella called Lawrence of Arabia. It's in one of the comics. I'll tell you later,' I said.

'Now, lads,' said Mrs Halligan, 'quit the clownin'. These young *gossins* are here to gather mushrooms and they have mothers waitin' for them back home.'

Dekkie Brady, Tommy's older brother, was waiting for us outside.

'I see you have another guest waiting for you, Larry,' said Dekkie with a grin. He was looking down at the Halligans' chicken-coop. It was a big cage, completely covered with chicken-wire, like an upturned shoebox. Just outside the coop, a beautiful fox lay stretched out, dead, a slim wire noose around his neck. Inside the wire, a big red hen stepped slowly along, pausing to peck uncertainly at the ground. She paused on one leg and looked up, letting out a long, slow cackling sound, as if thinking about something. A rooster strode about, as if he owned the place.

'Y'see,' said Larry, 'what chickens require is not just good-quality food but a sense of security. These girls,' he said, nodding towards the chickens, 'are happy hens and produce the best eggs for miles around.'

'How do you manage to catch the fox every time?' Dekkie asked.

Larry shook his head. 'For security reasons, I cannot disclose that information. Word gets around.'

Dekkie grinned. We all knew Larry was a frequent visitor to the garda station in town to collect bounty on his foxes' tails. He lifted the fox, undid the wire noose and threw the body into a little wooden shed.

'So, where do we get the magic mushrooms, Larry?' said Tommy, trying to sound like Dekkie.

Larry gave him a sideways look from under his hooded lids.

'The first thing you need to know is the mushrooms *not* to pick. Some would kill you as dead as that fox.' He nodded towards the shed. 'Let's go!'

We started straight across the bog. It was like walking across a giant sponge cake that had a well-baked crust on top.

'Hey,' said Larry. He dropped on one knee in the hip-high heather and signalled us to do the same. We went still as he was, waiting. Then he carefully pointed.

Two rabbits were silently frolicking in a clearing. They suddenly became still, as if enjoying the sunshine. Larry silently waved us down further into the heather then pointed again. It was a fox. Sliding around a turf bank, creeping almost on his belly like a cat, the fox edged in little stages towards the rabbits. We went still as stone. Larry carefully wet his finger and held it to the breeze. He waved his hand to show that we were downwind from the fox. Now he was reaching behind him. He gripped a dry sod of turf, stood up suddenly and heaved it at the fox. Rabbits and fox disappeared in an instant.

'Hey, what was the idea?' said Dekkie, clearly puzzled.

Larry grinned. 'They were *my* rabbits he was after. I'll be back for them tomorrow.'

That made sense. Larry supplied a lot of the rabbits for sale in town.

Yellow clumps of furze covered the rise so that the great deep basin behind it came as a surprise. We squelched across the marshy grass towards a grove of silver birch that shivered in the lightest breeze. Up on the left rim of the basin was a tiny shack. A white-bearded man sat smoking his pipe in front of a fire on which a little tin kettle was blowing steam. Behind him, three small children were turning turf. Two bigger boys were footing sods. A third was finishing a perfect rick. Larry waved and pointed ahead. The man waved back and nodded.

In the birch grove was a tiny, ruined cottage. Rough new thatch covered the end from which a tall stone chimney poked up through the trees. Larry pulled carefully on one of the rotted barn doors that closed off the space. Right inside was a new stone chimney breast, roughly made. Sitting on top, like a kettle on a hob, was a great big copper cylinder, like the one in our new bathroom. This one, though, had a strange, conical hood with a long, thin pipe curling away from it. It dipped down into a wooden barrel like a big swan's neck.

'Shit!' breathed Dekkie, clearly impressed.

'What is it?' Tommy asked.

'It's a still,' said Larry, surveying us now with a hard, cold look from under hooded lids.

'We didn't see a thing, Larry, did we, lads?' said Dekkie, bending a similar look on us.

'I didn't see anthin',' said Tommy. 'Did you?' he said, looking at me.

I shook my head.

'I didn't see a thing,' I said. 'I'll only remember gathering mushrooms.'

Larry nodded soberly at us. The man with the white beard arrived. He looked at us suspiciously then looked at Larry. Larry nodded reassuringly and the man relaxed.

'How many?' the man asked.

'Give us two,' said Larry. The man poked around in a pile of sacking and handed two bottles of clear liquid to Larry.

'Is this genuine holy water, Father?' demanded Larry, like a querulous housewife.

'Blessed by my own fair hand, my son,' replied the man with a straight face.

Dekkie grinned.

'Right,' said Larry, making to move, 'we'll settle up later!' He slid the clinking bottles into a little sack he'd had inside his coat.

'Right you are,' said the man.

'I'll get that basket from you now,' said Larry.

The man rummaged in the gloom and handed Larry a large, rectangular, butcher-boy's basket. He passed it to Dekkie.

We came up out of the basin onto a kind of high, flat plain. Tall, thin grass waved in the breeze. We headed towards another grove, with larger, older trees, beside a little stream. Larry was looking to left and right as we approached it. Suddenly he went down on one knee, parting the grass.

'See!' He pointed down. There was a little cluster of whitish mushrooms near a fallen tree trunk.

'What do you see?' he demanded of Dekkie.

'I'd say,' said Dekkie cautiously, 'they're not the right colour.'

Larry was nodding.

'Look closely,' said Larry to all of us. 'What colour would you call that?'

'It's slightly green,' I said, 'or yellow green.'

'Dead right!' said Larry, 'dead being the operative word. These are *death cap* mushrooms. Don't, on your life, ever eat them, or even pick them!'

We nodded solemnly. We saw hedgehog and milk-cap mushrooms, trumpets of death and all the warning signs to look for before Larry showed us the puffballs. He carefully cut one with his penknife.

'This is what you look for,' he said, one knee on the ground. He sliced the mushroom top to bottom. 'If it's white the whole way through, you're safe.'

We went home with a full basket of puffballs strapped to the carrier of Dekkie's bike.

I was in the kitchen doing my homework a week later when Peggy said, 'You're still scratching your leg, John-John!'

'Peggy, please, I'm not taking that medicine any more. It makes me vomit!'

I had ringworm behind my right knee and there was much discussion as to whether I had got it from Johnny Madden's pony or some cat that had it.

My mother came in. 'Is he still scratching?' she enquired of Peggy, as if I wasn't there.

'He is,' she said, and they launched again into the possible source of the infection. I got stuck into my sums until I realised they had stopped talking. I found them gazing at me speculatively. 'Will I have to take that medicine again?' I asked, trying to look as green about the gills as possible.

'No, you won't,' said my mother in her businesslike manner. 'Peggy is going to take you to someone tomorrow morning who'll clear it up.' With a nod at Peggy, she was gone.

I was puzzled next morning when Peggy, as usual, turned into Doyle's corner shop.

'Peggy, I thought we were going to see someone about my ringworm.'

'We are,' she said mysteriously. 'Just wait and see.'

Dermot Doyle came clumping out from the cold room. He was a great big, hearty, red-faced man, with fish-scales all up his red-raw arms. He wore a hat, a white shop coat and big black wellies.

'Peggy, my darling, is this a special visit or is it the usual pet rabbit for your stew?'

Metal bars ran the length of the plate-glass windows near the top. Rabbits hung upside down from them every few inches. Great big fish, on beds of ice, stared vacantly and unmoving below them on the tiles. Dermot claimed he did business on two streets from the one corner shop.

'No, Dermot,' said Peggy. 'I've come in today because John-John here has ringworm.'

'Well, here's the very man,' said Dermot, looking out the window. We saw Larry Halligan coming down the steps from the garda station across the street.

'Just wait here a minute, John-John,' said Peggy and she went out to meet him. I watched them from inside. Larry was nodding slowly, then they came in together.

'John-John,' said Peggy, 'Larry is going to look after your ringworm. I'll be back in a few minutes.'

I was too surprised to say anything as she went out the door.

'John-John,' exclaimed Larry, 'how were the mushrooms?'

'Great!' I answered dumbly, wondering what was coming next.

'Doctor,' said Dermot, 'have you brought that special

medicine for me rheumatism?'

'I have indeed, my good man.' So saying, Larry took out from an inside pocket one of the bottles of clear liquid we had got up the bog from the white-bearded man.

'Now,' said Larry, before handing it over, 'take two teaspoons before every meal or any time the missus isn't looking. Have you got that?'

'Thanks, Doctor. We'll settle up later. Now, do you want to take this lad into the back room?'

'That'll do. Come on, John-John, and we'll have a look at your ringworm.'

'Larry,' I said, in the back room, 'you can't be a seventh son of a seventh son.'

'Why can't I be?'

'You can't because there's only Danny and you and your mother.'

Larry nodded, as if he agreed.

'Let's have a look at your ringworm first,' he said.

He examined the itchy patch on the back of my leg.

'Yes, it's ringworm,' he said. He was rubbing his hands together slowly, staring vacantly, as if he had gone into a daze. As if he was miles away, he said, 'Show me that spot again.'

I turned around. A rough thumb gently traced the red ring behind my knee. He was completely still and silent for once. The whole hardened hand then wrapped around the back of my knee. I was interested enough in this new experience to remain still for a time, but nothing was happening and I was feeling the first stirrings of restlessness. Questions were beginning to form when a surge of energy up my spine created a strange heat that began to pour like liquid down into my legs. I was shocked but unable to move until I realised the hand was no longer at the back of my knee.

Larry had collapsed into a chair, face white and looking exhausted. He had the same faraway look.

'Are you okay, Larry?'

Slowly he grinned and turned his attention on me. 'I will be, in a minute.' He paused, as if assessing me. 'So will you be, in about a week.'

I sat on an upturned crate. I suddenly became aware of Dermot's loud banter in the shop outside.

'But your father has to be a seventh son, too,' I said.

Larry focused on me for some time. 'My father was the last of seven sons who emigrated. He was helping to rebuild Great Britain after the war when his pickaxe hit a gas main, digging trenches for cables. He was blown to bits, leaving a wife and seven sons at home in Clonown.'

I started frowning, unable to work out the seven sons bit.

Larry was nodding, looking at me. 'Three of my brothers went to Australia and one to Canada. Another brother was helping to make America great. He was working on the top of a big dam out in Colorado when he slipped and fell. It took a long time to dig him out of the wet concrete down below. He left a wife and four kids.'

He gazed at me with a slight smile, his eyes gleaming. The door opened and Dermot stuck his head in. He spoke softly, as if in church.

'Peggy is here, if you're finished.'

'We're finished,' said Larry quietly and we both got up.

Later, at home, Peggy said:

'You never said much about your trip last week up to Halligans' house. Did you enjoy it?' She gazed at me, smiling, as if expecting my usual detailed account of events.

'Oh, it was great,' I said. I told her all about the chickens and the dead fox. Then I described the rabbits playing and how the fox started creeping up on them. I told her in some detail about all the different kinds of mushroom, which ones were deadly, which ones you could eat and what you had to do to get them ready for eating. Then I ran out of things to say. She gazed at me steadily, a slight smile playing around her lips.

'So,' she said at length, 'you learned a lot from that trip?'

'Yes,' I said, 'I think we did.'

The Crotty Sisters

~

1952

In 1952 I was put on trial for a crime I did not
commit. I was eight years old. The injured parties,
two old spinsters in their eighties, also happened to be
prosecutors, judges and jury. They were, in addition,
the sole testifying witnesses to the alleged incident.
This could be stated as follows: that the accused,
myself, did conspire with a person or persons unknown
to cause serious embarrassment and loss of dignity in
a public place. The crime in question was perpetrated
in St Peter's Catholic Church, by the simple device of
dropping hard-dried peas into the broad brims of the
sisters' hats from the organ loft above. The injured
parties, the aforementioned elderly sisters, had been
engaged in fervent prayer in the course of an unduly
long high Mass. The real culprit was my erstwhile bosom
pal Tommy Brady. He had quickly assumed his original
place in the choir, along with an expression of shocked
innocence. I was left leaning over the balustrade, staring

down, wondering what he had been up to.

Never mind the injustice of it, my mother had advised. Just go down to the sisters and somehow put it right and don't forget to address each of them as Miss Crotty and not ma'am. We would deal, she said with a significant look, with Master Tommy Brady later.

So one day after school, I walked down the hill from our shop to where the Crotty sisters lived.

In the 1940s and fifties it was de rigueur for any institution or establishment worthy of the name to be regulated by the measured tones of a Faller clock. Suppliers of these timepieces, at least to our town, Athlone, were J. M. Crotty & Son.

J. M. & Son were long dead, but the legend of their commerce over generations still lived on, at least on the ancient sign above the shop, which creaked and swung in the wind.

Dust gathered on the clocks in the window, long stopped, but down the length of a long, tiled hallway, in the Crotty sisters' sitting room, the afternoon tea ceremony was drawing to a close. Flower-patterned china and chintz glowed in the dim light of lamps, but my attention was focused on the chocolate éclairs, cream doughnuts and butterfly cakes arranged round the rim of a doily atop a silver cake stand.

It's hard for an eight-year-old to sit up straight on a rigid kitchen chair, trying to look remorseful and at the same time respectful while salivating over a shameless display of confectionery. Oddly enough, some of the more elaborate offerings seemed to match the headgear the sisters were wearing.

They had kept their hats on, as if they had just come in from yet another visit to the church. Their coats and silver foxes had however been discarded. One fox was carefully draped along the top of an armchair, in crouching position, his eyes fixed intently on me. I had often been subjected to similar scrutiny throughout the course of an endless Mass in St Peter's. This one looked as if at any moment he could spring at my throat, but he continued to lie doggo, and every time I glanced at him, it seemed his face took on an increasingly cynical expression.

The other fox was similarly draped over another chair, but he had his back to me, and his tail hung halfway down the side of the chair, his black, useful-looking claws hung uselessly too, as if all effort at self-expression had long been abandoned.

The Crotty sisters, Laetitia and Elizabeth, otherwise Letty and Lizzy, in their eighties at the time, were two small, wizened, bird-like creatures, dressed all in black. They sat in matching carvers behind the vast mahogany table at the back of the room, like judges on their bench, and I sat on the chair provided, in the centre of the room, facing them. A tall, long-case clock stood behind each of them, like watchful sentries, ponderously dividing the silence of the room between them.

That tea was apparently over was signalled when the slightly older sister, Elizabeth, or Lizzy, delicately dabbed her lips with a large white napkin, and oh so carefully removed a crumb from the corner of her lips, as if giving a lesson in finesse. Letty's and Lizzy's napkins seemed to arrive at the same time, as if in tandem, onto their laps.

Letty looked at Lizzy, examining her face, and Lizzy looked back in like manner at Letty. This was how they communicated. They were deciding who should speak first, and I sat bolt upright in the witness box, looking from one to the other, trying to guess which one would speak first. It was, in fact, Lizzy who spoke first. She had been examining me with those unmoving, red-rimmed eyes for some time before making her first pronouncement. Turning to Letty, she said in that slow, croaking voice that was an exact replica of her sister's, 'I thought at first he was like the father, but do you know, I think now he's more like the mother.'

They spoke as if I were not in the room at all, and I was for a moment tempted to look over my shoulder to see if there was someone else behind me, to whom these remarks could possibly refer. But of course, I knew that was how adults spoke about children, especially if they were on trial.

Defendants in these cases were considered to have forfeited all rights. In fact, strictly speaking, they did not exist at all, except as problems to be examined and addressed. I suspected that certain laws were being abrogated but I was not in a position to contest this.

'And do you know,' said Letty, 'the parents are so hard-working. And his poor mother! How does she manage a business at all and she having seven children!'

'Oh, she's a saint!' declared Lizzy, gazing off into some distance behind my head. Or maybe she was staring at that china clock, with its tiny tick, that measured time in its own way on the sideboard behind me.

In fact, the whole room was a madness of clocks, ticking, tocking or chiming with a kind of syncopated, slow-motion frenzy. In the long pauses between the sisters' pronouncements, which seemed in keeping with the measured rhythms of the room, I found myself trying to identify and place, without moving or looking, each of the timepieces I had noticed before the sisters' impressive entrance.

'And the father,' said Letty. 'Sure the man is always working hard, trying to improve and increase his business.'

The clock behind Lizzy began chiming at this very moment, and a few seconds later, the one behind Letty went into its routine. The sisters consulted their personal timepieces. Lizzy extracted an ornamental fob-watch from some hidden crevice in the folds of her breast, and consulted it like a hospital matron checking on her patient, in this case, the tall sentinel of a long-case clock behind her.

'Mr. Dickens is behind time today, I see!'

'It's Shakespeare that's a bit fast, I think,' said Letty, having consulted the minuscule gold watch on her wrist, with much squinting and turning it towards the light.

Shakespeare? Dickens? I'd heard of those two.

I examined each of the clocks in turn myself, before turning my gaze on the sisters. They had both gone into musing mode.

'Ah!' declared Lizzy at last, clearly having given the situation much consideration 'They're great business people altogether.'

'Well, that they are,' agreed Letty, having thought about it for a while.

The clocks went about their business for some considerable time, and I listened to them carefully, until I realised that both sets of owls' eyes were examining me with a new intensity that I felt did not bode well for the outcome of the proceedings.

'So, what's to be done with this young man?' Lizzy said to no one in particular.

The clocks and I all waited for the answer to that one.

'You know,' resumed Lizzy, 'the dean used to talk about what a good voice this young man had.'

'Maybe as good as Louis Browne, didn't he say?'

'Do you remember Louis singing when he was a young man just like—'

'Oh, I remember him well. And Count John's voice, do you remember?'

Count John? I would certainly always remember him. It was the awful wet summer the year before. My Aunt Sarah lay dying of cancer at the top of that beautiful house down on O'Connell Street, next door to the old residence of the Bishop of Elphin. She loved the singing of John McCormack, but could not stand even that sound near her. My maternal grandmother, who was looking after the family at the time, installed the gramophone in the hallway, and the pure, reedy tones of Count John carried up the stairwell, three floors up the narrow winding stair, through the open door of her daughter's room, and that's how it was for the last two months of her life. I was sent up to help and was immediately put in charge of the gramophone. My grandmother's instructions were clear and precise, and she would issue them only once. She surveyed the world with calm severity through round steel-framed spectacles that sat firmly on her aquiline nose and made her look like De Valera.

It was the constant rain, the solemn silence of that house, the expectation of death and the reek of cabbage that filled the whole house that will forever be associated in my mind with the singing of Count John McCormack.

'The poor, poor dean!' Letty said, and her partner in keening took up the lament.

'Oh, if only he was still alive,' said Lizzy, the way the faithful responded to prayers given out by the priest in Mass.

I knew of course that that was how people went on after funerals, and that it could go on for some time, especially if they were in the snug of a pub after a few dry sherries.

'If the dean was here now,' Letty told Lizzy, 'he'd want to be listening to his favourite arias.'

I also knew what that was all about. The dean had been a founding member of the music society and was a frequent visitor to the Crotty sisters' musical evenings.

'What about some Verdi? Wouldn't he love to hear

some Verdi or Donizetti if he was here?'

'He would indeed,' agreed Letty, and so saying, rose unsteadily and made towards the gramophone in the corner.

That's when I suddenly saw the light. The glint on the cut-glass decanter behind the huge, flowered teapot and on the little delicate sherry glasses beside their cups gave the game away. More than afternoon tea, I'd say!

'Excuse me, Miss Crotty,' I suddenly blurted out, seeing my chance, 'can I do that for you?'

They stared at me in amazement, as if I had spoken out of turn. Lizzy looked at Letty, and Letty looked at Lizzy. It seemed it was Lizzy's turn to speak:

'Do you know how to manage a gramophone?' she asked stiffly. Judgement had not yet been officially handed down, you see.

'Oh, yes,' I said eagerly, and immediately launched into the whole story about Count John McCormack and my Aunt Sarah dying, and I could see that they were impressed by the fact that she had lived next door to the old residence of the Bishop. I placed special emphasis on my function as a changer of gramophone records, implying all the while that I was a lover of the great man's singing, and giving them clearly to understand that I appreciated the preciousness of each and every gramophone record and the necessity to place the needle of the arm with the utmost delicacy in the correct groove. In short, I laid it on thick, benefiting at last from my time as understudy to the redoubtable Tommy Brady.

I'm not sure that they were wholly convinced, but a potent mix of sherry, sentiment and salesmanship won out in the end and before they knew it, the strains of some operatic piece began to quietly emanate from the machine. It gradually swelled in volume and drama until the whole room, even the house, seemed to vibrate with what I began to realise was wonderful singing. It turned out to be the famous sextet from Donizetti's *Lucia di Lammermoor*. I had never heard it before, or anything like it.

When it was over, I found the sisters examining me with interest.

'Well,' said Lizzy very quietly in the deep silence of the room, 'it must be well past this young man's teatime.'

They looked pleased with me, as if the alchemy of the music had wrought some fundamental change. I think it had.

Unexpectedly, I felt a familiar movement inside. It was as if something had arisen from the subconscious to tug at my sleeve. My blood began to race, pounding in my ears, as if I could hear the drumming of myriad hooves across a plain. It was the call of the wild. I remembered the gang and longed to run with them again, even to watch the older ones smoking, spitting and talking about sex as we stood inside a barn watching the rain.

Suddenly I was on my feet.

'Thank you, Miss Crotty!' I said, sort of bowing slightly in Lizzy's direction.

'Thank you, Miss Crotty!' I said to Letty. I practically

curtsied as I did so but remembered myself in time.

'Forgot my tea!' I called as I bolted out the door. I left them smiling and nodding at each other, as if they understood.

Some months later, I arrived home just before dark. I was soaked, frozen and late. It had taken Tommy and me ages to clean down the ponies up in Johnny Madden's yard.

My mother and older sister stared at me as I entered the kitchen. They were standing still, holding forgotten cups of tea.

'What?' I said.

'Old Miss Crotty has died!'

'Which one?'

'Old Miss Lizzy Crotty.'

'Oh!' I couldn't take it in.

I could see old Miss Lizzy Crotty smiling benignly as I left their sitting room. What did dead mean? Just gone, empty, nothing?

'I want to talk to you about something later,' my mother said with her significant look.

After tea, my mother said, 'Old Miss Letty Crotty has asked for you to sing at the requiem Mass.'

'What?' I was shocked.

Tommy Brady and I had had to leave the choir. Tommy thought it did his reputation on the street no harm. I was sorry we had had to leave. There was the difference between us. We were the only two riders in our gang. His aim was to establish a reputation for bravado. I was considered the more skilful rider, but he was more daring. To my mind, the things he did were just stupid and dangerous. He jibed me for being too cautious. He had had a couple of quite serious accidents, of which he was inordinately proud. I simply had no wish to break a leg or risk injuring my spine.

All this was going through my head as I sat at the kitchen table.

'Sing in the choir, you mean?'

'No. Miss Crotty has asked that you sing "Panis Angelicus" solo.'

'I can't do that!' I spluttered.

My mother was gazing at me calmly, nodding her head. 'What would the gang think?' she said sarcastically.

I felt angry, because she had put her finger on it.

'That Tommy Brady is all about physical courage,' she said. 'Think about *moral* courage, son.'

After evening devotions, I went down to the church to see Miss Ryan, the choir mistress. I felt far from committed to the promise I had made my mother.

The church below the choir hummed with a large congregation for the requiem Mass. To me it was the sound of anticipation. It terrified me.

I had met Tommy Brady on the steps outside.

'So,' he said, smirking, 'you're singing the "Panis"?' His whole attitude expressed contempt. Would that be the attitude of the gang? I climbed the stairs to the organ loft in an agony of indecision.

Miss Ryan was just finishing her instructions to the senior choir. She fixed her steady gaze on me. She was small, bespectacled and calm. 'No need to be nervous,' she murmured. 'You can sing the "Panis". Just do what I told you to do.'

I faced the altar and waited. I had no idea if Tommy would be down below. I knew that Miss Crotty would be sitting just below the organ loft, my mother beside her. The crowd stirred like a seething sea.

The organ started, startling me. It resounded mightily through a vibrating church.

Miss Ryan was nodding to me. I counted, breathing as she had instructed.

The hymn was born somewhere in my lower abdomen. It swelled and grew in volume until my diaphragm and then my whole head seemed to vibrate with it. It opened up my tightened heart. It sang from my soul, turned it up towards something sacred, something infinitely higher. I was a particle in willing service to this infinity. My voice brought it to a close, leaving me cleansed by fire.

Afterwards, Miss Ryan patted me on the shoulder and murmured, 'Well done!', as if it was the most normal thing in the world.

My mother and Miss Crotty were waiting for me below. Miss Crotty stood completely still, her eyes wide open and fixed on me as I approached. Tears welled up, and she gripped my hands fiercely in her little claw-like hands, staring into my face.

My mother said nothing. Her smile was enough.

I need not have worried about the gang. Nobody even mentioned the requiem Mass when I met them later that week.

My mother was right about something else. Miss Letty Crotty, as predicted, followed her sister to the grave just three months later.

Vindication at the Ritz

~

1952

By the time I was eight years old, in 1952, there was already talk of pulling down the old Ritz Cinema in Athlone.

Clearly visible from the bridge, the cinema perched on piles rising from the river bank, the rear of its sagging bulk sort of leaning on the town's ancient ramparts. The Ritz legend blinked on and off in outsize red and yellow neon. It was a beacon in the dark and rain and fog of winter, a Hollywood come-hither in the balmy nights of summer. The stories of this cinema and its commissionaire, Mickser Daly, are inextricably linked.

Mickser stood sentinel at the back entrance. His dictum – 'No ticket, no entry' – paved or barred the way to the pit. Closest to the screen, the pit was the repository of the cheapest, fourpenny, seats. It was also host to the cinema's real entertainers, the group of local yokels known as the Town Criers. The speciality and assumed function of these characters was to entertain the audience when Hollywood's best, or worst, failed to do so. To Mickser Daly's mind, they represented chaos. He represented order. They were natural enemies.

B-movies were the Criers favourites, when the full range of services they offered could be brought into play. This could involve orchestrating raucous boos, cheers, slow clapping, or a chorus of whistles or heckling. Staples included advice shouted at full volume to favourite targets like Ronald Reagan, John Wayne or Mickey Rooney, who of course remained impervious to all remarks. This offered a forum in which the Criers competed keenly to deliver the wittiest remark, to howls of approval and laughter from the audience. They kept an eye on Mickser at all times, and made their comments on him sotto voce.

Mickser stood at the back. His lips moved under his fading moustache and the long torch clasped behind him wagged slowly like the tail of a dog.

The Criers free translation service was much appreciated, especially when applied to sequences featuring Tonto and the Lone Ranger. This could involve a curious melange of Amerindian and Wild West idioms – albeit tinged with the local accent – voice-over commentary, or macho dialogue delivered in a loud falsetto. Conversations between Roy Rogers and his wonder horse, Trigger, would of course include replies from the four-legged friend in a peculiar whinnying parlance.

Their best work probably was to be experienced when Indian chiefs spoke Indian and Indian Scout John

Wayne, or equivalent, would be obliged to translate for unaccountably dumb US Cavalry officers. These heavy-duty macho exchanges were not only naturally rendered in pure falsetto or mock-contralto with the usual voice-over commentary, but also featured additional dialogue that converted an otherwise lacklustre script to high entertainment status.

Sound effects provided by the Criers included vocal renderings of the theme music of the weekly serials, with special choral backing for the cliffhanger bits that ended each episode. Vocal hoof-drumming sounds were provided as a matter of course for galloping horses, as were renderings of steam train whistles disappearing sadly into the vast night. If the soundtrack quality was poor when John Wayne's fist connected with some villain's jaw, they made up the deficit. They had a field day when *Batman & Robin* featured, providing Pows!, Whams! and Splats!, for fist–jaw connections, as per the comic-strip version.

Kissing scenes were the house speciality. The commencement of this service was also a signal for Mickser to begin patrolling the aisles, his torch wagging slowly behind him. As heroine and hero closed in on each other, eyes closed, lips puckered in readiness for the climactic clinch, the Criers provided the background violins or anticipated the ecstasy of meeting lips with protracted tearing, ripping or sucking sounds, in case the audience was not sure what was going on. Sometimes, as a special treat at such moments, one of the Criers would loudly break wind, or in lieu of that, provide the appropriate sound effects to simulate same. It goes without saying that volume, purity of rendition and especially timing were of the essence at such opportune moments.

Mickser invariably resumed his watching brief from the rear at this juncture, as if he had given up.

The kissing couples up in the back rows of the balcony, referred to as the Gods, of course pretended not to hear any of this, but many a romance was ruined before it even got started by an inappropriate splutter of laughter as two pairs of puckered lips were about to meet in anticipated ecstasy. Privacy in those privileged seats was not guaranteed either if the Criers, in a lull between their activities, happened to turn their attention on them. And woe betide any girl whose name they knew, or whose reputation was known to them, because free advice, in graphic detail, would be offered on how to proceed. It was the same advice, freely offered, to the actors on the screen, be it Ava Gardner, Jane Russell or Lana Turner, as the heroine's puckered lips, with eyes closed, gravitated tentatively towards the hero's lips and waiting embrace.

Sometimes the detail of advice offered became so lurid that suddenly the house lights would come on and the black-and-white imagery on the screen flipped madly before stopping and the soundtrack distorted as it groaned to a halt. In tandem with the flipping images up front, Commissionaire Mickser, in his chocolate-brown uniform with brass buttons and visored cap, would come furiously limping down the aisle, flicking his now useless torch to left and right.

"Who's . . . who's . . .?" he would predictably shout.

His enquiry never got beyond those first two words. Faces of potential culprits, blinking in the spotlight, had become masks of exaggerated innocence and indignation.

So without the culprits being identified, the film resumed as the house lights dimmed, and a rising chant of 'Who's . . . who's . . .?' began to swell in the semi-darkness. And if it didn't overstep the mark, the status quo could remain in place, until the next infringement, in the form of intimate advice, once again too freely dispensed to Hollywood's finest, to raucous applause, cheers and whistles from the audience.

Sometimes, of course, a voice was recognised and Mickser would swoop from the darkness, catching the culprit in the full beam of his torch. Such successes, however, were relatively rare, but when they occurred, they resulted in the culprit being publicly frogmarched towards the exit and unceremoniously ejected, to a chorus of jeers, boos, whistles and slow clapping from the crowd. In a perverse way, the culprit thereby became a local hero and poor Mickser Daly the villain of the piece.

Once the show was over, two sets of double doors flew open to disgorge a blinking, hypnotised crowd into the harsh reality of daylight or winter darkness and driving rain.

Mickser would remain to close up shop. He would don his ancient brown tweed overcoat, mount his rickety bike and head for the cold comfort of home. The uniform then was curiously neutralised and he was no longer the demonised buffoon of the pit aisles. Mounting that bike was clearly a painful experience, pumping the pedals to instigate locomotion even more so and he looked just a frail old man, already a relic of another era. Vindictive queries about his alleged war wounds, albeit directed at him from the safety of the crowd, never elicited a single reaction.

Once, as he was departing after a matinee show, his famous peaked cap was whipped off by a vicious wind and landed at my feet. Instinctively I grabbed it and the residual respect for older people, inculcated by my granny, was suddenly evinced.

'Where are you going, John-John?' Peggy called. She was chatting and laughing with Mrs Maher after the Abbott and Costello film. I just waved as I headed towards Mickser.

The bike had shuddered to a halt, perished brakes protesting.

'Here's your hat, Mr Daly,' I said, proffering it.

He became completely still, wild wind tossing wisps of hair, and transfixed me with those red-rimmed eyes. 'You're a good lad,' he eventually croaked, with that peculiar, slight overlay of an English accent.

'Mr Daly,' I said hesitantly, 'where did you really get your war wounds?'

He looked at me for what seemed a long time, a peculiar ancient staring down at a small boy in short trousers, the forgotten cap clutched to the right handlebar.

'I got this leg,' he said, patting it carefully, 'in Suvla Bay, Gallipoli, August 1915.'

'Where's Suvla Bay?'

'Turkey, lad. Aye, Turkey.'

He had gone still as stone, staring out across the river, or maybe back into the past.

'I was with the 10th Irish Division, under Lt. General Sir Bryan Mahon – an Irishman, mind you! D Company of the 7th Dublins was our outfit.'

'And?'

'We set sail for Gallipoli July the tenth, landed Suvla Bay August seventh.'

'What's war like?'

He inhaled deeply, as if pondering how to seriously answer my question. 'We landed on the beach without maps or orders. Our Division's artillery pieces never arrived. We were so short of water that men nearly killed each other for a drink.' He licked his lips, looking deep inside, as if he were experiencing the whole thing again. 'Then our ammunition ran out, and we ended up throwing stones at the Turks.' He stared at me, as if to see if I could imagine such a thing.

'So how did you get that wound?'

He looked down at his leg contemplatively, as if trying to remember. 'There was a young lad at the end of the trench I was in. He was catching grenades and throwing them back at the Turks. Can you imagine that?' He paused to scrutinise my face.

I slowly shook my head.

'He caught five. The sixth blew him to pieces. And

bits of the same grenade caught me in the leg as I was climbing out of the trench.'

I told my mother the whole story when I got home. She always said that my reports of the goings-on at the Ritz were better than the productions themselves, but this story she took seriously.

My mother knew everybody who was anybody in town. She had known Mr Begley, the manager of the cinema, since they were going to dances together, and she went to see him. They came up with a plan that had an impact on several people's lives.

My mother felt strongly that Mickser's story called for recognition. After much discussion it was decided that Mr Begley would put on a special film show, featuring old Pathé newsreels, from his father's collection, which dealt with the whole Gallipoli and Suvla Bay episode. The declared purpose of the show was to honour all those Irishmen, long forgotten, even reviled, who had died in that campaign. It was also to acknowledge the part played by one local survivor, Corporal Michael 'Mickser' Daly, on the occasion of his retirement as commissionaire.

The Ritz was packed for the special show. We saw reel after reel of old black-and-whites, with the same plummy BBC-type voice-overs. We saw the bodies, the trenches, the hopeless situation, the hardships and the incredible bravery.

There was dead silence in the pit that night. When the two sets of double doors at last flew open, it was to disgorge a much-subdued collection of individuals, each immersed in deep thought. There was some discreet rubbernecking, curious eyes seeking out the normally ubiquitous commissionaire, but Mickser Daly was nowhere to be seen.

Mickser died peacefully at home a year later. I wrote a poem at the time in which I imagined one of the myriad little white crosses on that hill above Suvla Bay marking the spot where Mickser's own youth had died.

Scorched Earth

1953

The banshee wail of the air raid siren tore the night in two. Three pairs of feet hit the attic floor at the same time. Befuddled by sleep, we pushed the wooden table under the open skylight, making a loud scraping sound. I slammed the chair on top, my older brother already climbing up.

'What do you see, what do you see?' we called.

'Holy God!' he cried.

'What?' I could see the sky above all red and moving.

'It's the whole of Clonown, one solid blaze!'

'Lemme see, c'mon!' He stepped carefully down and up I scrambled.

'Holy ...'

'C'mon, what do you see?' It was my younger brother this time.

A massive wall of flame was moving steadily across Clonown bog. The midsummer sky was still light to the west behind it. Black, oily smoke billowed up in ragged waves.

The siren dipped down to a hopeless wail then started up all over again. You would think the German or British bombers were coming. The siren had been installed on top of the castle wall during the Emergency, in case of invasion by either side. That never happened but the siren stayed where it was. It just became the town fire alarm. To hear it go off in the middle of the night was the most exciting sound I knew.

The old fire engine joined the din below in the square. We heard it clanging into the hollow chamber of Barrack Street then wheezing its way up Pearse Street hill. When it turned the corner at the top, we raced down the winding attic stairs and ran to the sitting-room window to watch it come up Connaught Street, the bell clanging like a noisy toy. This happened at least once every single summer and it was all we would see because we were never allowed anywhere near the bog fires up Clonown.

Faintly in the distance came another fire-engine sound, clanging up the hill from Magazine Road. Both engines must have met. There was a pause, then the two engines roared and whined with effort, as they tightly turned up and over Battery Bridge. We heard them faintly repeat each other as they gradually melted down the bog road and out towards Clonown.

Men had come out of the pubs and stood in the street below. Some were pointing at the rosy sky above the rooftops. Others were shouting up the length of the street to men from another pub. We couldn't make out what they were saying.

Above the noise, I heard the familiar fire-engine sound, faintly in the distance, from across the river. The bell sound became louder as it got onto the bridge, echoing across the water. The engine banged lustily across the square, followed by a second engine! The whole thing was repeated as two more fire engines roared up our street, crossing Battery Bridge and getting swallowed up in the distance that was Clonown bog.

'Jeepers,' said my older brother. 'Let's go down in the street!'

'You'll do no such thing,' said my mother crossly, coming in behind us. 'You'll go straight back up to bed!'

Peggy came quietly in behind, smiling at our excitement. She was in her long nightdress, her wavy hair all loose. We trooped reluctantly out.

I said quietly to Peggy in the doorway, 'Peggy, I won't be able to sleep. Can I have a glass of milk or something in the kitchen?'

'Would that be all right, ma'am?' she said to my mother.

My mother nodded curtly, following my brothers to the stairs.

'What about the Halligans up Clonown?' I said to Peggy in the kitchen.

She nodded seriously, as if she had been thinking the same thing. 'We'll know soon enough on Monday.'

On Monday, Mrs Halligan stood over the washboard in the sink as usual. But she was strangely quiet. Every movement was thoughtful and she seemed sad. When

Peggy carefully asked her about the bog-fire, she said, 'Oh, we were all right, well away from it. But neighbours of ours were wiped out, just wiped out altogether.'

We thought she wasn't going to tell us, but slowly it came out: 'The first we knew of it was when Danny looked out the door because the birds were making an awful racket. We saw hundreds of birds rising up, as if pushed up by this big black cloud of smoke. Underneath was this long line of flame, licking up the gorse bushes. We saw a fox running for his life and two rabbits running all over the place.' She slapped the wet shirt onto the washing-board and blew down on her cigarette.

We watched her for a while.

'Is your house all right, Mrs Halligan?' I asked.

'Our house,' she said drily, 'is all right. The wind was goin' the other way.' She turned around massively and shook her finger at me. 'Now, none of ye young *gossins* are to come anywhere near Clonown until after the rain. The air is full of ashes and it's pure *pizen*.'

We waited patiently while she thumped the washing-board in silence. Slowly, in dribs and drabs, the story came out. The biggest problem was the high winds that came up suddenly. They whipped the fire into a roaring frenzy that was soon three miles wide. Men working on the bog had to run for their lives. They had to leave behind nearly everything they owned; turf carts, wooden turf barrows, *slanes*, turf forks. Tim Pat Dervan, the man who had given the bottles of clear liquid to Larry, just managed to save his pony by unyoking him from his cart. He had to cover the terrified animal's head with a sack and run. He had been trying to rescue the still.

'Tim Pat, as you know,' said Mrs Halligan, with a sideways look at me, 'is the lad that does be making a drop of the *craythur* for the local population.'

I said nothing. I knew she was talking about *poitín* making. Dekkie had explained everything on the way home from picking mushrooms. Tim Pat was Larry's cousin.

'Is his house okay?' asked Peggy quietly.

Mrs Halligan spoke without turning around. 'It's not,' she said drily. 'A shower of sparks got into the thatch. The whole roof is gone. But there's another four houses the same. There's hardly a shed left standing. There's people lost pigs and chickens. Ah!' Mrs Halligan waved her hand, as if to clear the whole thing out of her mind.

'What will Tim Pat's family do this winter?' asked Peggy.

'Ah, that's not the worst thing. They'll stay with cousins. Sure the neighbours will have that roof back on in a few weeks. It's all happened before. What can you expect, when most of the houses up Clonown have thatched roofs.'

'Lord, what could be worse than that?' said Peggy.

Mrs Halligan turned to face her. 'If you only seen the place now. There's maybe hundreds of acres destroyed. It burned everything in its path – turf bridges, stands of timber, houses, sheds. Ricks of turf that they were saving all summer are just heaps of ashes. There's families up Clonown that's been sending turf on the canal boats up to Dublin for generations. They'll have no income at all this winter.'

She turned away to smoke and think and pound the washing. Before we could say anything, she turned around again and said quietly, 'But thank God, even if some of us have little or no income, haven't we our health. And we can grow our own food. We have meat and eggs and milk. We have a roof over our heads and we're warm in winter.' She turned back to the sink, leaving us nothing to say. I had a feeling that there was something she wasn't saying.

'When is the funeral for the child?' asked Peggy quietly.

Mrs Halligan seemed to stiffen then go completely still. She said nothing for some time. I felt some very strong emotion coming from her. When at last she turned around, it was as if something had been pulled out of her, leaving her empty. I thought there were tears just behind her eyes, but she held on to herself.

'Larry went to help Tim Pat, to try and put out the fire in the thatch. Larry was up a ladder and the children were all running around with buckets. They emptied the water butt and they ran to the stream. One little lad went across in the dark to the bog-hole. They heard only a splash when he slipped and fell in . . .'

Peggy went still and pale. She knew all the children. Tears seemed to slowly swell and stand out on her eyelashes.

My mother came in, quickly took in the scene and went out again.

The hot dry spell came to an end. We woke up one night

in the attic when a massive clap of thunder seemed to shake the house. Rain began to hiss then bucketed down.

'Get the skylight!' yelled my older brother.

I was already on my feet, dragging the table under the skylight and clapping the chair on top. Up I went like a monkey. The skylight closed with a loud clump and rain danced a fandango on it. It drummed mightily on the glass and it went on for a good half hour. Only a few big drops, gathering themselves slowly on the frame, dropped heavily and splattered on the bare boards below. I lay in bed, listening to the noise on the roof and remembering what Mrs Halligan had said about not going up to Clonown until after the rain.

Tommy Brady told me next day that his brother Dekkie had the answer. We would go up to Clonown and see if we could help with Tim Pat Dervan's house. But there was a problem. The bike I shared with my two brothers was being used that day by my older brother.

'Peggy,' I said, 'will you please, please lend me your bike to go with Tommy and Dekkie?'

Peggy gazed at me with a slight smile, as if considering something.

'You can have the bike, as long as you bring it back clean!'

'It'll be as clean as a whistle, Peggy, I promise!'

Clonown was a wasteland that struck us dumb. The stench from drenched, blackened land hung in the air. Gorse on hills, the sharp outlines of cut turf banks, the lines that marked little shaded boreens were all wiped out, buried under black ash. Tim Pat Dervan's house was almost unrecognisable. Beds and dressers and tables had been pulled out. They were piled all together near the house, partially covered with a big tarpaulin. Larry was up a ladder, looking down into the blackened ruin of the house. There was a loud scraping sound inside, like someone shovelling something across the concrete floor. Larry called down something to him and the scraping stopped. 'Ah,' he exclaimed when he saw us, 'here comes the *gossins* brigade. Sure they'll get us out of trouble, lads.'

The men stopped working and grinned at us. It seemed to change the mood. One man went on working, as if he hadn't heard a thing. I recognised the beard. It was Tim Pat Dervan. He sat on a milking stool, away from everyone else, absorbed in cutting and trimming canes that he measured absentmindedly against the length of his arm. I noticed that Larry kept giving him sidelong glances as he carried on his banter. When Tim Pat had finished trimming the canes, he paused a moment, gazing at them thoughtfully. Then he picked one up again and starting paring the end with a penknife to sharpen it.

'What's he doing?' I murmured to Dekkie.

'He's making scallops to hold down the thatch.'

'How do you mean, hold it down?'

'Look, you bend it like a horseshoe' – he showed me – 'then push in the sharp ends.'

It was only later, when I saw it done, that I really understood.

'Listen, Tim Pat,' called Larry from the top of the ladder, 'we could do with another pair of hands up here!'

Tim Pat looked up, startled. Then, as if coming out of a dream, he got to his feet like an old man. 'What do you want me to do?' he asked quietly.

Larry was brusque and businesslike. 'We need to prepare the top of the wall to fit the cross-timbers. If you get the other ladder, we can work together.'

'Right you are!' Tim Pat began to move as if life was slowly coming back into him. I could see that the men were keeping a careful eye on him.

'What'll *we* do, Larry?' asked Dekkie.

'Ye can start by cleaning down that furniture. But use these wet cloths, lads. Don't raise any dust or ash.' He passed two buckets of water with cloths in them.

'Oh God,' I said.

'What?' Tommy said.

'I need to get to a toilet, fast!'

'What was that?' called Larry from the top of the ladder.

I explained my urgent need.

Larry laughed. 'Listen, go up to the house,' he said, 'and ask Danny where to go.' He waved towards something.

Across the flatness of the bog, I was surprised to see the Halligan house on the familiar hill in the distance. I walked at first and then started running. Ash and dust rose up and I slowed down. As Halligans' house came nearer, I noticed an astonishing thing. The black, burnt earth ended in a jagged line a few hundred yards short of Halligans' and then I was walking across the springy, dry crust of the bog, with yellow gorse all around. It was like returning to the real world.

I looked in across the half-door to see Mrs Halligan cooking at the fire.

'Hello, Mrs Halligan. I'm looking for Danny.'

She stood up erect, surprised. 'John-John, hello! He's beyond in the byre, milking'

'Right. Thanks.' I fled.

As soon as I threw open the door of the cow-byre, Danny put a finger to his lips.

'Shh!' he said, pointing to the cow above him. He was on a tiny, three-legged stool, milking the cow. She turned and stared in mid-chew, long lashes framing large, surprised eyes.

'Mildred here,' he said in a loud whisper, 'is in a very nervous state after the fire. She can hardly give any milk.'

Beside him on the floor there was a steaming bucket of water and a cake of carbolic soap on a saucer. I knew that Danny always washed his hands and the cow's udder and teats before milking. I looked at the empty bucket beneath her.

'What's the matter with her?' I whispered.

'All the noise of the fire engines upset her.'

'Danny,' I whispered urgently, 'I need to use your toilet.'

'Toilet, you say?' he said, frowning. 'I'm afraid that's not a word we use in our house and Mildred mustn't hear it.' He rose and pretended to cover Mildred's ears.

She looked up briefly then went on chewing. 'To be polite, we say *reading room.*'

I knew he was clowning but my need was great. 'Where is it, Danny?'

'Just follow me,' he said, giving Mildred a pat. 'Back in a moment, darling,' he said. But she was busy, her head down in the trough.

The haggard was built right up against the gable wall of the house and was twice the size of the house itself. Around the corner, where we were, the cow-byre extended from the haggard. Tacked onto the byre at the end was a tiny building with two doors. One door was marked No. 1 and the other No. 2 in black on the peeling green paint. Ivy had formed a dense bush across the corrugated roof and tendrils of it dangled down against the tiny windows. Danny threw open the door of No. 2. 'And here we have,' he exclaimed like a guide on tour, 'reading room No. 2.'

Along the length of the little room was a foot-high concrete trough, on top of which was a wooden cover, thick and wide. Neatly cut into it were two holes like large pot lids. Built into the wall below each hole was a little wooden door. I knew straight away that it was a dry toilet but I had never used one. In our house it was easy. You just pulled the handle on the chain and the water came cascading down. I looked down one of the holes to see if there was water there, but I could see only white powder.

As if reading my thoughts, Danny said, 'This facility is of the non-flush variety. It depends largely on nature. You sit, nature provides movement and she also deals with the results, with a little help of course from a bit of lime and earth.' He pointed to a long-handled spade against the wall. Under the window were two small concrete cubicles, one containing earth, the other, lime. 'For this is a place of tranquillity, a place to withdraw from the world and sit in quiet contemplation. It is where we put the world to rights and return refreshed.'

'Danny, I really need to –'

'In the meantime, you can catch up on your reading and world events. We stock back numbers of the *Irish Independent* and the *Irish Press*.' He pointed to a stack of neatly folded newspapers on an upturned crate. 'We don't keep *The Irish Times* of course, unless the mother reads it secretly next door in No. 1.'

He slammed the door on me and I heard him tramping away. I sat as instructed and surrendered to nature. A tendril of ivy hung outside the window. The breeze stirred and gently tossed it against the glass, as if reminding me of the life outside. The heavy ivy moved on the roof then sagged into stillness again.

Distant birdsong celebrated summer. I realised how silent it was in that little room. It was peaceful too, as Danny had said. The rough-plastered walls gleamed white in the gloom, with the sharp, clean smell of new whitewash. I laughed when I saw the neatly cut squares of newspaper skewered on a nail near the door. I wondered what Danny would have to say about those. Anyway, it was time to put them to good use.

Tommy and Dekkie were still busy cleaning the furniture when I got back.

'God,' I said, when I saw Tommy, 'look at the state of

you!' Tommy's clothes, his face and arms were smeared with black ash. I laughed.

'All right for you,' snorted Tommy. 'It's about time you did something.'

It wasn't long before I was in much the same state.

'God bless the work!' sang out a strong woman's voice and Mrs Halligan came around the barn, a big cloth-covered basket in the crook of her arm.

'Howya, Missus,' one or two of the men murmured. There were five of them altogether.

'Well,' she cried, when she saw us, 'will you look who's here! Well, that's a mighty *meitheal* ye have there, lads,' she said to the men, nodding at us. We knew she meant *team of workmen.*

We grinned sheepishly but also in relief. We were not sure if we were really supposed to be up Clonown as yet.

'Well,' she said in the same bantering manner, 'I only brought enough fodder for the regular troops and there'll be precious little left over when these lads have had their fill.'

'Oh, it's all right, Mrs Halligan,' said Dekkie, 'sure we'll be off home for our tea soon.'

'Well, there'll be a cup of tea for yiz, anyway, and maybe a cake or two.'

'Oh, they won't go hungry,' said Larry as he came down from the ladder. Everyone had stopped working.

'Well now,' said Mrs Halligan, 'I won't delay. I'll stay goin'. And you might bring home the basket, Larry.'

'I will!'

The men all washed in the stream and we did the same. Then Larry uncovered the basket. There was a big round loaf of bread, raisins bursting out of it, and it was still warm from the oven. In a corner all by itself was a glass dish of yellow country butter, glistening with salt. There were rough slices of ham and hard-boiled eggs, a clutch of scallions and a stack of warm potato cakes. Tied up in a tea towel, still steaming, were a dozen rock-buns with currants embedded in the crusts. Without a word, Larry handed out the rock-buns to Dekkie, Tommy and me. There were at least six large white cups, clean as a whistle, and a big corked bottle of tea with milk and sugar. But Larry had a better idea. Turning to Tim Pat, he said, 'Haven't you a little something you've kept aside to bless this start we've made on the house?'

'I have indeed,' said Tim Pat, smiling wanly. He was almost back to his usual self. He went over to the pile of furniture, rummaged in a sack and brought back a bottle of clear liquid. A generous drop was poured into each man's cup.

'These lads,' said Larry, nodding at us, 'have all taken the pledge so they won't be having any. They can have the tea.'

The tea was strong, hot and poisonous with sugar. I thought that that tea, combined with the rock-buns, was the most delicious thing I had ever tasted. We were seated on a stack of long, smooth trunks, like telegraph poles but not as thick.

'What are these for, Dekkie?' I asked.

'These will be the main roof timbers, and what you see coming will go on top.'

We saw a horse and cart, piled high with what looked like straw, turn in at the end of the long, twisting boreen that led to the house. Two men sat up front, legs hanging down sideways from the shafts on each side.

'Hey, it's Danny Halligan,' said Tommy.

'And that's Seán Dempsey driving. He's bringing in a load of reeds from the Shannon,' said Dekkie. 'He's the thatcher but he'll only come to finish the job. Larry and Danny can do most of it.'

They stopped below at the barn and started to unload. We were all watching them when we heard, faintly in the distance back in town, the bells of St Peter's chiming six o'clock.

Dekkie jumped to his feet. 'Jeez, lads, we'll be late! I said I'd have ye back by teatime. Larry, we're off!'

Larry laughed and the men waved and we headed back to town as fast as we could. On the way home, we pointed at each other's filthy clothes and pretended to laugh at the dressing-down we were going to get.

As soon as I got into our yard, I saw how dirty Peggy's bike was. I got a brush and started cleaning it at the tap outside the shed.

'Lord!' said Peggy, when she saw the state I was in. 'We'll have to get you into a bath straight away. And you'll have to take off every stitch you're wearing.'

'But, Peggy,' I said, 'there's no hot water upstairs yet!' I was talking about our new bathroom.

'I know that very well, mister,' said Peggy, 'so you'll

just have to have a bath in front of the range as you've always done.'

I was aghast. It wasn't Saturday night and anyone might walk into the kitchen. Besides, I had begun to feel stupid squeezing down into that little tin bath. Supposing Tommy called, or even one of my sister's friends?

'Oh, Peggy, I'm far too big–'

'Now, John-John, supposing your mother comes in and sees the state you're in?'

I knew from the set look on Peggy's face that her mind was made up. I did the only thing I could think of doing in the circumstances; I put on the most miserable face I could and let my whole body slump. I kept an eye on Peggy until I saw a tiny smile start up.

'But,' she said, with that growing smile that revealed her tolerance of my strange ways, 'I'm going to put up a little screen so you can be nice and private in there.'

I watched Peggy dragging out the big wooden clotheshorse that was folded out around the range when Mrs Halligan finished the washing on Mondays. She put down the tin bath on the floor in front of it with a clang and draped a sheet over the clotheshorse.

'Now, sir, your bath will soon be ready,' said Peggy, 'but I must ask you to help fill it up.'

I poured in two cans of cold water from the sink and Peggy heaved the great big iron kettle off the range and poured it in. She poured in half the other kettle as well and splashed her fingers around in it.

'Now,' she said, 'see if it's hot enough.'

'It is,' I said.

Peggy placed a cake of carbolic soap on a dish beside the bath and said, 'Now you can take your clothes off and get in.'

Peggy adjusted the clotheshorse once more then started bustling around the kitchen.

I got undressed and eased myself down into the water. I hardly noticed Peggy scooping up my clothes. I lay still for a bit, enjoying the warmth of the water and the heat from the range. I was reaching for the soap when the door behind flew open.

'Hiya, Peggy! Is Mari in?' said Steffi's voice. I froze in the warm water. There was a definite pause, when I felt two pairs of eyes attempting to penetrate the thin barrier of the sheet draped over the clotheshorse.

'Oh, em,' said Peggy, 'I think she's upstairs.' And I heard her feet moving towards the door, followed more slowly by Steffi's.

'Mari!' called Peggy up the stairs. I heard a faint voice replying. 'Steffi is down here!'

I was in agony. Would they come back into the kitchen? I heard my sister's feet running down the stairs.

'Now,' said Peggy's voice in the hallway outside, 'you can stay over in Steffi's until eight o'clock, no later, okay?'

The door to the yard slammed and I let out the long breath I'd been holding. I heard Peggy's footsteps coming back in and she must have stood still in the middle of the floor. 'Are you still in there, John-John?' she called in a quiet voice.

'Peggy, are they gone?' I asked, haunted by the possibility that they might suddenly return for some reason.

Peggy came around the screen, gazed down at me in the soapy water and burst out laughing. She laughed and laughed, throwing her apron up against her face as if to contain the laughter.

I was not amused. I rose from the cooling water feeling vaguely wronged, and wrapped myself safely in a big rough towel. What really worried me was that Steffi might have suspected it was me in there, keeping quiet, pretending I wasn't there at all. If she and my sister got hold of that idea, I'd never hear the end of it!

Lie Down, You're Dead

~

1953

Silence reigned in the little valley. We lay flat on the ground, gun barrels poking out through the wagon wheels. Two crows wheeled lazily on a warm breeze way above in the blue sky.

Low, regular chanting and a steady drumbeat, swelling in volume, rose from behind the steep hill in front of us. Then with eerie, frenzied howling the savages erupted over the top and poured down the hillside towards us. I shot the nearest painted devil squarely in the chest when he was almost on top of me, but he failed to fall down.

'Hey!' I shouted. 'Lie down, you're dead!'

But he ran on regardless, sinking his tomahawk into Tommy Brady's neck.

'Hey! You're not supposed to do that!' yelled Tommy and gave the savage a whack of his popgun across the backs of his fleeing legs.

'Ow!' yelled the savage, tumbling this time, as he

was supposed to, and losing several eagle feathers in the process.

'That's just typical of the Parnell Square gang!' said Tommy in disgust as we watched the savages tomahawk the remaining settlers inside the circled wagons. 'They never play by the rules.'

The 'wagons' were several farmers' turf carts, the high-crated sides covered with canvas stretched across bent bamboo. There was Jack Kerrigan's ass and cart, a dray-cart from the Guinness yard, old Mrs Webb's dogcart and Johnny Madden's pony and cart.

We hardly noticed at first the rhythmic drumming of horse's hooves, so fierce was the hand-to-hand fighting. Tomahawks halted inches from necks with the first blood-curdling whoop from the galloping rider who circled the wagons, reins in his teeth, rifle in right hand, six-gun in left, spitting death to left and right. I couldn't believe it; he was controlling his horse with only his legs. He came to a sudden halt right in front of me. Beneath the big white Stetson, I saw Mickey's big teeth exposed in the mouse-like grin that gave him his nickname. Reality immediately reduced his galloping steed to Johnny Madden's pony doing a smart little canter.

'Shit, Mickey!' said Tommy, his mouth open in admiration. 'I never knew you could do that!'

I knew, because we had both been learning in Johnny Madden's yard.

Practically every redskin and settler had gathered around, some stroking the pony, others wanting to see Mickey's two guns.

'God, Mickey,' I said, 'where did you get the chaps?'

Mickey grinned again. 'Me mother made them from the legs of Daddy's old trousers. And she sowed on all these big buttons.'

'Right, lads,' said Tomsie McGee, coming up, 'time for peace to break out.' Tomsie was the organiser of this An Tóstal event. 'So, where's the Big Chief?'

'Me Big Chief,' boomed Dinny Hoctor, thumping his chest.

'Whataya talking about?' shouted Tommy. 'I'm supposed to be the chief. Tomsie gave me the headdress.' He triumphantly held up the wide leather belt with chicken feathers cleverly glued all along it and with little coloured ribbons that fluttered in the breeze.

'No, me Big Chief,' rumbled Dinny, and he made a lunge for the headdress.

Tommy snatched it away but not before Dinny's big bony hand had grabbed one end of it. A tussle followed in which chicken feathers flew in the wind and Tommy got a thump that sent him flying.

'Now me Big Chief,' said Dinny triumphantly, waving the belt that now had just two feathers clinging precariously to it.

'Listen, lads,' said Tomsie, knowing full well that Dinny was a bit simple, 'Dinny will be a perfect chief and he knows how to smoke the pipe of peace.'

Dinny was persuaded to sit cross-legged in front of the homemade wigwam, a construction of poles with an old tarpaulin draped around them. The peace pipe was a pipe borrowed from one of the farmers, with a bit of bamboo stuck onto the end. Dinny gravely accepted the peace pipe in both hands, looking very serious, as chiefs are supposed to. Two feathers stuck up at wayward angles out of the belt on top of his head. In his dignified, chiefly manner, he accepted the coloured blanket that Tomsie draped around his shoulders. Dinny never missed a cowboy picture at the Ritz and he knew exactly what to do.

'Where my squaw?' rumbled Dinny.

'Yes,' said Tomsie, scratching his head, 'you'll need a squaw. Tommy, you'll have to be the squaw.'

'I don't want to be a bleddy squaw,' squawked Tommy. 'Why doesn't *he* do it?' he said, pointing at Mickey.

'Can't,' said Mickey calmly. 'I'm Roy Rogers.'

'And *I* can't,' I said. 'I'm the colonel in charge of the United States Cavalry.'

'Look, Tommy, just do it for the moment, then we'll get someone else,' said Tomsie.

Much discussion and reluctance followed but eventually, glowing with resentment, Tommy gave in. Tomsie quickly dabbed a spot of red paint on each of Tommy's cheeks, followed by two white stripes on either side. Two long black wool stockings, sown together to look like hair, were slapped on Tommy's head and held in place with a coloured headband that had a single hen's feather sticking up at the back. The feet of the stockings, bound with coloured ribbons, hung down his back like plaits. A coloured blanket draped across his shoulders completed the picture. That's when the photographer from the *Westmeath Independent* arrived.

'Just hold it there,' said Frankie Simmons, as he lifted his camera. The shutter clicked and solemn chief and glowing squaw were forever captured in print.

'Gosh,' said Mickey, twitching his thumb at Tommy, 'doesn't he look pretty?'

'Hey, I'll friggin' get you when this is over,' growled Tommy, his face like an oncoming storm.

'Me smoke pipe of peace,' declared Dinny, and everyone wondered what was supposed to happen next.

Tomsie was pushing me forward. 'Start making peace,' he muttered in my ear.

'White man wish make peace,' I declared to Dinny, trying to remember the kind of thing John Wayne said over in the Ritz. I needn't have worried. Dinny knew the game inside out.

'White man,' he replied, glaring at me, 'speak with forked tongue.'

That stopped me for a moment. A light bulb went on in my head. 'Hey,' I said, 'why don't we smoke pipe of peace?'

'Big Chief,' replied Dinny, 'light pipe,' and he started fiddling with a box of matches.

But he was holding too many things and the box slipped out of his fingers and matches scattered all over the ground.

'God, look what you done, ya big eejit,' said the squaw beside him, making a grab for the matches.

'Squaw,' said Dinny, 'have much long tongue.'

Tommy shut up and I helped Dinny to get the pipe lit. I had no idea if this was supposed to be part of the plan.

Eventually, he got the pipe going and was puffing away until he started spluttering and took a fit of coughing. Tommy saw this as an opportunity to make a grab for the pipe. There was a loud cracking sound and the pipe of peace lay in bits on the ground. At this moment, the farmer who had lent his horse and cart and pipe to us came over.

'Well, if ye've broken me bleddy pipe, I'll skin the lot of yiz,' he promised. He bent and lifted his pipe, carefully fitting together the two bits that had come apart. 'Just as well it's not broken.' And off he went with his pipe. Only the bamboo extension had been broken.

Dinny was sitting in his Indian chief pose as if nothing had happened. Over at the railway station, a loud whistle announced the departure of the Dublin to Galway train.

'White man's iron horse kill all buffalo,' announced Dinny.

The wind suddenly changed and the little turf fire that Tomsie had lit to make things more Indian-camp-like blew choking smoke right into our faces. Everyone was coughing and moving away when Johnny Madden came over with old Mrs Webb. She spoke immediately to Mickey: 'Mickey [she pronounced it *Mick-ayh*], I've just been watching you ride. Johnny tells me you've been training in his yard for the past six months.' She spoke with such a posh accent that we could hardly understand her. *Yard* sounded to us like *yawd* and *past* sounded like *pawst*.

Mickey was clearly taken by surprise but he managed

to answer. 'Yes, that's right, Mrs Webb. There's three of us training.'

We all knew about eccentric old Mrs Webb from Johnny Madden. Horses had been her whole life. Now that she was retired from the hunt, she had started a kind of retirement home for ponies on the old Webb estate outside town. Johnny knew her well because he had always bred a few hunters that he sold occasionally to members of the hunt.

'Of course,' said Mrs Webb, 'it'll be winter before the polo ponies arrive and then some months before I manage to retrain them. But then I shall need young riders to take them out on hacks. Now, who would be willing to do that?'

Our three right hands shot up in the air and we stood tense and silent, watching her face. Mrs Webb turned to Johnny, smiling.

'I think we're in business, Johnny,' she said and she beamed on us.

I was surprised to see Mrs Webb take Mickey aside. They were both small and wiry. She was dressed in her tweed jacket and slacks and smoked from a well-worn cigarette holder. She gave the impression of being both tough and kind. They seemed to be having a friendly chat, as if they were old friends.

We were still clearing up as Mrs Webb climbed into her dogcart. Mickey came wandering over to us. He looked relaxed and happy, or maybe content. I didn't ask him anything.

We walked silently down Connaught Street, on a

cushion of air. I could see the excitement on Tommy's face. Gone was the flushed, sour look of the discontented squaw. No amount of teasing about the photo to appear in the *Westmeath Independent* could dampen his spirits now.

'Hey, did you hear the way she said polo ponies?' Tommy said.

'Poh-loh poh-knees!' Mickey exclaimed.

'No,' I said, 'it was more like pow-low pow-knees.'

'No', said Tommy, 'it was poe-loe.'

We got as far as Jimmy the Barber's, trying out different versions. Peter Murray from our class was coming up the street towards us.

'Hey, lads, where are ye coming from?'

'Pow-low,' Tommy replied.

'What?'

'Pow-low,' said Mickey.

'What are ye talking about?'

'We're talking about pow-low,' I said.

He looked at us as if we were mad.

'Ye're mad as hatters!' he told us to our faces and he walked on up the street. He was almost out of sight when he turned around and called back:

'Ye're cracked, the lot of ye!'

'Pow-low,' we shouted back and the sound echoed all along the houses.

Mickey was glum and silent on the way to school.

'Hey,' I said, 'who died?'

But Mickey kept his eyes down, kicking a stone along.

'No one died,' he said quietly. He glanced over.

'Me Da went on the tear last night.'

So what, I thought. Men seemed to do that occasionally. The only thing I knew about it was that women clearly didn't like it.

'Okay,' I said carefully. He had gone silent again.

'I never saw him do that before.'

'You mean; never?'

'He promised me mam, when they got married, he'd never touch the stuff.'

'Why?'

'Why do you think,' said Mickey, 'he never became a jockey?'

I shook my head.

'It was because of the drink.'

Mickey came into our kitchen after tea that evening.

'Hello, Mickey,' Peggy said, raising her eyebrows. We all knew it was a bit late to be calling.

'Can John-John come with me, Peggy?'

'Go with you where?'

'Mam sent me out to find Daddy.'

'Where's he gone?'

'He's in one of the pubs. She sent me out to bring him back.'

Peggy had gone still, gazing at Mickey, as if working out the meaning of what he had said. She glanced at the clock then at me.

'I want you back here, John-John,' she said quietly 'by nine o'clock.'

I nodded. She started putting on her cardigan. My mother came in but stood at the door, taking in the situation. I sat down at the table and Mickey took his cue from me. I had already got permission from Peggy. I wasn't going to ask my mother too.

My mother looked at Peggy, her face all question. There was decision and determination in Peggy's every movement.

'I'm going up to Lily Maher for a few minutes, ma'am,' said Peggy.

My mother glanced at Mickey. It was as if a message had passed between the two women. My mother nodded and went out again.

We waited until we saw Peggy going out through the archway. I could hear my mother moving about upstairs.

'Let's go,' I said.

We started up at the Battery Bridge end with McNeil's pub and worked our way down Connaught Street, crossing over and back. Sometimes we had to go in through the grocery part first.

'Can I help ye, lads?' we were asked once or twice. We shook our heads and scampered out. We got to FitzGerald's, at the other end of the street, and stood in their archway, wondering what to do next.

'What started your father off on this batter?' I asked. Tommy shrugged.

'You remember Mrs Webb took me aside to have a talk?'

'Sure!' I said. I was still curious about that.

'Well, mainly she was remembering what a great

young jockey my father was, especially at the hunter trials and the point-to-points. She was wondering what had happened to him and said she hoped I would follow in his footsteps.'

'Is that it?'

'She wondered what he was doing now and said she'd be very pleased to meet him again.'

I looked at Mickey. There seemed to be some special meaning in what he had said.

'Were you telling your father all this?'

'Yeah,' Mickey sighed. 'I thought he'd be pleased.'

'But he wasn't?'

'He got really mad. He started shouting. I thought he was going to belt me. He told me never, ever to talk about his business to someone like Mrs Webb again. Then Mam came in and started arguing with him.'

'They had a row, you mean?'

Mickey shook his head and sighed.

'I never heard them having a row before. Out he went, slamming the door.'

From Connaught Street, we went to Lenehan's pub down O'Connell Street. Tommy Lenehan came into the grocery part when he heard the bell pinging above the door.

'Well, lads?' enquired Tommy.

'I'm looking for me fader,' said Mickey.

Tommy gave him a long look. 'You're Jimmy's young lad?'

Mickey nodded.

The men's voices from the bar behind suddenly seemed louder. Smoke rose lazily above the partition, up to the yellowed ceiling.

'Quiet now, lads!' called a deep male voice. A complete hush fell on the men inside.

'Come inside a minute,' Tommy whispered. He opened a connecting door and pointed Mickey and me to the low bench just inside.

Men in caps and boots sat on high stools at the bar, pints of porter within reach on the counter. They sat on benches all along the wall across the room from us, balancing their pints and managing their pipes or cigarettes. All attention seemed focused on one small, square-set man in the middle of the bench across from us. I knew the man, Padhraic Nestor, because he sometimes sang in our pub too.

They were all waiting for something. I noticed that the pot-bellied stove still dominated the space in the centre of the room. Instead of the suffocating heat it gave off in winter, a cool draught was coming from an open door or window somewhere.

At first, there was only silence. Nestor stared ahead into some unseen distance, his hands limply folded. He started in a low, wobbly voice. Suddenly, as if the sound had awakened him, the man beside him with the long greasy hair, whose head had fallen forward onto his chest, looked up. His staring black eyes fixed on me and the hair almost stood on my head. It was Jimmy the Barber! His stare shifted to Mickey. I felt the sharp movement beside me as Mickey reacted too.

The singer's voice gradually rose. It increased in volume until it seemed to fill the whole space above and around us. It was a rasping, rough voice, but the effect was riveting. The song was sad but beautiful, torn from the depths of a soul.

There was silence when he finished. Jimmy's head had dropped onto his chest again. Feet shifted. A few dry coughs and then there was a spatter of clapping and murmurs of appreciation. One of the men began sawing at a fiddle. Then off the wild music went, shaking Jimmy out of his trance. He stood with an awkward, jerky movement and came over to us.

'Did your mother send you out looking for me?' He hiccupped and he could hardly speak.

'She said you were to come home for your tea,' said Mickey, looking down at his shoes.

The three of us walked in total silence down Connaught Street. Jimmy halted at our house and said:

'You go on home, Mickey. Tell your mother I'll be along in a while. I need to talk to this man's father.' I knew he meant me. Mickey walked on without a word. I went in through the pub with him because the side-gates were closed. My father took one look at Jimmy and came out from behind the counter. Only three of the regulars sat on high stools with their backs to us. An old farmer had fallen asleep on the bench near the stove.

'Jim,' Jimmy said. 'I'm in no state to go home yet. Could you fix me up with a bit of grub?'

It was strange to see them together. My father towered over Jimmy.

'Sit over there by the stove, Jimmy, and we'll look after you.'

Jimmy walked over carefully and sat on the bench opposite the sleeping old man. My father followed. I had sensed the immediate understanding between my father and Jimmy. My father loved horses and admired anyone who was good with them. Jimmy clearly respected something in my father. They sat side by side. My father had a loud, commanding voice but in situations like this, when he gave someone his whole attention, he could carry on a conversation in such an undertone that even I couldn't hear. I waited, because I knew what he'd want me to do.

'John,' he said – he never called me John-John – 'go into the kitchen and ask Peggy to get us a few ham sandwiches and a pot of tea.'

'Right,' I said and left. He only ever seemed to speak to me to give commands.

Peggy looked up from her sewing, her whole expression expecting an explanation.

'Peggy, Daddy wants some ham sandwiches and a pot of tea out in the bar.'

She put down her sewing, expecting more.

'Jimmy Maher is out there, looking for food,' I explained.

'Is he drunk?'

'Not so bad.'

Peggy rose and, without another word, started preparing the tray. I got out the cups and saucers. As soon as the tea was made, she said:

'I want *you* to take this tray in, John-John.'

'Okay.'

She opened the kitchen door for me then held the bar door, with its strong spring, until I got through. My father glanced up briefly, took in the situation, but said nothing. I put the tray on top of the stove then dragged over a low stool and placed it in front of their knees. They watched me transfer the tray to the stool.

'Good man; you're a dowser!' my father said, with scarcely a glance. It was the nearest he ever got to praise. I had no idea what a dowser was until I asked Peggy. Even then I couldn't see any connection with praise. But in his language there was.

Without being told, I went in behind the bar and started washing glasses, in case that was expected of me. My father glanced over but said nothing. He was listening intently to Jimmy, nodding, looking down at his knees or into Jimmy's face. I couldn't hear a word.

'This must be the new barman,' exclaimed Mick O'Gorman from across the counter. He was already half-drunk and I often wondered how he managed to stay balanced on the tall stool. My father was looking over.

'It's all right, John; you can go on in now,' he called.

'Right,' I said and promptly left.

Peggy was sitting completely still at the table. I guessed she had been staring into space. I felt that I had noisily intruded into the deep quiet that was in her and even around her. But she began her slow smile.

'Well, what's happening?'

'The sandwiches are gone. The tea is gone. Now they're talking.'

'They probably will be half the night.' She sighed. The clock ticked loudly in the quiet of the kitchen.

'So, what were you thinking about?' I asked.

That made us both smile because it was the question she usually asked me. She reached across and took my hand.

'Promise me something,' she said.

'Sure; anything!'

'Promise me that, no matter what happens to you in your life, you will not regret anything.'

I stared at her.

'I don't understand that, Peggy.'

'I know you don't, but promise me at least that you will remember what I said.'

'I promise!'

I knew immediately that she was talking from her own experience. But was she also talking about Jimmy's? I couldn't tell.

That Summer

1954

Johnny left us right in front of the Webb house. He turned the pony and the trap and rapidly disappeared down the tunnel of trees that overhung the avenue.

Six stone steps ascended to the front door. The brass lion's head, which I thought must be the knocker, had turned a mouldy green. Two panes were missing from what I knew was a Georgian fanlight. There was one exactly the same over the door of Steffi's house, across the street from us.

'Jeez,' said Tommy, 'this place is empty!'

A horse whinnied somewhere behind the house.

'Betcha it's not,' said Mickey.

Angry March light glinted on uneven glass in the windows two storeys above. We gazed up in silence at the mighty moss-covered roof. Crows slid on the slates and fidgeted around the chimney pots. Their hoarse cawing echoed around the ancient trees that crowded around the building. The trees sighed and heaved in the wind. The front door opened with a dry, scraping sound and there stood Mrs Webb, tiny in the big doorway, cheerful and waving her ancient cigarette holder.

'Morning, boys!' she sang out.

'Good morning, Mrs Webb,' three voices responded.

'We're just finishing breakfast, if you'd like to come in.'

We traipsed after her across a massive hallway. It was round, with four pillars that went up to a ceiling, way above us somewhere. Rising off the black-and-white tiled floor was a great carved stairway of the kind I had only seen at the pictures. We nearly stumbled into each other, craning our necks to try and take in the sheer size of the place. 'We have some visitors, Kitty!' Mrs Webb called out loudly to someone unseen ahead of us. A woman, who was certainly as old as Mrs Webb herself but completely lacking her energy, padded out of a doorway in her slippers. The dull, cold gaze she gave us was somewhat short of welcoming.

'I've hardly a rasher left to feed ourselves, let alone visitors,' she said sourly in the strongest country accent.

'Oh, come now, Kitty, I'm sure you can work your magic and conjure up a wonderful breakfast for these hungry young riders. I take it you *are* hungry,' she said to us.

'Well, actually–' I began.

'Well, of course you are! Boys are always hungry. Now, I'm just going to finish mine while Kitty–'

But Kitty had other ideas. She sank down heavily on a chair across the table from Mrs Webb. 'Mrs Webb,' said

Kitty emphatically, 'me lumbago is just killin' me this morning and the oul shoulder is crucifying me again.'

Mrs Webb put down her knife and fork. She rose from her place and immediately came over to Kitty, arranging her features in what seemed to me a comical look of contrition, like some Hollywood actress.

'Oh, Kitty, how very inconsiderate of me!' She gently put her hand on the crucified shoulder. 'You just sit there and I'll cook up something. Mine's gone stone bloody cold anyway.'

I was a bit shocked to hear a woman, a lady no less, using language like that. I realised that the large room we were in had been roughly adapted as a kitchen. We learned later that the original kitchen was in the basement. We were sitting around what had once been a fine carved table, the top of which was now stained with rings from tea mugs and burn marks from hot plates. It was beside a battered range on which something was frying in a pan. Mrs Webb moved the pan to one side and reached for a bowl of eggs. She cracked in four of them and started draping big slices of bacon across another pan.

'Ridiculous, when you think of it,' she remarked to us in an aside. 'I had more expensive cookery classes than one needs in a lifetime when I was a girl (she pronounced it *ghel*). Now I can just about fry an egg and a piece of bacon.'

We heard the sound of tyres on gravel and two dogs started barking.

'Oh,' said Mrs Webb, 'would someone please take

over?' and she looked appealingly at me. I stood up as she abandoned the pan to greet her visitors.

'Here,' said Kitty, suddenly coming to life and taking over from me, 'I doubt you know what you're about,' and she started moving stuff around on both pans with a large spatula. We sat and watched.

'How come ye're out here at the Webbs' anyway?' she asked, turning around. She said it as if we had no right to be there, as if we were invading her territory. The other two looked at me and I explained the circumstances that had brought us to Mrs Webb's door. Kitty divided her attention between the pans and me, squinting at me as if in suspicion. She grabbed three plates and banged them down on the hob. One egg and two rashers landed on each.

'Now!' she said and slapped a plate down in front of me. She did the same with Mickey and Tommy. Between mouthfuls, I continued the explanation.

'Don't I know you?' she suddenly interrupted. 'Your mother runs that bakery and the tearooms in Pearse Street.'

'That's right,' I said, wondering if I should have confessed the relationship.

'Ah, sure I know your mother well,' she said in a considerably warmer tone, with something like a smile beginning to break out on her face. 'Sure I've known Babs this twenty years. And who are these other gentlemen?'

She was larding butter onto doorsteps of toast, with a dry, scraping sound. One landed on each of our plates in turn. Then she lifted a steaming kettle over a big brown teapot.

Tommy and Mickey, as they chewed, gave their family details and Kitty's whole being seemed to gradually warm up. Sure, she knew the parents well, hard workers all of them. She'd get into town more and see people again if it wasn't for the cursed lumbago and having to wait hand and foot on her ladyship.

She was pouring the tea when the front door opened to loud barking and we heard three sets of footsteps approaching across the hallway. The voices were loud and hearty and they were accompanied by a peculiar tic-tic sound. The mystery was solved when the kitchen door was thrown open and two large dogs rushed in. On their heels came Mrs Webb and – shock of shocks – Dr Nolan and his daughter Steffi.

Dr Nolan broke off his conversation with Mrs Webb to call out heartily to Kitty. 'And how's Kitty today?'

'Kitty's just fine,' she called back, just as heartily, 'if she could only find a doctor that would cure her lumbago.'

We had quietly put our knives and forks down, suddenly feeling shy.

Dr Nolan laughed. Clearly he was a frequent visitor. He was a tall, handsome man with a moustache. Steffi waved to us but said nothing. Her look lingered on me a moment and she smiled. She looked very smart in her jacket, jodhpurs and high boots. I don't know about Mickey and Tommy, but I certainly felt that we looked like anything but riders.

Mrs Webb addressed us all: 'Well now, boys and girls.
Steffi, Prince is already tacked up for you, and you and
the other two *ghels* can take them out on a hack, as
usual. Now, boys, the ponies are already tacked up in
the yard and ready to go. I'll be with you in a moment.'

She left with Dr Nolan. We bolted the rest of our
breakfast.

Dr Nolan was leading a beautiful horse out of the
yard as we arrived.

'That's the doctor's racehorse,' said Mickey.

'Jeez,' said Tommy, gazing around at the buildings.
The stable block was a quadrangle, with a little bell tower
above the arched entrance. But weeds and nettles came
up through the cobbles and whole sections of slates were
missing above some of the stables.

That spring, we took every opportunity to cycle out to the
Webb place. The summer holidays came in no time and
then we were out there every day. When we got used to
the ponies, we started going out on hacks with Steffi and
the other two girls, who were clearly from the same stable
as Mrs Webb. They were friendly enough but managed
to keep their distance. I realised that Mickey, Tommy
and I were certainly as good as these more experienced
riders, and better, I thought, when it came to jumping. I
was surprised to find myself competing with Steffi. For
some reason, I wanted to be not just as good, but better.
I was well aware that Mrs Webb kept her sharp eyes on
our progress, sometimes trotting or cantering alongside
us on the fat little cob she called Fuzzy.

That summer we became real riders.

I was walking in through the bar one day after coming home from the Webb place when my father looked up from the paper he had spread on the counter.

'Well,' he said, 'how are you getting on out there at the Webb place?' My father's way of talking to me was to ask questions or give commands. It was best to let him ask the questions that led to the answers he wanted to hear.

'Oh, good, I think.'

'So, what stage are you at now?'

'Mrs Webb says we're ready for a cross-country competition she's organising. Her cross-country course has nearly a hundred flights.'

My father didn't just love horses; he seemed to admire the gentry that went with them. I often wondered if he was a snob. He was looking me up and down.

'How do the others dress for riding out there?'

I knew where this was leading. I told him about jodhpurs, high boots, jackets and hard hats.

'Well,' he said, 'there'll be a right crowd out there. You can't be in the competition looking like that.' He made it sound like it was my fault. I already knew that there was no point in asking him to get me properly kitted out until he himself felt that I should be as good as anyone else out in a place like the Webbs'. It really had very little to do with me. It had to do with some image that had to be protected.

I dreaded the next bit. I didn't mind him being

tight-fisted. A journey to Galway or Dublin to the right outfitters was out of the question, as he wouldn't leave the business for a whole day, even with the ever-reliable Betty Carton in charge. First he took me to Burgess's over in Church Street to see if he could order the stuff, but they started talking about long delivery times. Then he thought of Tommy in Heaton's just up the street. He liked doing business with Tommy when he wanted a new suit or shirts and ties. Tommy was the kind who would do his best to get him exactly what he wanted. Tommy said he knew someone in Dublin who supplied that kind of thing and he immediately got out his famous tape measure. I had my neck, chest, arms and legs measured while they talked about farming and the weather. I might have been a mannequin, to be twisted and turned and told to hold out my arms.

'The only thing now,' said Tommy, 'is that this man in Dublin won't supply the boots.'

I felt my heart drop. Boots were the most important thing!

But, he said, if we went down to Mr Sharp, below in Parson's shoe shop, he'd see us right.

Mr Sharp, below in Parson's, was always dressed in a fine dark suit. He had a small, grey moustache and his manner was courteous and grave. But he was obliging. Having measured my feet, he went to the telephone and within minutes was able to assure us that the boots would be with him in a couple of days. I was exhausted after that outing and felt somehow in debt.

'My God,' exclaimed Peggy, the following week,

when she saw me dressed in my outfit, 'don't you look a real gentleman!'

'Peggy, please, please say you'll come out and watch us in the competition.'

Peggy's face fell. 'Lord, John-John, I won't be able to. I have to be here to get your brothers and sisters their lunch and tea. But look, I'll cycle out after tea. Won't you still be there?'

'I suppose.' I was disappointed. I knew that neither my mother nor my father would be there.

From the very beginning – apart from the endless mucking out, cleaning tack, grooming the ponies and taking them out on hacks – Mrs Webb really taught us. She rarely explained anything; instead she demonstrated, and that suited me perfectly. For example, as soon as she had seen how well we did over the jumps, she took us straight out onto the cross-country course. She stopped in front of a single line of hurdles on a flat piece of ground.

'Now boys,' she said over her shoulder, 'you've all gone over flights this height. Just get in behind me and do what I do.'

She set off at a terrific pace and went over the first, then the second and the third. To our amazement, we went over just as quickly, impressed at how keen our mounts were to keep up with her lead. We went over the last and pulled up behind her, breathless and full of wonder at what we had done. From then on, our confidence knew no bounds.

I thought the scariest thing of all was cantering down a wooded hillside and going over a jump with a big drop behind it. Mrs Webb did it several times first. "Lean back, heels down, keep your legs on!" she called as she sailed over and down. Mickey did it first and very nearly came off. He did it a few times until we all got the idea. Tommy was next and he came off three times. He just laughed and got right back up. I knew he was proud of his toughness and persistence. I came off once but got right back up again.

On the day of the competition, we were all at the Webbs' early, even though the event didn't start until 2 p.m. There were entries from all over the county and beyond. Members of the hunt had been around the place for days, helping to erect a marquee and string up bunting and microphone wires between the trees. We groomed and cleaned tack as never before. I was finished before Mickey and Tommy, so I decided I needed a warm-up hack on Samson. He was my favourite and I had asked to have him for the competition.

The Webb place was magnificent. The house stood on a rise, overlooking the distant Shannon. The land was all green valleys and wooded hills. I was enjoying Samson's loping canter, the sun and the breeze, when I saw Steffi coming down out of the trees on a hill to the left, leading her pony. Even at that distance, I could see that one knee of her jodhpurs was stained. Clearly she'd had a fall. I reined in and waited. As she approached, I saw that she was close to tears. I got down.

'You all right, Steffi?'

She nodded, as if in pain. I could see she needed a moment.

'It's just,' she said now in her normal voice, 'that Candy here refuses nearly every second jump.'

'Well, you know she was a polo pony?'

'I know.'

'Are you riding Candy today?'

She nodded, looking distressed again.

Suddenly I remembered Mrs Webb's methods. 'Listen,' I said, 'let's go over the first flight together. I'll go first, you follow.'

We went over the first flight without a hitch. Candy seemed eager to follow Samson. We went over a good part of the course, including the water jump, and there was no problem.

'John-John,' said Steffi, 'please, please let's ask Mrs Webb if we can be paired together for the competition.'

'Okay,' I said as casually as I could. I didn't want her to know how delighted I was.

There was one thing about Steffi that really made me think. As soon as she walked into the yard, every horse's head, sticking out over their stable doors, turned towards her. Horses loved her. I loved horses too, but they responded in that way only when I stroked them and talked to them. They certainly loved Mickey but were mostly indifferent to Tommy.

Mrs Webb said there was absolutely no problem. She looked at her list, scratched out something and wrote something else. We were entered for the under-fourteen section and of course we would only do the part of the course specially marked out for us with coloured, numbered placards. Our particular section was familiar to us by then. Competitors were to be run off in pairs, jumping the course against the clock, and there were twenty pairs. Tommy and Mickey were each paired with one of the older girls. Each pair was given two sets of numbered placards, one to be pinned on the backs of our jackets, the other on the chest.

Mrs Webb's voice echoed and bounced from the microphones strung out between the trees. We sat our ponies close together on the little wooded rise that was the starting point, listening to her commentary on the progress of pair No. 6. We were next. A steward stood close by, ready to give us the signal.

The pair finished to a scattered round of applause, as Mrs Webb read out their times. Steffi and I looked at each other, eyes lit up in the shade, knowing we could beat that time. We were trembling, but it was the trembling of eagerness, not fear.

The steward was looking at us, slowly raising his coloured handkerchief, tensely listening to Mrs Webb's announcements. 'Go!' he shouted, forcefully bringing the handkerchief down.

'Pair No. 7, John and Steffi,' echoed Mrs Webb's voice calmly in the trees, 'and they're off to a good start.'

We thundered down the incline, the first part of the big horseshoe shape of our course. Mrs Webb, armed with binoculars, sat erect in her camp chair midway between the starting point and the finish line. The echoing loudspeakers and the thudding hooves kept my mind empty but wide awake. We leaned back mightily as we cleared the two downhill jumps, my ears sharply attuned to the thudding hoof sounds behind.

At the turn of the horseshoe bend, we went as one rider over the poles and down into the water with a mighty splash. The crowd cheered and clapped and we were up and out the other side.

'Good on ye!' someone yelled, then we were going up the steep incline and over the 'little cottage' jump. Mrs Webb said something about John and Steffi and then we were in the home straight, urged on mightily by unknown voices. We went smoothly over the last jump then trotted around in circles, sweating and breathing heavily.

Mrs Webb read out our time. Steffi and I held our ponies still and looked joyously at each other. Neither of us had ever completed the course in such a good time. Steffi kneed her pony alongside mine, put her arm around my waist and pressed her head hard into my shoulder. I gripped her shoulder awkwardly in what I thought was a hug. When she released me, there were tears of joy on her face.

We both knew well that Mickey and his partner would win the competition. He had become such an outstanding rider that he was really in a different league. No one doubted that he would become a professional jockey. So far as we were concerned, the competition was really between the rest of us. Steffi and I had way and ahead the best time so far.

We dismounted and started taking the tack off the

steaming ponies, our ears all the time attuned to Mrs Webb's commentary on the next pair of riders. Our training obliged us to rub down the ponies and sponge them, to cool them. The possibility that another pair of riders could beat our time kept us silent. Thirteen pairs of riders followed us. By the time we had turned our ponies into the paddock, there were only two pairs left. We went and sat near Mrs Webb and waited out the agony.

At last it was over. So far as we could tell, our time had been the best. Steffi and I sat on camp chairs outside the marquee. We looked at each other silently, eyes luminous with anticipation.

'And the winners are,' boomed Mrs Webb's voice, 'Mickey and Louise, in first place.'

Everyone cheered and clapped. We did too.

'And second, with a really excellent time, John and Steffi.'

We rose from our chairs and properly hugged this time. I was vaguely aware of the announcement that Tommy and partner had come in fourth. I knew he wouldn't mind, that in fact he would probably be pleased. Then it was over, bar the presentation of rosettes in the marquee.

I had been somewhat shocked to catch a glimpse of Jimmy the Barber chatting away, apparently happily, to Mrs Webb. Who had persuaded him to come? Could it have been my father? To my further surprise, he appeared on the dais in the marquee to present the rosettes, first to his own son, Mickey, to appropriate humorous remarks that produced brief bursts of laughter and clapping from the audience.

Mrs Webb strode onto the stage as he finished and he held the microphone out towards her. She stood still a few moments and the audience went completely silent.

'I hope, one day,' she began, 'to see one member of the winning pair today, young Mickey Maher, ride over the jumps at Cheltenham. I know that his partner of today, Louise, will not mind my saying this–'

'I don't mind!' called Louise, and everyone laughed and clapped.

There was a curious silence then. I was watching Jimmy's face. It was as if things rippled across his features as he stood very still, eyes down. Mickey glanced at him.

'I am saying this also,' continued Mrs Webb, her voice low and husky, 'for the benefit of another pair of young riders, John and Steffi.' There was some brief applause as she beckoned us over. She hooked the microphone on its stand and put her right arm across my shoulders, her left across Steffi's.

'In any other competition, without an exceptional rider like Mickey, these two young riders would have been the winners. I never saw them ride as a pair until today. What I saw was a real team, each anticipating the other's move, always aware of where the other was. And,' – she paused and looked around her audience – 'they have that rare thing in young riders – style!'

We were cheered as we floated back to our places. Jimmy squeezed our shoulders and said, 'Well done!'

Kitty, clad in white coat and cap, waved us over from her station at the tea urn. She frowned down at us, her eyes wide as if in disbelief. 'Well, didn't ye do well,' she exclaimed.

Then someone was waving, to catch our attention. It was Peggy, brandishing a Brownie camera. She struggled through the crowd, grabbed us both and gave us a big hug.

'Well, congratulations, both of you! Now, I'm going to take your photo.'

She instructed me to put my arm across Steffi's shoulder and Steffi to put her arm around my waist. We did so self-consciously, producing the smile demanded. Peggy took several photos, just to be sure. We stood waiting, clasped together.

'It's okay, John-John,' Peggy joked, 'you can let her go now.'

I grinned as I released Steffi. The truth was I didn't really want to.

I could have gone in under the archway but decided to go in through the bar. I was feeling bullish and triumphant. My father stood behind the bar, the newspaper spread out on the counter.

'Well?' was all he said.

'I came second,' I said, showing him the rosette.

He stared at me coldly and sniffed. 'Aah, second is no good. Only first place counts.' He went back to his newspaper, as if he had a bad taste in his mouth. I was rooted to the floor, feeling as if I had been slapped hard across the face. He didn't look up, and I found myself moving towards the door into the hall. The spring slammed it hollowly behind me.

I was numb as I stared into the wardrobe mirror in the attic. I was looking at a sad clown, dressed in an outfit that was utterly meaningless. I began to take off each article very slowly, watching myself disrobe the ghost within. Each item had been paid for in humiliation in Heaton's gentlemen's outfitters. I took off the boots, remembering the facial expression of Mr Sharp in Parson's shoe shop. I laid each item sadly on the bed, like dead friends.

My father might be tight-fisted, but when, after careful consideration, he bought a suit or a shirt or a property, it had to be the best, because it was an investment. Is that how he saw me, a poor investment? I felt anger burst like a sudden storm in my chest and I grabbed the riding gear off the bed and threw it on the floor. I was still staring at the mess when there was a gentle knock on the door.

'John-John, are you in there?'

'I'm getting changed, Peggy,' I called in a voice I hoped was normal.

'Bring down anything you need washed.'

'Okay.'

It brought me back to normality. I carefully examined the riding gear and could see that the jodhpurs certainly needed a wash. Then I carefully wiped the boots at the wash-hand basin and put the jacket on a hanger in the wardrobe.

I probably looked sheepish as I came into the kitchen. Peggy was at the table, sorting out clean clothes. She looked at me curiously.

'I heard you coming in then going up the stairs.'

'Oh,' I said, hoping to sound casual, 'I just had to get out of that outfit.'

Peggy left what she was doing and looked at me long and hard.

'What's the matter?'

I had to take hold of myself and put a lid on my emotions. I started relating what had occurred in the bar, as if it had happened to someone else. I listened carefully to my own voice. I began to feel pleased that there wasn't even a tremor in it. It even helped that Peggy's eyes were getting wider with shock, as if she was feeling the full impact of what I was saying.

'John-John,' she said in a voice that was close to quavering, 'that's . . . that's terrible.' She stared at me in horror and seemed for once to be at a loss for words.

I started talking about all the things that troubled me. I talked for a long time and she listened, nodding and absorbing everything.

The kitchen door opened and my mother came briskly in. She stood for a moment. 'What are you doing, sitting there in the dark?' she said. She switched on the light and we blinked in its harshness.

'Oh, we just got talking, ma'am,' said Peggy cheerfully, 'and forgot about the time.'

My mother looked at Peggy strangely. I often thought that she was jealous of the way Peggy and I got on together.

'God,' I said, 'I forgot to bring down the jodhpurs.' I rose and left. I could hear them talking as I went up the stairs.

In the attic, I was lifting the jodhpurs when the rosette tumbled onto the floor. I stared at the rosette a moment, grabbed it off the floor and stuffed it in my pocket. I went down the stairs as quietly as I could. Peggy and my mother were talking in the kitchen. I went into the yard and out through the archway, like a thief in the night. A red sky was the background to the roof of Steffi's house and all the roofs across the street, but grey shadows were closing in, down in the street below. I went up past Jimmy the Barber's, thinking of Mickey and the joy there must be behind their door that evening.

I turned down the lane towards Micko and Johnjo's forge. It was strange to see everything closed up and shrouded in shadow. There was a kind of empty doorway to the right-hand side of the forge. I took the rosette out of my pocket and threw it right inside.

'Where have you been?' said Peggy, frowning anxiously.

We talked for a while. Eventually I told her what I had done.

'You did what?' she exclaimed. She was angry this time. She got up and put on her cardigan. She rooted around in the press until she found her bicycle lamp. 'You come with me, John-John.' There was no question of refusal.

We went up to the forge and, with the help of Peggy's lamp, found the rosette.

Back in the kitchen, we were silent for some time, as if there was nothing to be said.

'Why is he like that, Peggy?'

She looked at me, her old, calm self. She had been thinking deeply. 'Well,' she said, 'you saw for yourself what happened to Mickey's father. Some people have big disappointments in their lives, deep frustrations, talents that never get to be used.' She became thoughtful again.

Was she talking about my father? What disappointments and talents was she talking about? I realised that I knew nothing about my father. What I knew about my mother was like a family legend that she and her sisters preserved.

Later, in the attic, I stood in the dark at the window, staring across the street at Steffi's house. The roof and chimneys were black against a pale summer sky. The light in her window was amber behind the curtains. Did she dream of me, I wondered, the way I dreamed of her? I stood there a long time.

Fire!

1954

Our stables burned down the night of the annual horse fair, which took place on the third Sunday of January on Connaught Street. I would never forget that winter's fair. The horses started coming up our street as soon as Mass was over. Ice had turned the whole street to glass. We knew how dangerous that could be because there were always so many horses that the fair spilled over into O'Connell Street and down Pearse Street hill. It meant that our vet, Frank Martin, and his humane killer had to be on hand to put down horses with broken legs.

I was having breakfast after Mass. For some reason Mrs Halligan was there that day. The wind moaned in the chimney but flames danced merrily in the kitchen range. Suddenly the outer door crashed open and an icy blast of air seemed to throw in the little man who entered the kitchen proper.

'Boss says I'm to get a feed o' rashers an' eggs in here!' he shouted in a thin aggressive voice. Mrs

Halligan turned massively from the sink and pointed a huge finger at him.

'First thing you do, you miserable little calf-jobber, is go back and close them two doors!'

Left speechless by this unexpected attack, the little man obediently closed the doors. He came back to face Mrs Halligan, hands on hips, glaring balefully down on him.

'Now, ferret-face,' she said, 'you sit down there like a good little man, until we find out what the boss ordered.'

The little man sat down obediently on the edge of a chair beside the table. He glanced at me, finishing my breakfast at the top end, then looked longingly at the roaring range. Mrs Halligan and Peggy consulted quietly. Peggy seemed shocked, and her expression gave the impression that she was still wrinkling her nose in disgust. Glancing warily at the little man as she passed, she went out, and I heard the bar door swing open and shut.

The little man indeed had ferret-like features. A greasy peaked cap was pulled hard down on a bony head. A filthy tweed coat reached almost to his ankles and was belted with a twisted rope of material. His long nails were black with dirt, and he stank.

My father breezed in, Peggy trailing behind. He stared down severely at the little man. 'How far did you walk the cattle?'

'Listen, boss,' he said in a whining voice, 'I was up before six this morning and I must have walked them cattle a good thirty mile–'

'Don't tell me anything about miles! From where to where did you walk them and' – he raised a large threatening finger – 'don't you tell me any lies!'

The little man seemed to shrink into the chair. 'I tell you, boss, I had to walk out to Fuerty for two of them cattle then back to Roscommon and from Roscommon to here. And if that isn't thirty–'

'That's twenty-five miles. Where did you put the cattle?'

'I put them in the cowshed abroad in Kiltoom like you told me. Then I walked in that horse. And I tell you, boss, that took half the morning, because that horse is pure lame.'

'Where's the horse now?'

'Sure, he's below in the stable like you told me.'

'Right, when you've had your feed, come into the bar and you'll be paid.'

My father consulted quietly with Mrs Halligan, who nodded several times, and my father headed for the door.

'Boss,' called out the little man and my father turned. 'Sure, you'll give us a couple o' pints o' porter along with the few shillings?'

My father faced him. 'You'll get what was agreed and no more!' He looked at Mrs Halligan. Mrs Halligan nodded severely, as if in agreement. My father went out.

Peggy looked enquiringly at Mrs Halligan.

'It's all right, Peggy, *a grá*. Boss says I'm to look after this lad. I'll start frying as soon as the other lad comes in.'

She had hardly spoken before the door from the yard flew open again and this time a tall, skinny countryman with a battered hat blew in. He too was made to go back and close the outer door but he was not as easily cowed as the calf-jobber.

'Lord God, Missus,' he said, marching confidently up to the range, rubbing his hands, 'it's freezing out there. When are we going to have the feed?'

'It's not a feed you'll get but a pan over your head if you don't get your skinny arse away from that range this minute!'

'Lord God, Missus—'

'And don't you "Missus" me! You two blow-ins won't be eating in the kitchen either. You'll be fed in the room below.'

So saying, she threw open the door to the right of the chimney breast. Two steps led down into the high-ceilinged, whitewashed room that used to be used as a dairy. I knew it was freezing in there. There was only a deal table and a couple of benches.

'Lord, Missus!'

'In ye go, the pair of ye!' She held the door open.

The little man got up without a word but the tall skinny one was standing his ground.

'I'm having a word with the boss about this, Missus.'

'I've had a word with the boss,' she said, 'and he said that if ye're any trouble at all, ye'll be out on yere arses in the yard in a minute!'

Reluctantly, the pair of them went down the steps and into the room.

'There's an oil heater in there,' she shouted after them and closed the door. She smiled at me and then at Peggy as if the whole thing was a big joke.

Peggy kept her nervous smile in place and said, 'I'll go upstairs and look in on the girls.' She smiled at me in passing.

'What were you drawing?' asked Mrs Halligan and came over to look. She started laughing. 'Well, there's no doubt about it. He looks like a ferret all right.'

'Who's that other man, Mrs Halligan, the tall one with the hat?'

'Oh, him! He calls himself a horse doctor and he's here to try and fix that lame horse. Well, we'll see if he does.'

The two doors crashed open again but this time it was Mickey.

'Howya, Mrs Halligan,' he sang out and came over to see what I was doing.

'Well, how's young Mickey? Go out and close the doors behind you now, there's a good lad.'

He closed the doors and came over again to look at the drawing. He laughed. 'Who's that?'

'Ah, no one.'

'Will we go out and look at the horses?'

'Yeah, let's go!'

Mrs Halligan was frying at the range. 'Close the doors,' she called.

Connaught Street on a fair day was like an obstacle course. When it was cattle, they mounted the pavements, leaving steaming green dung everywhere and filling the echoing ravine of the street with a bedlam of bawling. When it was sheep, it was all wooden pens and a madness of bleating. With horses it was different. Mickey and I made a game of ducking under all the ropes that farmers used to tie their horses to the long metal bars that ran across the shop windows to protect them from the surge.

The wooden shutters that were attached to the bars during cattle fairs were hardly needed with horses. They stood patiently for hours on end, sometimes shifting restlessly or backing away, eyes and nostrils wide when some prospective buyer prised open their jaws to look at their teeth, a good way to find out what age they were.

Other farmers stood in the street holding their horses, willingly going through the fine points with anyone willing to listen or who showed an interest in buying. Other horses and ponies were tethered to telegraph poles, often with a nosebag of hay conveniently at their feet, enough to inform any passer-by that its owner had gone down the street for some liquid refreshment.

Suddenly Mickey was laughing and pointing. A donkey had carefully positioned itself and proceeded to urinate mightily on the footpath in front of us. The tall, thin farmer lightly holding his halter lifted his studious gaze from the steaming fountain.

'Anyone for hot lemonade?' he enquired.

We laughed and shook our heads. The donkey's ears were covered with woollen socks, full of holes.

'Why has he socks on his ears?' Mickey asked.

'Oh, this lad feels the cold,' the farmer said, quite

seriously. Suddenly farmers were pulling their horses aside to clear the street and we heard the sound of galloping. We saw a fine young hunter flash past between the watching farmers, with the famous redheaded 'Carrot Ward' on board. He was putting the horse through its paces for someone interested in buying. Ward went to all the horse fairs, showing off horses to interested buyers. He was loud-mouthed and boastful and generally a nuisance, but the farmers used him because he was the best.

'I could do that,' said Mickey quietly, gazing after the rider. He looked serious and I knew he meant it.

'God,' I said, 'that horse could slip and break a leg.'

'Ah, he'll be all right. The council put grit down this morning.'

'Hey, there's Tommy,' I said.

Tommy was waving from the other side of the street. As soon as the farmers started filling up the street again, Tommy started across, picking his way between the piles of dung.

'Did ye hear that Mrs Webb has horses here she wants to sell?' he said.

'You mean the old horses she wants to sell off?' said Mickey.

'Where are they?' I wanted to know.

'Johnny Madden has two of them up outside FitzGerald's pub. And by the way,' he said to me, 'Johnny says they'll be staying in your yard tonight.'

'God. Nobody told me that. Will some be staying in Johnny's yard?'

'Let's go up and talk to him,' said Mickey.

Johnny was holding the halters of two fine old hunters, past their prime. He was talking to a farmer interested in buying them. We stroked the horses and hung around until it was time to go home for tea.

The calf-jobber and the so-called horse doctor were talking loudly in the middle of our yard as I came in through the archway. The calf-jobber was so drunk that I couldn't make out a word he said. Clearly they were arguing about something.

'Well,' said Peggy, smiling, 'I thought you had got lost out there.'

'I see those two fellas are still here,' I said, watching them through the window.

'Yes,' said Peggy, frowning darkly. 'They've asked your father if they can sleep in the hayloft tonight.'

'What did he say?'

'I don't know.'

'I'm sure he told them not to smoke anywhere near the hay,' I said, watching them closely. The calf-jobber was waving his cigarette about and the lighted tip made red arcs in the gloom. As if he had heard me, he squeezed the lighted end of the cigarette between thumb and forefinger with a drunk's careful movements. Then he spat on it to make sure it was out and put the butt slowly into his pocket.

Peggy had the table set and as I sat down to my tea I realised that the loud voices outside had stopped. Shortly afterwards, I saw Johnny walk the two horses past the window and down to the stables. Then the yard lights went off and we heard him walking back out through the archway. I was telling Peggy, as usual, all about the fair when I was surprised to hear Tommy outside in our yard, calling me.

'Hey, John-John, can you come out here a minute!'

Tommy was standing outside the back door, looking down the yard.

'Can you smell something?' he said. I paused to see if I could smell anything.

'I sure can. That's smoke and it's from the stables. Let's get the lights!'

I switched on the yard lights and we stared in silence down at the stables. At first there was nothing but when we got used to the light, I could see the tiniest wisp of smoke drifting skywards from the roof of the stables. Without a word, I bolted back into the house.

My father was behind the bar, serving pints.

'Daddy, I think there's smoke coming out of the stables!'

He stared at me, put a pint glass firmly on the counter and grabbed me by the shoulder. 'Come with me,' he said quietly.

Out in the yard, he stared down at the stables. 'Right,' he said, grabbing me by the shoulder again, 'go across to Dr Nolan and get him to phone for the fire brigade. And you,' he said to Tommy, 'go up to Jimmy Maher's house and get him to come down here right away. Run, the pair of ye!'

We ran.

I rang Nolan's doorbell and Steffi came out. We

stared at each other in surprise. 'John-John,' was all she could say. I told her tersely what was needed. She turned and strode down the hall. She gave a single knock and we walked in on Dr Nolan, who was on the phone. He turned and stared at us, glasses halfway down his nose. Steffi wordlessly pointed at me.

'Listen, I'll have to call you back,' he said and slammed down the receiver. 'What?' he said to Steffi. She pointed to me. As briefly as I could, I explained what was wanted. He turned and dialled a number. There was a pause then a terse explanation. 'Right,' he said and replaced the receiver.

'Thanks,' I shouted and ran. I saw Tommy and Jimmy the Barber coming down the street at a run. Jimmy had no tie on and he had clearly just pulled on an overcoat. The fire alarm rose to a high wail as we came in through the archway. Jimmy had what I thought were two leather pouches clutched in his hand.

'Here,' he said to me, handing me one of them, 'hold on to that until I call for it.'

As soon as I had it in my hand, I realised what it was. We had used them countless times for fire drill with the ponies out at Mrs Webb's place.

Our yard was bright as day with both yard lights on and flames pushing up through the stable roof. Shadowy figures had formed a chain, passing buckets out the kitchen window and from the tap in the yard to someone up a ladder against the stable wall. Shouts mingled with the screams and whinnies of frightened horses and thumping, kicking sounds from the stables. My father emerged from the stable door leading a terrified horse that immediately reared. My father turned, trying to hold on, and the horse's hoof struck him on the shoulder, throwing him to the ground. Immediately a great big man rushed forward and grabbed the halter. He leaned all his weight into pulling the horse's head down then he rapidly walked him around in circles, gradually moving him up the yard, scattering the chain before him. He was talking soothing nonsense and the horse was calming down when he saw Jimmy.

'Paddy,' called Jimmy to the big man, who I now saw was Dinny Hoctor's father, 'how many horses are out?'

'There's three out,' shouted the big man, 'and two more inside right at the back. They're Mrs Webb's two horses.'

'Right,' said Jimmy calmly and started moving down the yard. The big man stared at him aghast, holding hard onto the horse, whose eyes were still rolling wildly.

'Jimmy,' shouted Paddy Hoctor after him, 'you can't go in there! That roof is about to give!'

Jimmy kept on walking. I saw him disappear through the stable door and I followed him as far as the door. My father was still on the ground. I was surprised to see Dr Nolan kneeling beside him.

'You and you,' said Dr Nolan to two of the bystanders, 'help me get him into the kitchen.'

My father was gasping, clearly in real pain, with his eyes closed. Something was wrong with his shoulder. I stood staring helplessly, then I felt the leather pouch in my hand and remembered that Jimmy would need me there when he called for it.

Two men carefully lifted my father, following the doctor's instructions, but still he let out a terrible groan. When they had him steadily between them, they carried him slowly up towards the kitchen.

The fire bell was clanging noisily out in Connaught Street, then the fire engine was coming slowly and carefully in through the archway. Paddy Hoctor moved the horse out of the way and then Jimmy was walking out the stable door, calmly leading a big hunter with a black hood over its head. He swiftly walked the horse up to Paddy Hoctor and wordlessly handed over the halter. With a gesture of his hand, he signalled that I should give him the other hood.

Clumps of burning hay were falling around him as he walked out the second horse. I was right beside the door when I saw the burning hay that had fallen on the horse's back, and without thinking I sprang forward and swept it away. The horse whinnied briefly but didn't spook. One of the farmers took the horse from Jimmy and walked it up to Paddy Hoctor. Johnny Madden was there now and he took hold of the second horse. The firemen were shouting at us and we all backed well away from the building as the roof began to cave in. The firemen were there immediately, training their hoses on the blaze.

As we watched the blaze and the firemen at work, I thought again of how we used to laugh behind her back at old Mrs Webb's eccentricities. As well as endless mucking out, cleaning tack and taking the ponies out on hacks, Mrs Webb had insisted from the beginning on our practising her very own version of fire drill for ponies. That was when she introduced us to the little leather hoods that could be used to quickly and easily cover a pony's eyes in the event of a rescue from a stable fire. Not only that; she would light a fire with damp leaves or old cloths in the yard so the whole place was full of smoke. Then we had to put on the hoods and lead the ponies out.

The next time we did the exercise she added something that made us laugh. She insisted that some of us bang on big oil drums and make as much of a racket as we could. To the next stage she added shouting and ringing the bell in the bell tower. By the end of that summer, the ponies seemed a bit bored by it all. It goes without saying that hay was stored well away from the ponies' stables, which of course involved more work for us. One day she explained it all. As a girl, she had witnessed horses being burned to death at her aunt's stables in Sussex, England. She never wanted to see that happen again.

Jimmy Maher was sitting on a chair in our kitchen while Dr Nolan examined his head and shoulders. His hair was singed and he had burn marks on his neck. I learned that my father had been taken to hospital with a broken shoulder.

Jimmy was having a cup of tea while Dr Nolan attended to one or two more people.

'Jimmy,' I said, 'how did you know to do that with the horses?'

'You must have done the fire drill out at Mrs Webb's?'

'Yes, we all did.'

'Well, so did I, before you were even born,' he said, somewhat mysteriously.

'Hey,' I said, 'the guards are in the yard!'

We both looked out the window. Sergeant Kelly and another guard were talking to the calf-jobber and the skinny man who 'fixed horses'.

'Yeah,' murmured Jimmy, nodding his head, 'a right pair of customers, them two.'

Immediately I had a vision of the calf-jobber putting the cigarette butt into his pocket.

'Of course,' said Jimmy thoughtfully, 'I told your father about a loose slate above that stable. And there's nothing like wet hay to start a fire.'

I decided there and then not to mention what I had seen. Giving information like that to my father could easily backfire.

The Democratic Process

1954

Everyone, even my mother, seemed different on the day of the election. There was a lot of activity in the courthouse across the street from my mother's shop that day. The district court was not in session, but Justice Michael Carney came into the tearoom before casting his vote. At least that's what I picked up from the conversation he was having with my mother while I did my homework at a corner table, more or less hidden behind the large potted plants.

I was in the tearoom that day for a specific reason. It was doughnut day. On that day every week, Katy Kiernan, the best baker my mother ever trained, made doughnuts. But I had to await a signal before entering the bakery.

Katy, in her white cap and coat, came swiftly into the tearoom with a loaded tray, eyeing me cheerfully as she passed.

'Now,' she said, as she carefully placed a teapot

between my mother and the judge.

'Oh, thank you, Katy,' said my mother, gazing up at her with theatrical sincerity.

'We don't usually see you in here, Katy,' said the judge heartily.

'Well,' said my mother quickly, 'Katy is just helping out on the floor today as we're a bit short-staffed.'

'I'm sure, Katy,' said the judge, 'that you'll have time to cross the street later on to vote.'

'Oh, who knows?' said Katy in her cheerful, hearty fashion as she turned and left. She winked mischievously at me as she passed.

I could see a cake stand with our nicest cream buns and some neatly cut ham sandwiches between my mother and the judge. He had unfolded a starched white handkerchief and spread it across his knees. My mother did most of the talking, a phenomenon unfamiliar to me. I was impressed at the skill with which her interlocutor could neatly eat and at the same time precisely time his replies.

I stared once again at one of the mysteries of maths challenging me from the page as my mother's suddenly more cultivated tones mixed with Justice Michael Carney's baritone rumble. The large mirrors on the walls, combined with the mirror behind the pair, provided a choice of impressions of the room. If I narrowed my eyes and tried to absorb all three views, the bentwood chairs seemed to float upwards and the white napery on the tables became lilies floating in a jungle of oversized potted plants.

I was hearing about a part of my mother's childhood I had never known about. She was a young girl, calling into McLoughlin's on the way home from school in Roscommon. She had to pass through the bar to get to the grocery part, and the aggressive, drunken shouting of the Black and Tans in there, with their ugly, Cockney accents, terrified her. She could still feel the trembling in her hands as she threw the groceries into the basket on the handlebars and cycled home like the wind, as if the devil himself was after her.

I looked over. Justice Carney was nodding his head in deep sympathy. He looked as if he was soaking in her experience with his whole body. Then she spoke about her famous namesake, Father O'Flanagan, who had campaigned against the Tans contrary to the wishes of his bishop. In the same breath she spoke about her pride when she heard Dr Douglas Hyde speaking in Roscommon dialect on the wireless, on the occasion of his inaugural speech as president, in 1938. Of course, she assured Justice Carney, to her Michael Collins was the great hero of the War of Independence. But she too, like De Valera and his followers, felt bitterly disappointed that only the twenty-six counties had gained independence. That was why she would vote later that day the way she had always voted.

Three loud bongs on a metal tin roused me from my stupor. Then I was on my feet, bolting for the bakery. Katy stood there waiting for me, grinning.

'I thought you'd hear the summons, all right,' she said. 'Now, you know what to do.'

'I do!' I said. I took the tin of whiting and the little
pastry brush and immediately ran out the shop door.
Carefully, in large capitals, I inscribed the legend 'Hot
Doughnuts' high as I could on the plate-glass window.
Then I went back inside and stuffed myself with as many
hot doughnuts as I could, washing them down with
Katy's strong black tea. This was a new arrangement
because some weeks previously I had accidentally
dropped a doughnut from the tongs into the boiling-hot
oil. The oil splashed up and gave me a bad burn on the
arm. Katy had refused to let me anywhere near the oil
after that.

'Are you going to vote when you're finished here,
Katy?' I asked between mouthfuls.

She turned away, busying herself with something.
'Ah,' she said, throwing up a hand as if to dismiss the
thought, 'maybe.' She turned around, as though she had
felt me staring at her.

'I thought everyone had to vote,' I said carefully.

Katy fixed me with a look. Tough, cheerful Katy
looked serious now. 'No one *has* to vote,' she said
quietly, 'and I have to wonder what voting has to do
with me.'

'What do you mean?'

'I have six brothers. They're all in England, working.
I might be the next. And when you're on that boat to
Holyhead, you're not thinking of Fianna Fáil or Fine
Gael, John-John.'

'Why would you be the next, Katy?'

'I get on great with your mother, John-John, but

you know she let two of the girls go last month. So who knows?'

Katy poured herself a cup of tea and sat down opposite me. I noticed for the first time that her face was white with tiredness.

'God, it's great to get off my feet!' She sighed and took a packet of Woodbines from her apron pocket and lit one. She blew out a long jet of smoke and smiled at me fondly. It seemed sad to me that her teeth, in that good-looking face, were not so good.

'So you're not going to vote?'

'I'm not. Politicians are only interested in votes. They're not interested in the thousands of Irish who end up in England. They can't vote any more, can they?'

'Why did your brothers go there?'

Katy studied me. Her look was kind but I felt shy under her steady gaze. 'Well, John-John, you'll probably grow up to be a doctor or a solicitor. It'll be different for you. None of my brothers had any education.'

'What do you mean?'

'Well, let's put it like this: on his first day in London, my brother Michael stood outside a famous pub called the Elephant and Castle at six o'clock in the morning. A load of green lorries roared up the street and this great big man in boots and a cap jumped down from the front one. He looked over the bunch of Irish lads waiting there in the street the way a farmer looks over cattle at a fair. He pointed at my brother and shouted, "You, jump on!" My brother got up on the back of the lorry. Six or seven more lads followed.'

'What was happening?'

'They were being hired for the day. They were day labourers – navvies is what they're called.'

I felt somehow shocked and insulated from the world. Katy kept her eyes on me as she slowly ground the butt of her cigarette into a saucer. 'I'm the only one in the family,' she said quietly, 'who has any kind of certificate. Thanks to your mother, I'm a qualified baker.'

'Would you emigrate?'

She shook her head. 'My mother is getting on and she's not well. I don't want the life my brothers have.'

'Why?'

'I went to see my brother once. The boat was packed with Irish lads going back after Christmas. They were all drunk out of their minds, lots of them being sick all over the place.'

'Why was that?'

Katy took a deep breath that seemed to lift her shoulders in a shrug. Her face was a sad grimace. 'They couldn't wait to get away from their bits of farms and fishing boats back in Kerry and Mayo and Connemara. But they hated going back to what was waiting for them in England.'

'Was it that bad?'

'My brother shared a big bare room with two other lads in a place called Camden Town. You had to put shillings in a gas meter in the bathroom down the hall just to have a bath. These lads came home at night exhausted and covered in dust from demolishing the bombed-out buildings left after the war. Of course, some of the Irish got rich doing that. Not many, though.'

Katy told me a lot that day, about the train journey through the night down to Euston, seeing the miles of factory chimneys belching smoke and fire into the black sky. A vision of hell, she said. She spoke of crowds of people, hurrying and swarming like ants around the trains as dawn was breaking. She waited an hour at the main gate and Michael never came. She realised he mustn't have got her letter. But she had his address, and with only a few pounds in her pocket she went to get a taxi. The driver was Cockney and she couldn't understand him, so she showed him the piece of paper with Michael's address. They drove through miles and miles of streets. Where was this stranger taking her? She imagined all kinds of things. The driver kept glancing at her in the mirror. Suddenly they were in a quiet street and he was staring up at a huge four-storey terraced house with steps leading up to the front door. Surely Michael couldn't be living here? The driver got out, opened the boot and left Katy's suitcase on the footpath, saying something she couldn't understand. As she paid the man, a window was thrown up and Michael was suddenly shouting and waving down to her. She was shaking so much that she and Michael sat on his bed for an hour without saying a word to each other.

She said they went to the Emerald Ballroom, where she heard stories of savage fights in places like Cricklewood and Kilburn, swarms of police arriving in Black Marias and Paddywagons. She remembered the signs in boarding-house windows that said 'No Blacks. No Irish'.

The names and places meant nothing to me but when she mentioned jokes about the Irish and comedians on the wireless imitating Irish accents, I interrupted: 'Why would they do that?'

Katy shrugged. 'They looked down on us the way they look down on the blacks.'

'Why?'

At this moment, my mother came in. Glancing at me, she said, 'Katy, I've been thinking. If your mother isn't well, why don't you finish up now and go home. You can take tomorrow off and come back in after the weekend.'

'That'd be great, ma'am, thanks.' Katy just sat there, as if too tired to move. There was silence for a moment.

'I know,' my mother continued, 'that since Sheila and Mary left you've had to do everything.'

There was another pause, full of things unsaid. Katy watched her stubbed-out cigarette on the saucer. A thin spiral of smoke rose straight up from it.

'Oh, they'll be all right, ma'am. They both got jobs in the new factory.'

My mother thought about that for a moment. 'Well, isn't it great that the Lenihans brought that factory to town after the woollen mills burned down?'

Katy let it hang in the air. 'Yes,' she said, 'I believe young Mr Lenihan is standing for Fianna Fáil.'

'Oh, he is indeed,' said my mother warmly, 'the best man for the job.'

I couldn't help but feel that a strange sort of game was going on. My mother and Katy were each saying one thing and clearly thinking something else.

'You probably don't remember,' my mother said, 'the night of the woollen mills fire. There was no fire brigade at the time, so the army was called in. They started blowing up the buildings around the mill in case the fire spread to the gas works.' She broke off to laugh. 'Everyone thought the Germans were bombing the town because that was back in 1940.'

Katy smiled wanly but didn't seem to know what to say to this. She became thoughtful. 'All I remember about the woollen mills, ma'am, is that my father cycled in every day from Cornafulla to the job he had there. After the fire, he went to England. He sent money back every month but we only ever saw him at Christmas when we were growing up.'

There was a strange little silence. Then my mother turned to me and said, 'You'd better go back in now and finish your homework, John-John.' To Katy she said, 'There's nothing much left here to do, Katy. You go ahead and I'll finish up.'

'Right you are, ma'am.'

I went back into the tearoom and got stuck into my homework. My mother and Justice Michael Carney immediately continued their interrupted conversation.

I saw the judge discreetly glancing in my direction, but my head was already down. When he lowered his voice, my ears became trumpets.

'I see the guards are keeping an eye on that young Ó'Brádaigh character,' he said.

'No harm either,' said my mother. 'I saw him walking down past the shop this morning, brazen as anything.'

For a minute, I thought they were talking about Tommy Brady, because that was his name in Irish. *And* he was always in trouble. Then I remembered another Ó'Brádaigh.

Suddenly the judge turned in my direction. *'Tá cluasa fada ar mhuca beaga.* What does that mean, John-John?'

'It means,' I said shyly, 'that little pigs have big ears.' I noticed my mother looked pleased with me. I was surprised the judge even knew my name.

My mother got to her feet. 'Excuse me a moment, Michael,' she said with respect. To me she said in passing as she walked out into the shop: 'I want you to go up to Miss Nelligan and get the paper.'

Her strong will seemed to pull me along with her as far as the till. She pulled out the drawer with its tinkling-bell sound and counted out the exact change I would need. I frowned and grimaced at her in protest. She knew I hated going in to Miss Nelligan.

'It won't take you a minute,' she said severely.

I went up the hill and around Grenham's Corner into Connaught Street, dragging my feet. I stopped and stared, as I did every time, at Miss Nelligan's shop window. Surely people must have thought Miss Nelligan strange, but I never heard anyone say anything. The entire plate-glass window was covered from inside with ancient yellowed pages of the *Irish Press*. De Valera stared stonily at me from several of them. I prepared my opening words and entered the shop.

'Dia duit ar maidin, a bhean uasal,' I said, with as much enthusiasm as I could.

'*Dia is Muire duit, a leanbh!*' she replied, with her usual scowl. '*Cad tá uait?*'

'*Ba mhaith liom an nuachtán, le do thoil,*' I said. There was no need to say which newspaper as she only ever stocked the *Irish Press*. We all knew she was some kind of fanatic. No matter what the weather, a large brown beret completely covered her hair. A long, faded black coat encased her tall, spare frame, and rimless spectacles seemed embedded in the bridge of her nose. Her father, we knew, had fought in the War of Independence and on the anti-Treaty side in the civil war that followed.

A well-dressed young man with glasses stepped down from the street onto the wooden floor behind me. I was handing over the money and receiving the paper when he called out heartily, throwing his head back to show off a smile full of teeth: '*Dia duit ar maidin, a Mháire!*'

'Well,' she replied, a warm smile banishing her scowl, '*Conas atá tu, a mhic?*'

I left them, realising it was the first time I had seen Miss Nelligan smile. It struck me that this stranger and Miss Nelligan must believe in the same thing, like members of the Legion of Mary or the Knights of Saint Columbanus. It was like they were the opposite of Katy.

I also felt puzzled because it was the second time in a week this stranger had crossed my path. The first time was during a Fianna Fáil rally in the square. From the Palace Bar to the bridge and from the castle walls to the front of St Peter's Church, the square was packed tight with people. Tommy and I leaned against the castle wall, watching his father, Jack Brady, standing on the back of the open lorry in front of the church gate. Men we didn't know sat on the chairs behind him, and Fianna Fáil posters made the lorry look like a circus wagon. Tommy's father was making a performance of adjusting the microphone. Each adjustment crackled and echoed loudly around the speakers placed high on the castle walls and on the upper storey of the Palace Bar. It seemed to me that the sound even bounced up behind, to hang suspended between the twin steeples of the church.

'Ladies and gentlemen, *a chairde gaeil,*' Jack Brady's voice boomed around the square. The crowd became silent. 'Today I would like to present to you Fianna Fáil's candidates for the fifteenth Dáil.'

He paused for a moment and the crowd, seemingly taken by surprise, produced a hesitant scattering of applause. But Mr Brady was getting into his stride now. 'First of all,' he boomed, 'I would like to introduce a new candidate, standing for the first time – Mr Brian Lenihan – from the well-known Athlone family, who have done so much and are doing so much for this town. Ladies and gentlemen, give him a big round of applause.' He ended with a flourish, waving Lenihan forward.

Brian Lenihan stared silently at the crowd a moment as he gripped the microphone. I was struck by the mass of wavy hair that covered his head like a bonnet.

'Hey,' I said to Tommy '*is* he from Athlone? I've never seen him before.'

'Sure, he is. He went to school over in the Marist Brothers. Now he's a barrister or something up in Dublin.'

'What exactly is a barrister?'

'Oh, like a solicitor or something. I dunno.'

'What Lenihan family is he talking about?'

'They own the Hodson Bay Hotel, that's who. Hey, let's hear what he has to say.'

Tommy set himself up as an authority on anything to do with politics but I wondered if he knew as much as he thought he did.

'The Fianna Fáil government,' Brian Lenihan's voice boomed and echoed, 'in 1935 put down the foundations of a true democracy by banning both the Blueshirts and the IRA—'

'De Valera,' shouted a man from the back of the crowd, 'promised to break up the big farms and give land to smaller farmers. Instead he sends in the Broy Harriers to take our cattle!'

'I can see, my friend, from that nice blue shirt under your jacket, which side you're on, and all I have to say to you is what we've always said – that there should still be no free speech for Blueshirt traitors.' There was an outburst of laughter and appreciative clapping. Heads turned towards the back, to see who he was talking about.

Tommy was laughing, shaking his head. 'That lad will go far,' he said to me knowingly.

But my attention had been taken by what was happening at the far end of the castle wall, from where the heckling had come. Several guards had appeared. They weren't from our barracks and I hadn't seen them before. One of them was speaking seriously to the man who had been in Miss Nelligan's shop. He was protesting to the guard who was questioning him. His two companions had been taken aside and two of the guards were earnestly talking to them. Suddenly, a group of guards surrounded the man from Miss Nelligan's and walked him purposefully along the edge of the square in the direction of the garda barracks. I nudged Tommy but he was already watching the incident.

'Who's that?' I asked him.

Tommy wore something like a self-satisfied smile. 'He teaches Irish in a school in Roscommon.'

I looked closely at the man being walked away. He looked no different from any of the teachers in our school. 'C'mon, Tommy, what do you know about him?'

Tommy became the man who has inside information. 'They say he's also the commander-in-chief of the IRA west of the Shannon.'

I looked closely at Tommy. He could only have heard his father say something of the kind.

'What's his name?'

'It's the same as ours – Brady – but he calls himself Ruairí Ó'Brádaigh.'

'What'll the guards do with him?'

'I'd say they're taking him in for questioning.'

My mother and the judge were still talking when I got back.

'Grand,' she said, glancing up as I put the *Irish Press* on the table beside her.

The sandwiches were all gone and the confectionery had been reduced to a solitary cream bun. I put my beady eye on it, marking it out as already spoken for. The judge glanced at me with a faint smile, as if he knew what I was thinking.

I heard Katy coming down the stairs and I slid off my chair to say goodbye. Katy stood in the middle of the bakery, transformed. Her hair was brushed and her lips dark red. She carefully put on her headscarf, smiling at me.

My mother came in. 'Katy,' she said rather breathlessly, 'I want to give you something for your mother.' She moved out into the shop and Katy followed.

'Sure there's no need, ma'am.'

'Oh, I know she loves a bit of cream sponge with a cup of tea.' As she spoke, she lifted the sponge cake out of the glass case.

I was watching Katy's face, trying to read her expression. That morning I had seen her place that self-same sponge, which she had baked and filled with cream, into the case.

'Oh,' said Katy uncertainly, 'I'm sure she'd be delighted.'

My mother seemed to ignore the comment, swiftly wrapping the sponge in a sheet of tissue paper and sliding it carefully into a cardboard carton. Without pausing, she took a brown-paper bag and started filling it with Scots Clan chocolate toffees, followed by two bars of Cadbury's chocolate. She was wise to Katy's sweet tooth.

Katy sort of chuckled, looking embarrassed. 'Oh, Lord, ma'am, no – that's far too much! I couldn't–'

'Not at all, Katy. Sure it's only a little token,' she said, thrusting the bag at her almost aggressively. Katy reluctantly took it, looking uneasy about the whole transaction, but my mother was definite and determined.

'Now Katy,' she said, lowering her voice to a somewhat brusque but confidential tone, 'I need to look after Justice Carney, so I'll see you Monday!'

'All right, ma'am!'

My mother left. Katy stood holding the brown-paper bag. Slowly she opened it and looked inside. 'Lord God,' she said to me, 'it's way too much!' She lifted out the two bars of chocolate and grinned at me. 'Eating two bars of chocolate would be like eating mortal sins. So, John-John,' she said, 'you'll have to share the guilt,' and she shoved one of the bars into my hand. She laughed at my expression as I stared down at the unexpected windfall. Then she gathered up her things, being especially careful with the carton containing the sponge cake. She squeezed my arm and walked swiftly out through the shop. She waved as she passed the entrance to the tearoom. 'Bye now,' she called out.

'Goodbye, Katy,' rumbled the judge.

'Take care, Katy,' my mother called. 'Hope your mother is better soon.'

Back at my homework, I kept the chocolate bar out of sight. The talk was still of politics. The last cream bun, looking curiously isolated on the cake stand, was still intact.

'Well,' said my mother to Justice Michael Carney, as if clinching an argument, 'no matter how bad things get, I will never let Peggy or Katy go.'

Corpus Christi

~

1954

I knew it was a dream. But the watcher in me didn't want to wake up. I was crossing the square when the bells of St Peter's started booming above me. I was the watcher, behind me, observing my every move. I broke my stride in the middle of the square to genuflect and throw my right hand to my forehead, my belly, my left shoulder and my right shoulder, the way I'd seen an old man do. The watcher behind me laughed, because the genuflection and the sign of the cross hardly broke my stride.

A hand grabbed my shoulder. I looked up into the angry face of Father John, wiping the spilt red wine off the white sleeve of his vestment.

'Get off the altar!' he snarled at me. 'You can't even ring the bell in time!'

I looked across at my brother, kneeling sanctimoniously in his surplice and soutane. His sly look told me he had given me the wrong signal on purpose.

But the hand gripped my shoulder even more tightly.

'Wake up, John-John, wake up!' Peggy's smiling face hovered above me like the sun.

'You need to get up, John-John – Corpus Christi procession day!' Then she was gone.

Bells were in fact ringing in the silent, sunlit morning. The Shannon split the town into two counties, two provinces, two parishes and two dioceses. I wondered if we really had seven churches in the town. St Peter's below in the square was loud, deliberate and majestic. Across the river, St Mary's had a higher, lighter tone, at the mercy of the wind. Just across the bridge in Church Street, the Protestant bell had a quiet, more discreet tone. Across the street from it and down a lane the friary bell had a light, musical tone that seemed to linger on the river. If the tiny Presbyterian church down on the docks had a bell, I never heard it. Nor did I ever hear a sound from the Methodist church over in Northgate Street.

All four church bells were in action that morning. They made for a strange, disjointed harmony. In between, twittering birds sang their own, separate song in the yard below.

There was another, discordant sound. I held my breath, straining to hear, the familiar wrench in my gut. It was my parents arguing. The voices rose, ugly with hatred. It seemed to be coming from the hallway between the kitchen and the door to the bar. I decided to stay where I was and block out the sound. Suddenly it ended and the bar door slammed. That was my father gone. The kitchen door was next, followed by murmuring voices. Next, the door into the yard closed hollowly and quick steps went across the gravel to the archway, after which they gradually faded. That was my mother gone.

I got cautiously out of bed and slowly began to dress. I stopped when I heard the bar door again. My father's voice was in the kitchen and the murmuring could only be Peggy answering. Then I heard the bar door again.

Ten minutes later, Peggy stood in the middle of the kitchen, a grave expression on her face. 'Well, John-John,' she said with a wan smile, 'you're up!'

'What's going on, Peggy?'

My words seemed to galvanise her and she moved towards the table. 'You know what's going on,' she said quietly. 'Will you have porridge?'

'Just a bit. Can I have tea and toast?'

Normality seemed to return with Peggy's routines. A bowl of porridge was put before me as I sat down.

'Peggy,' I said, as I watched her fill the teapot, 'what about flowers for this house?'

From the attic window, I had seen Steffi and her mother finishing off their bottom windows. Pots and urns of flowers already covered the three stone steps that led up to their Georgian doorway. The gate to their archway was closed. The four windows above were brilliant with banks of tall flowers in jars, standing on tables draped in white, enclosing holy pictures with little candles flickering in glass containers. White drapes hung behind, with bits of greenery pinned to them. Brady's, closed for business, had magically been transformed overnight or very early that morning.

Peggy glanced at me, a little smile on her face as she put the lid on the teapot. 'I thought you would think of that,' she said. 'It was exactly what I was talking about to your father.' She sat down opposite me, ready to pour the tea.

Tommy Brady and I once counted all the buildings on Connaught Street. There were seventy, and sixty-seven of them were shops or pub-groceries. Although most shopkeepers and their families lived above their premises, we knew that the better-off ones had houses and farms out the country. Johnny Madden's family was one of them. His business on the street went back five generations, and Jack Brady's went back six. That bit Tommy told me. A tall, gaunt building housed the one disgraceful family on the street. So far as I could remember, it was the only building that never had a single flower to show for the procession that passed up Connaught Street every Corpus Christi. I experienced some unaccountable horror at the thought of ours becoming the second.

'Your mother,' said Peggy, breaking into my thoughts, 'has ordered all the flowers she needs for the shop in Pearse Street. But there must have been some mix-up about getting flowers for the house here.'

Peggy and I gazed at each other, neither of us saying what we both knew – that there had been a row over who should take responsibility for decorating the house. Peggy didn't say what I knew she would say if I asked her – that my mother was far too busy running the bakery and tearooms and decorating one premises. On the other hand, men were never expected to look after such things. That was a woman's job. Peggy fetched a deep sigh.

'Your father,' she said, 'asked me to see what I can do to decorate the front windows.' She gazed at me and shook her head hopelessly. 'There isn't a spare flower to be had on the street.'

Her expression made me think of Steffi and Pauline, the Nolans' housekeeper, Peggy's friend. Steffi and Pauline would have organised the whole flower thing a good week in advance. Our disgrace would be Peggy's disgrace too. A light bulb went on in my head.

'I know where we can get flowers,' I said, feeling suddenly smug.

'Where would you get flowers at this hour?'

'Out at Mrs Webb's place.'

'John-John,' said Peggy, with a disapproving little smile, 'let's be serious, because this *is* serious.'

'Peggy,' I said earnestly, 'Mrs Webb has a huge rose garden just running wild!' I examined Peggy's face to measure the effect. 'She hasn't had a gardener in *years*,' I added, just to hammer the point home. I thought I saw some kind of glimmer in Peggy's expression. But she was slowly shaking her head.

'John-John, how could we possibly get the flowers in time? Not to mention decorating six windows and one doorway before the procession comes up Connaught Street?'

'The procession doesn't start until after twelve o'clock Mass and it isn't even eight o'clock yet!' I said.

As if to bear out what I was saying, the bells of St Peter's began to toll below in the square. It was ten to eight. The faithful were being summoned to eight o'clock Mass. We both became thoughtful, listening to the sound.

'Well,' said Peggy, as if coming out of a dream, 'maybe it could be done.' Suddenly she seemed to have a worrying thought. 'But isn't Mrs Webb Church of Ireland? What would she know about Corpus Christi processions? And how well do you know her?'

'Peggy,' I said, shaking my head tolerantly, 'Mrs Webb isn't like that. Besides, I've known her for years.'

Peggy went still, gazing straight into my face with a faint smile. I began to feel distinctly uneasy. The thought occurred to me: just how well did I know Mrs Webb?

'Well,' said Peggy at length, 'I suppose it can't do any harm to try. And *some* flowers would be better than no flowers at all.'

'Can I have your bike, Peggy? I could go straight away.'

She thought about that for a moment. 'You won't get much into the front basket, that's for sure. But if I gave you one of the big baskets, we could strap it onto the carrier at the back. That might do it.'

Out in the yard, we tried various containers that might be secured by the strong spring-loaded clamp on the back carrier of the bike. Anything that would fit was far too small. In the end, we strapped a large basket to the carrier and I ran the bike out through the archway.

It was a beautiful morning, just like the best summer mornings out riding at Mrs Webb's. Cocks of hay stood in stubble fields. Heavy trees hung over the road, dappling the sunshine as I whizzed along, listening to the birdsong from the shadows above. I was hot and sweating as I laboured up the hill to the house. The first thing I saw was Kitty, Mrs Webb's housekeeper, wandering through the flowerbeds with a large scissors. She swung around, frowning suspiciously at this unexpected arrival.

'Well, well,' she said with her vinegary smile, squinting at me as I came into focus, 'if it isn't young master John-John!' She stared at me and the big basket strapped to the bike's carrier did not escape her attention. 'Well, what brings you out here this fine morning?'

Now I had to think fast. Telling the bald truth would be unwise. The story would be around the town in no time. 'Well,' I said, as if laughing it off, 'Mammy ordered flowers for the shop in Pearse Street and for the pub but we only just realised that she didn't order enough for the pub, so . . .'

'Oh, right,' she exclaimed, in a peculiar, drawn-out manner as she examined me carefully. 'For the procession, you mean?'

I could almost see her interpreting what I'd said. At that moment, I heard the click of metal on stone and Mrs Webb came around the corner aboard her favourite cob.

'Hallo, John-John!' she sang out cheerfully as she swung down near the stable door. 'Kitty,' she gasped, 'I need about a gallon of good, strong coffee. Would you mind?'

'You've been overdoing it again, Mrs Webb,' said Kitty disapprovingly. 'What will you have with the coffee?'

'Oh, I know I have! And I wouldn't say no to a soft-boiled egg and some toast.'

'Would you take a fry – a few rashers and a fried egg?' demanded Kitty querulously.

'Oh, Kitty, you're a real darling! There's nothing I would like better.'

Kitty went off into the house, muttering something. Mrs Webb looked at me and winked slyly. All her exhaustion seemed to drop away and she immediately started fitting a cigarette into her ancient cigarette holder. She lit the cigarette, inhaled hungrily and blew out a cloud of smoke before she was ready to talk. I was used to that.

'Now, John-John, would you mind helping me to get the tack off Polly and then you can tell me why you're here.'

We undid the buckles in companionable silence and I took each piece into the tack room. I sponged down the cob and Mrs Webb absentmindedly brushed her down. Mrs Webb clearly was tired. She pulled out a crate, collapsed onto it and indicated that I should sit on another one. She seemed in no hurry to get back to the house.

'Well,' she said with her mischievous smile, 'tell me all.' She blew out a great cloud of smoke and gazed at me.

I made up my mind straight away to tell her the situation exactly as it was. She listened seriously, nodding gently every so often. When I finished, she was thoughtful.

'How many windows do you need to decorate, or doorways?'

I went through each one and she nodded.

'Look,' she said, 'no problem with the flowers. Take as many as you want. It's a jungle now but we still have beautiful roses, lovely lilies and oodles of lilac. How did you propose to get them back? On that bike?'

I nodded, touched by her instant generosity and uncomplicated way of doing things. I was also a bit embarrassed now by my idea of taking the flowers on the bike.

Mrs Webb was shaking her head. 'You'll never manage to get all the flowers you'll need onto your bike. Now, I have an idea. But first things first: I'm going in to have my breakfast whilst you, John-John, go up the field and catch Sylvie for me.' So saying, she rose with her cheerful smile, lifted a bucket and handed it to me. 'If you put a few handfuls of oats into this, Sylvie will come running and she'll be your best friend, at least for this morning!'

I laughed, already feeling better because I knew she was up to something. I went up the field as Mrs Webb disappeared into the house. I felt touched, realising what she meant to do. She was clearly going to take the flowers into town in her pony and trap.

Sylvie responded to the oats exactly as promised and she behaved like a lamb. She wasn't in any hurry, though, and by the time we got back to the yard, Mrs Webb was coming out of the house.

'Right, John-John,' she said, all business now, 'you harness Sylvie whilst I look out some gloves and secateurs for the roses.'

By the time I had Sylvie harnessed, she was back. We pulled out the trap together and backed Sylvie into the shafts. We left her with her nose in a nosebag while we tackled the roses. By the time we'd finished, my hands and arms were covered with little scratches. Mrs Webb just laughed.

'Don't say I didn't warn you!' was all she said. She worked very quickly but without hurrying. I ended up loading the trap, under her direction, until only the central part of the driver's seat was free from flowers of every kind. Finally, Mrs Webb straightened up, looked the trap over and decided it was time to carefully place the best roses in the basket on the back of Peggy's bike. And that's how we rode into town, Sylvie clip-clopping down the empty streets, me following on Peggy's bike.

Mrs Webb pulled up at the footpath outside our house. 'John-John, I'll wait out here. Would you mind getting Peggy to help you take the flowers inside?'

Peggy's eyes were enormous as she gazed at the trap. 'Hello, Mrs Webb,' she said.

'Hallo, Peggy,' said Mrs Webb, once more inserting a

cigarette into her cigarette holder. She lit up and calmly surveyed the street, her eyes moving from one house to the other. We came and went in silence, carefully handling the delicate plants. Peggy seemed to be in a daze. She had already filled every available vessel with water in the kitchen and she took the precious loads from me and placed them thoughtfully in the most appropriate container. As I took the last bunch from the trap, I turned uncertainly towards Mrs Webb.

'Mrs Webb–'

Immediately she put a finger up to her lips. 'No need to say anything, John-John. Glad to do it. Sylvie, walk on!' She shook the reins. Sylvie tossed her head, walked a bit then broke into a trot as they disappeared down the street.

Up the aisle, in front of the priest, Tommy, Mickey and I stepped slowly and solemnly along. Old Dean Crowe, his voice cracked and hoarse, tried to keep up with the choir, and the organ ground out its echoing sound, filling the space above us. I held the cross aloft with aching shoulders, flanked by Tommy and Mickey, holding big brass candlesticks that flickered on their shiny faces. My brother brought up the rear, swinging a smoking thurible.

Outside on the steps, the light was blinding, the heaving mass of humanity in the square like a seething sea. Twin shadows of steeples cooled the square, while the sun baked the castle walls. The noise was tremendous. The bells above boomed and bonged as the dean halted on the top of the steps, dwarfed by the massive pillars. Four members of the Knights of Saint Columbanus held the canopy above him.

Little girls in white Communion dresses ran up the steps, scattering rose petals from their small, white baskets as they backed away towards the gates. The dean slowly held the monstrance aloft and one of the altar boys rang the bell three times, with solemn pauses in between. A great murmur rose from the heaving crowd and the prayers began. We stood waiting, sweating in our surplices and soutanes. From the new loudspeakers in the steeples above, as soon as the bells stopped ringing, the recorded voice of Canon Sidney McEwan burst into 'Bring Flowers of the Rarest' and it echoed all around the square.

The faint rhythmic sound from down Grace Road grew louder. A brass band suddenly blared into the canon's song and we saw the first of the soldiers march smartly into the square. A great loud voice barked out some instruction and the soldiers suddenly halted, as boots came crashing down in unison. Another barked instruction and they turned smartly right to face the dean. As if he had been waiting for this moment, the dean slowly and solemnly descended the steps, his white head protected by the canopy above.

As soon as the dean turned right, outside the gates, the Army Brass Band started up again and the soldiers fell in behind. The procession had begun.

The square was like a patchwork quilt of uniforms. Banners were unfurled and men in uniform fell in behind, in ordered ranks like soldiers. First were the Knights of Malta, followed by marching ranks of the St John's Ambulance and the Red Cross. Members of St Mary's Pipe Band had been standing around, wilting in their kilts. Now they were scrambling to get the bass drum strapped to the drummer's big chest as they shuffled into line.

The enormous serpent of the procession edged into Barrack Street, beneath the fluttering bunting strung across the street. The colours were alternating white and pale gold, like the papal flags stirring listlessly above the Palace Bar. We three altar boys led the way, my older brother trailing behind.

'Slow down,' he snarled, every so often, glancing anxiously behind him at the slow-moving canopy, some ten yards to the rear. 'The dean will bleddy well kill us! Ow!' he shouted as the heavy thurible once more banged off his knees.

To my right, Tommy's face was boiled beef. Every so often, the heavy brass candlestick tipped towards him, threatening to set his hair alight. Mickey looked as close to melting as the candle near his face.

Behind us, the Army Brass Band struck up the 'Tantum Ergo' and the voices of the boys' choir swelled up to fill the shadowed canyons between the houses. The crumbling brick chimneys above Doyle's Corner were gilded by the sun, above the baking slates. The second- and third-floor windows above my Aunt Sarah's shop, The Arcade, were all thrown up. Behind were little white altars, heavy with flowers. At a second-

floor window, in the gloom behind the flowers, sat my
granny. Dressed in black, her glasses gleamed. She was
mouthing Rosaries, fingering beads and gazing down.
Below her, her daughter's two plate-glass windows
had been transformed. All winter, mannequins had
stared left or right into the distance, with sophisticated
disdain, clutching the beautiful fur-trimmed coats to
their throats while frosty tinsel sparkled on their little
hats. More recently, they had displayed arms and legs in
cool cotton in the fashions of Milan and Paris, cities my
aunt had never visited. Now the left window was draped
in white, full of flowers and candles. A blue and white
Madonna looked directly out, hands seeming to reach
out to the whole world with compassion. In the right-
hand window, in the midst of the flowers, an agonised
Christ stared at the passing crowds.

Somewhere back near the post office, the women
of the Legion of Mary started the first decade of the
Rosary and the deep murmur of the Men's Sodality
responded as they passed the garda barracks.

Way behind somewhere, the girls' choir had started
into '*Panis angelicus*', Miss Ryan's strong soprano urging
them on, while behind them again, St Mary's Pipe Band
had launched independently into 'Faith of Our Fathers'.
Immediately behind us, the dean, in an old man's high,
quavering voice, started singing the words. In ones and
twos, other voices around him joined in uncertainly,
creating a curious out-of-sync medley.

We laboured up Pearse Street hill, a narrow gorge,
deep in shadow. The bass drums of the Army Brass

Band seemed to echo off the formal facades of the courthouse and the Munster and Leinster Bank. Now 'Sweet Sacrament Divine' dominated, washing to and fro in the stirring breeze. The hymn seemed to be trying to come to grips with 'Faith of Our Fathers' down behind in Barrack Street. My mother's bakery and tearooms held no surprises. Her flowers and statues and candles were every bit as good as her sister's below in The Arcade.

As we emerged into the sun at the top of the hill, the Misses Murphy had their sunblind down, even though the ice cream parlour was in deep shadow. We could see the gaunt face of Angela Murphy, standing solemn and still in the shadows behind her plate-glass window, fervently fingering beads and breathlessly mouthing the Rosary.

Around Grenham's Corner we turned into Connaught Street, a praying, singing, marching machine, bristling with banners. Shoes met the tarmac with a shuffling, slapping sound. Windowsills and doorways were packed with flowers. Candle flames fluttered and curtains billowed. Commerce had gone into hiding. Gone were the galvanised buckets, rakes and cans tied to the bar outside Hannon's Hardware. Egan's Salt Store window was cleared of pigs' heads and trotters and glowed with candles and flowers. Hanging signs advertising tobacco or porter were draped with papal flags. The air was heavy with the sweet smell of roses.

Some heads turned to see the one house of shame, door closed, windows down, not a face to be seen. My nervousness grew as we approached our house. I focused my gaze on Steffi's house until the last moment. Then I whipped my head around to discover a completely transformed house. Peggy had done it! I kept looking back, almost braining Tommy with the heavy brass cross.

'Hey, watch out, ya eejit!' said Tommy. 'What are you doing, anyway?'

'Oh,' I said casually, 'just checking to see if I left Peggy's bike outside.'

The tightness in my chest had suddenly melted and the sun-trapped street, the babble of prayers, the heavy perfume of flowers, the echoing brass and the singing choirs all seemed wonderful.

The procession flowed across the little humped-back Battery Bridge, winding towards Battery Hill. The road was white with dust. The sycamores baked in the heat and listless crows stirred in their shade. Our voices and the bands seemed distracted now, taken this way and that by the breeze. The Rosary's rhythm rumbled on, driving us forward, a wilting, moving mass of humanity. A huge wooden replica of an altar stood silhouetted on the hill before us as we climbed. To me, this was Calvary brought to life.

'Bleddy sheep!' said Tommy, suddenly stepping aside. The grazing sheep were gone but they had left their souvenirs behind.

We stood to one side of the altar and waited, watching the slow approach of the canopy. The old dean at last reached the foot of the altar. He was red-faced and breathing hard. There was a murmured conversation with the knights bearing the canopy before he slowly mounted the steps. Someone had yoked up ancient loudspeakers to the telegraph poles along the road and to the nearest trees.

Now the dean began to give out the prayers and they echoed around the little valley in meaningless gibberish. Everyone knew the responses anyway, and back they came, unsynchronised, the timing all over the place. It didn't matter. It seemed to me that the overwhelming fervour remained intact. It was clear that the old dean considered Corpus Christi the crowning glory of the religious year.

Later, Peggy slumped at the kitchen table, clutching a cup of tea, exhausted but happy.

'Peggy, you did a fantastic job with the flowers!'

Peggy smiled. 'Your father was happy with it anyway. I told him what you did.'

My father never said anything to me. It was as if it had never happened.

The Floods

~

November 1954

I snapped awake, wet with sweat. A vicious wind had thrown a handful of hailstones against the attic window. The whole street outside had come alive. I lay absolutely still, listening to the sounds of a rising storm. Every hanging sign seemed to be creaking or groaning. I tried to identify each in turn. Hannon's Hardware sign, like a mighty pendulum, swung slowly back and forth. The sign over Craven's, advertising Sweet Afton cigarettes, was the squeakiest, ready to excitedly flip over with every gust. I slipped out of bed and went to the window, shivering all over.

Hidden in the dark was a whole orchestra of hanging signs advertising plug tobacco and every kind of porter and stout. The only things I could see in the driving sleet were the pools of light around the tops of the telegraph poles that bestrode the narrow street like shadowy totems, joined by swaying, sagging lines. Halfway down the street, McGee's shop blazed like a cheerful beacon in the gloom.

The bedroom door opened behind me. Peggy stood there, her face a mask of horror, a steaming cup on a tray held against her chest.

'What are you doing out of bed?' she cried. 'Get back in straight away!'

Peggy had her crossest face on. I scampered into bed and pulled the sheets right up under my chin. When I heard Dr Nolan's voice on the stairs the day before, I knew things were serious. He clapped a stethoscope to my chest and back, told me to breathe in deeply, and told my mother I had come as near as damn it to getting pneumonia. My mother looked at me severely, told Peggy about hot water bottles and hot drinks and left. Peggy fussed around, tucked me in and asked me how it had happened.

I never lied to Peggy. We both knew that it was because of the floods that I had nearly got pneumonia. But how could I explain that the sights and sounds out near the floods had made me forget that I was wet and frozen to the marrow? And how the whole thing seemed to begin that October when we were crossing the square to look over the parapet of the bridge. That's when we saw the three army trucks standing under the castle wall, rain glistening on tarpaulin covers.

'Look,' said Tommy, 'isn't that what's-his-name from our class?'

I couldn't believe what I was seeing. The old people and the women had already been lifted down. Now one of the soldiers was lifting down Timmy Dervan from Clonown. We ran over, our schoolbags bumping on our backs.

'Hey, Timmy; what's happening?' I called.

Timmy looked around in a daze, the rain running down off his hair.

'Jeez,' he said, as if relieved to see me. 'The soldiers got us out of the house. The water was nearly up to our knees with the floods.'

'Where are ye all going to stay?' Tommy asked.

Timmy pointed behind him, up at the castle wall. 'There'll be three families staying here tonight. The rest will be down in Custume Barracks.'

'Timmy!' called his mother. His brothers and sisters stuck close to her, soaked and shivering.

'I'm coming!' he called. He headed towards them, throwing us a wordless wave.

'C'mon,' said Tommy, pulling his coat up over his head as the rain came bucketing down. 'Let's get in the church!'

We ran, splashing, across the square and took the steps of St Peter's two and three at a time. We stood, panting, under the portico, and watched the slanting sleet and rain. Lights were coming on and glistened on the water running down the massive granite pillars before us. Above us, the bells began to boom, doling out four strokes to tell the time.

The heads and shoulders of the soldiers were barely visible behind the wall as they walked the families up the steep sloping ramp to the castle. The line of walkers began to snake around the sharp turn at the top and the figures disappeared, one by one, up towards the entrance gate. It was already getting dark.

Day by day, we watched the river rising, as we went

across the bridge, to and from school. We had moved that year, from Connaught Street over to Mardyke Street on the Leinster side. The river we crossed had become the centre of our lives. The floods around Athlone that year made us the centre of attention for the whole country. The water had begun to rise faster than usual in October. It had been a disastrously wet summer, which greatly affected the lives of people in Clonown. We were still in our old house in Connaught Street then, so every Monday we heard all about it from Mrs Halligan.

'Well,' she said once, at the sink as usual, 'the way it is now, Peggy, there isn't a dry sod of turf to be had up Clonown.'

'And are you okay for the winter?'

'Oh, we're okay. My two lads always make sure we have the haggard full of turf to see us through two winters, if needs be.'

'And is the water anywhere near you yet?'

'Oh, nowhere near us. Sure, we're as dry as a cork way up on that hill. Danny brought the boat up from the Shannon all the same, just in case we might have trouble getting into town.'

I was at the table, doing my homework, but listening as usual. To me she said, 'If there was no boat to take me in, my fine young *gossin*, there'd be no clean shirt on your back and you going to school.' She laughed her big hearty laugh, blowing down on her cigarette.

Tommy Brady never crossed the bridge to the Leinster side except when we went to the pictures at the Ritz. But by November, as the river continued to rise, he insisted on coming with me every evening after school so we could lean over the bridge and read what the meter below the Bank of Ireland steps said.

'It's up to sixteen foot, nine inches,' he cried one evening in excitement.

'What does that mean?' I asked.

'My father says the last time it was that high was in 1925.'

'It said on the wireless that it was seventeen foot, one inch in 1925.'

'See what I mean?'

The torrential rains of 8 December brought the flood level way above that of 1925. We stopped running to the bridge after school. The newspapers and the wireless kept telling us what we already knew – that we were witnessing a major disaster. A light plane zoomed in low over our school one day and we all stood up in excitement.

'Sit down, sit down,' said Mr Finneran. 'They're taking photographs of the floods for the newspapers.'

We could hardly wait to get home that lunchtime to see what was happening.

'Peggy, Peggy, can we go up to Clonown after school?'

'I can tell you this,' said Mrs Halligan, turning from the sink, 'ye won't get further than McQuaid's bridge because the guards are stopping everyone there. They certainly wouldn't let any young *gossins* up.'

'Anyway,' said Peggy, 'Clonown Road is under a few feet of water just after the bridge, isn't it, Mrs Halligan?'

'The only thing you'll see,' said Mrs Halligan, 'is the

tops of hedges and water, water, everywhere.'

'But how big are the floods?' I asked. 'Is it just Athlone and Clonown?'

'Ah, sure, it said on the wireless,' said Mrs Halligan, 'that it's stretchin' the whole way from County Cavan down to County Clare, so it is.'

'Yes,' said Peggy, 'it's supposed to be fifty square miles and Athlone is right in the centre. It's affecting Westmeath, Offaly, Galway and Roscommon.'

'And Longford,' said Mrs Halligan. 'Don't forget Longford.'

'Gawd,' I said. 'I'm going to look it up in the atlas.'

I was tracing the area with my finger on the map of Ireland when Peggy said, with a smile, 'You don't have to frown when you're reading, you know.' She leaned across and brushed back the hair that was always falling across my forehead. 'And you're going to need a haircut again soon.'

'Well, look at the time,' said Mrs Halligan, turning and gazing up at the clock.

'Oh, we'll just get the news,' said Peggy and she switched on the wireless. The news had started and we heard a familiar voice. It was Mr Dillon, the minister for agriculture.

'And my department has offered to relocate farmers from Clonown who are most affected by the floods. But what we have found is that in every case, those farmers would not leave the callow lands of the Shannon basin, where their families have lived right down through the generations.'

Mr Dillon went on to praise the tenacity with which the people of Clonown clung to their holdings, but he uttered a word of caution concerning official handling of the situation: 'We must not go a step further beyond providing for these people and force them against their will to leave, when it is perfectly clear that they have prudence and a right to decide for themselves what is best to do.'

Mrs Halligan roared with laughter when she heard this. Peggy switched off the wireless.

'Well now,' exclaimed Mrs Halligan, wiping away tears of laughter, 'it's clear that that minister has never heard of Mary Jane Fallon of Clonown.'

Peggy smiled. We all knew about Mary Jane Fallon. Larry had rowed across in the boat after the deluge of 8 December to Mary Jane's house, to see if she was all right. He found her sloshing around in her kitchen in her wellingtons in a foot of water, rapidly rising. He also found one of the six army units assigned to the floods trying to persuade Mary Jane to leave. Mary Jane was eighty years old, had her own teeth, all four of them, and as she put it herself, not all of them to the front either. She was a tiny bag of bones, with a big man's laugh, and had a voice, as the neighbours put it, that would take paint off a door. She wasn't going anywhere, she told the army, and that was that. When the officer in charge insisted, she told him to feck off and he, no doubt mindful of what the minister had said, backed off. Larry laughed his head off but the officer apparently was not amused.

'Well, if you're a neighbour,' said the officer, 'are you going to take responsibility?'

'Listen,' said Larry, 'let's have a word outside and I'll explain something to you.'

Larry and the officer stood outside in the wind and rain, the water up to the tops of their wellingtons. What Larry explained to the officer was that Mary Jane's stubbornness would make any mule doubt himself and that the only way to get her to move would be to get the parish priest up in a boat to talk to her.

Tommy, Mickey and I stood at McQuaid's bridge the day the army rowed the parish priest up towards Mary Jane's house. There was nothing to see but the green uniforms and the parish priest's black coat and hat gradually disappearing into the distance. The sky was a great grey bowl with ragged dark blankets of rain shunting in from the west. Over to the left on the Leinster side, St Mary's Church steeple tolled the time, faint and distant in the scouring wind. The river was over there somewhere but you couldn't tell it from the great open expanse of water that covered everything as far as the eye could see. Most winters, the raised road that led up to Clonown Church was like a causeway across an endless lake. But that winter, it had disappeared below the waters. Either side of where we knew the raised road to be was a checkerboard pattern of hedge tops and trees that marked the *callows*, or river meadows, near the town. Beyond that was the vast open space of the bog.

A gunshot rang out, echoing across the distance, and

clouds of birds rose off the water with a great squawking sound.

'Hey, look,' said Tommy, pointing upwards. A flock of wild geese flew high overhead in arrowhead formation, making their peculiar hoarse honking call above the whirring of their wings. I listened intently as the reverberation of the gunshot died away. A distant cloud of birds still circled above, and the waters below them were dotted with the white shapes of hundreds of wild geese. Their haunting calls in the keening wind created something ancient, wild and free. Across the river, lights began to come on faintly in the town.

'Hey, what's that?' said Mickey, pointing across the water. We could make out the dipping of oars in the distance. Barbed wire, uneven ground and brambles made the use of an outboard motor impossible. A Red Cross vehicle came down the sloping road from town and stopped just beyond us where the bog road began to disappear below the water. Three or four men in uniform got out, laughing at something. We knew that no one involved in the flood relief work – St John's Ambulance Brigade, the Knights of Malta, the Garda Siochána or the fire brigade – could go beyond that point. Only Colonel Collins-Powell's six special army units were equipped with vehicles that could pass through any floods on the roads. And of course they used boats to rescue stranded families and to deliver fodder to isolated farms. They always had a vet or two with them, including Frank Martin from down our street, because of the danger of fluke. We were dying to see them swimming the cattle out to safety but we only heard it second-hand from the Clonown lads in our class.

'Hey, look,' shouted Tommy, pointing at the dipping oars in the gathering gloom, 'I think they have Mary Jane in the boat!'

The winter's evening was closing in but the occupants of the boat were still clearly visible. Another car came down the road from town. We recognised the battered Ford belonging to Frank Simmons, photographer for the *Westmeath Independent*. He got out immediately, clutching his camera. He shoved his untidy shock of hair back up as usual and pushed his glasses up on his nose, ready for action. He stood still, fixing his eyes on the approaching boat. The Red Cross men were still laughing but one of them was pointing at the boat. We heard Mary Jane's strident voice carrying across the water but we couldn't make out the words. Whatever she said had started the Red Cross men laughing again. Suddenly she stood up in the middle of the boat, which started to rock dangerously from side to side. There were shouts for her to sit down but she was angry about something and ignored the calls. What we hadn't seen was a second boat coming up behind the first. In the middle was an old man and she was shouting abuse at him.

Mickey laughed. 'That must be the poor oul' husband,' he said.

'Will ya listen to her!' said Tommy, laughing.

I couldn't hear what she was saying except that she was calling him an *amadán* and several other juicy words, which must have galvanised the parish priest to intervene.

'Mary Jane, Mary Jane,' he exhorted her, in tones more suited to the pulpit, 'what is the matter?'

'His bleddy teeth, fader! The eejit is after leavin' them in a tin back in the house! Stop the boat, stop the boat!' she shrieked.

The Red Cross men roared with laughter and Frank Simmons got his photo of Mary Jane and the parish priest in the boat. The boat in fact was almost up to the road by then and Mary Jane was still shouting.

'Go back to the house! Go back and get them!' she shrieked at the soldiers. The soldiers had shipped their oars and were looking, some with nervous grins on their faces, to their senior officer. He in turn was looking at the parish priest. It was a story that went the rounds of the town when Frank Simmons' photo appeared in the *Westmeath Independent* later that week.

We watched for a while as the soldiers got Mary Jane and her husband onto dry land. Then we saw two of the soldiers get back in the boat and head out across the darkening water, having promised to recover the missing teeth.

There was nothing more to keep us after the army truck departed with Mary Jane, followed by the Red Cross vehicle.

'Come on, let's go,' said Mickey, shivering and pulling his coat up around his neck. Tommy was already ahead, skimming stones across the water from McQuaid's bridge. The sinking sun was a great red presence behind us, turning the floodwaters to liquid fire. I lingered, listening to the honking of the geese, the soughing wind and the bells of St Mary's tolling in the distance.

A fog rose off the river. Dim lights glimmered in clusters where the town had been. I could easily imagine the campfires of two opposing armies, Queen Maeve's and the Ulstermen, who from dawn to dusk had watched the ferocious fight between the Brown Bull of Cooley and the White Bull of Cruachan, in the ford of the river. The Brown Bull had won, leaving the 'loins' of the White Bull scattered about the ford. The legend had given our town its name – the Ford of the Loins, *Ath Luain* in Irish – later becoming Athlone. That was the story Mr Finneran had told us. There was another version, according to which an innkeeper called *Luan* had kept a tavern by the ford before the Normans came, but I preferred what Mr Finneran had told us.

Tommy and Mickey were already far ahead. I called them and they waved me on. That's when I realised that I was frozen to the marrow, feet wet and teeth chattering.

It was well into spring before the waters receded enough for our gang to venture up to Clonown. The rancid smell that rose up from the ground as we squelched along was like no other smell. When the silt, deposited by the floodwaters, had settled down and the ground temperature began to rise, nothing could stop the fresh green grass that came bursting through, to become the tall, waving meadowlands of summer.

Time and Tide

1954

St Peter's Church was packed. The voice from the pulpit was from a distant planet. It mesmerised me, insulating me in a kind of bubble. Securely sandwiched between Tommy and a big countryman, my body was still as stone. I watched motes of dust spinning in a coloured shaft of sunlight that slanted down from the stained-glass window.

Tommy nudged me with his shoulder. Without moving his head, he said out of the side of his mouth, 'Hey, there's your sister up there. Who's that beside her?'

'That's Marcie Coleman,' I whispered.

'Jeez, she's gorgeous!'

Occasional words or phrases penetrated the insulation around me. There was something about the Marian Year, the Legion of Mary and, with a change of tone, quite a lot about Father Peyton.

'The family that prays together,' old Dean Crowe

now said distinctly, 'stays together.'

The dean disappeared and I was immediately transported to our kitchen of the previous evening. The light had been switched off. In the dark, left and right on the wall above the range, two little lamps glowed. A red one was under the picture of the Sacred Heart, a blue one under the Blessed Virgin.

'Our Father, who art in Heaven,' my mother began, giving out the first part of the prayer.

'Give us this day our daily bread,' responded all the girls who worked for us.

Decades of the Rosary rolled back and forth like a deep-voiced tide. All were kneeling on the floor, elbows resting on the seats of chairs. Beads clicked quietly and elbows shifted. The tide washed over me. Then Peggy was shaking me awake. I blinked in the harsh kitchen light. 'Well, John-John,' she murmured, smiling, 'you'd sleep in the middle of a blackthorn bush.'

Tommy elbowed me in the ribs.

'Look,' he said, nodding slightly to his right.

I looked. Peggy was gazing at us from a crowded bench in the side aisle, a slight smile on her face.

'Hey,' said Tommy, 'there's your other mother watching us.'

I turned and looked him straight in the face. Tommy knew that look meant he would get a puck in the gob if he said another word. He shut up and looked straight ahead.

I looked across at Peggy. Her head was bowed, listening to the priest. Unlike the other girls who worked for us, she never wore a headscarf. She wore a little plain hat with a bit of black netting that came down over her eyes. With her gloves and her good coat, there was something of my mother's style about her. She was young and good-looking and I wished once again that she really was my mother.

The dean folded his notes on the pulpit in front but didn't move. The congregation waited. When the dean spoke again, it was in a very quiet voice. The silence of his listeners was complete. 'There is just one more thing I would like to say.' He paused significantly and his gaze seemed to take in the whole congregation. 'We are living in a time of great change in Ireland. I have spoken from this pulpit before about the need to embrace this change. I have spoken the last few Sundays about the need for every parishioner, whatever his or her financial situation, to seriously consider committing to the rural electrification scheme. I speak especially to the people of Clonown.' Here the parish priest paused. 'I speak to them especially, knowing full well the poverty caused in recent years by bog fires and the most disastrous floods experienced this century. I say to them simply this: electricity is the future. Electricity is what can change your lives for the better, for you and your children. I urge the *backsliders* especially to think about it again. May God bless you all.' He raised his hand high to bless us and the whole church rustled with the sign of the cross. The old dean turned and descended.

Outside the church I said to Peggy, 'What exactly does "rural electrification" mean?'

'Well now, John-John,' she said with a smile, 'what do you think it means?'

'Well, it must mean getting electricity to people, and no one has electricity up Clonown.'

'That's it exactly.' Peggy walked ahead, looking serious.

I was puzzled by Peggy's attitude. 'But what did Dean Crowe mean by *backsliders*?'

We were walking up Barrack Street. I had trouble keeping up with Peggy. She seemed to be in a hurry to get home and she was taking her time about answering my question. She suddenly came to a halt outside the guards' barracks and looked down at me. 'I'll be going home after we have something to eat. Would you like to come?'

I stared at her. I knew she cycled home most Sundays. I hardly knew what to say.

'Johnny Madden showed us your house when he was bringing us out to his place.'

'So, would you like to come?'

'Yes, Peggy, I would.' I was surprised more than anything else.

It was a warm July afternoon as we cycled out the Galway road. Sudden breezes heaved in the gorse, waving their gold in the sun. Our bikes waltzed close, then danced apart, spinning wheels throwing up the hot-tar smell.

'What's that steeple, Peggy? Is it a church?'

'No, that's Summerhill Convent. It's a school. Whew! It's hot! Let's stop a minute.'

We stood in the shade of a big oak tree, letting the breeze cool our legs. Peggy took off her cardigan. The bell in the convent began its tinny yet gently musical pealing.

'Oh, I love that sound,' said Peggy, with sudden feeling. She had gone still, listening.

'Did you go to school there?'

Peggy turned and looked at me, as if coming out of a dream. She shook her head. 'John-John, I left school when I was fourteen.'

She gazed at me a moment then looked away. I didn't know what to say. I realised that there was a whole lot about Peggy I didn't know.

'I have an aunt who's a nun and she teaches music in the convent. I used to go and see her on Sundays when I was about your age.'

There was so much respect and longing in what she said that I suddenly saw Peggy as a nun, complete with veil and wimple. The sighing leaves above us cast a patchwork shadow across her face.

'Did you learn music with her?'

'I would love to have learned to play the piano.'

A car went quietly past on the dusty road and we watched the sun glinting on its roof.

'Why didn't you?'

'When you come to our house, John-John, you'll see that there's only my mam and Dadda at home. I'm the youngest. My brothers and sisters are all gone.'

'Gone where?'

For the first time, Peggy smiled. 'My two brothers

are in the United States. I have a sister married in Liverpool and another sister nursing in London.'

'Why?'

'Because there's just no work around here.' She smiled.

We were silent for a while. Peggy gazed towards the convent and I was in deep thought.

'Peggy, why is this electrification thing bothering you?'

Peggy turned and gazed fondly at me. 'You don't miss much, do you, mister?' She turned away for a bit. 'Yes, it's bothering me a lot.'

'Why?'

'There are farmers, neighbours of ours, who badly want to get connected to the electricity–'

'Is Johnny Madden one of them?'

'He is. We, and the neighbours around us, are just not in a position to get connected.'

'Why is that?'

'We can't afford it. We haven't the money.'

'What did Dean Crowe mean when he talked about *backsliders*?'

Peggy lowered her head and looked very sad. 'Some communities like ours said they would do their best to raise the money and when we weren't able to, rumours started up saying that we were going back on a promise.'

'But why does that bother you so much?' I could see she was close to tears.

'The rumours have nearly destroyed my father. My father and my grandfather were always held in the greatest respect by our neighbours. Whenever there was a dispute over grazing rights or the use of the common land, they always came to my father to settle things.'

'Peggy, I'm glad you didn't marry Johnny.'

Peggy looked for a moment as if I had struck her. Then she took my hand and just gazed at me. It seemed to me that every kind of feeling passed like clouds behind her eyes. 'We'd better get going,' she said in a hollow voice. 'Mam is expecting us.'

A dog was barking fiercely as we turned up the boreen. I saw him running alongside us behind a hedge. Then he jumped out ahead of us. Peggy got off her bike, laughing as the dog attempted to jump up and lick her.

'Shep! Down, Shep!' But she started rubbing his ears and I held her bike. A man in the field ahead was backing a horse and hay cart up against a haycock. He raised a hand in greeting but went on working as another man started putting the chains around the haycock. The first man wound a handle, and we watched the haycock being slowly pulled onto the lowered back of the hay cart.

'That's Dadda,' said Peggy as she went on stroking the dog.

As soon as the hay cart was righted and the haycock secured, Peggy's father said something to the other man, who nodded and started leading the horse out of the field. We walked our bikes to meet him as her father walked towards us, taking off his cap and wiping his brow.

'Well now, girl, how have you been keeping?' He grasped Peggy's hand and wrist in his two great big hands and the look on his face and hers told of the deep affection between them. He was almost a head taller than Peggy, his face burned by wind and sun. The little whitish lines around his eyes showed that he was a man who liked to laugh. As he came across the field, I saw that his hair had receded to a widow's peak.

'And who's this little *maneen*?' he said, breaking off the complete attention he gave his daughter. He looked at me coolly, the way a farmer sizes up a young bullock.

'Oh, this is John-John, Dadda. Remember I told you about him?'

'So, this is the man! Well, how do you do, John-John?' he said, extending his hand.

'I'm fine, thanks, Mr Hannon,' I said, remembering my manners and preparing to have my hand crushed.

'Oh, now,' he said, 'we don't have too many misters around here, so you can call me Michael.'

I looked to Peggy for help. According to my mother, every adult had to be respectfully addressed as mister, miss or ma'am. Peggy just smiled and nodded her head.

'Well now,' he said, 'we'll be forking up the hay abroad in the haggard, so I'll see you in a while.'

'Okay, Dadda. Oh, look, there's Mam waiting for us at the door.'

With a wave he was gone.

A smaller, older version of Peggy was standing in the doorway of a neat, thatched house. She waved and we waved back. Six or seven, mostly thatched, houses were clustered around the top of a small, round hill, with stone walls and gravelled spaces in between. A huge chestnut tree sighed from behind a wall and cast a shadow over Peggy's house, which was near the top of the hill. Her mother waited for us at the door.

'Peggy, *a stór*, well let me look at you!' she exclaimed, grasping Peggy by the wrist, much as her father had done. She gazed into her daughter's face with the same deep affection as Peggy's father had. 'And who have we here?' she cried, as if she had only just noticed me.

She gazed with smiling interest until Peggy said again: 'Mam, this is John-John, that I told you about.'

Her mother gazed at me, smiling but with the same sizing-up look.

'Hello, Mrs Hannon,' I said, waiting to be corrected. Peggy and her mother just laughed.

'Well, you must be famished after the long cycle out,' said her mother, suddenly looking concerned.

'Well now, we wouldn't mind a cup of tea, would we John-John, and one or two of those beautiful buns I can smell.'

It seemed dark in their kitchen after the glare of the sun outside. But it was lovely and cool. Mrs Hannon left the door open, with the half-door across to keep out the chickens pecking at the gravel outside. A fire was burning in the hearth and the big black kettle hanging from a hook on the crane above it gave off steam like a train. The griddle on a tripod one side of the fire had buns arranged in a ring, and raisins glistened juicily in the firelight. The table had already been set, and the blue-patterned cups matched the shining oilcloth.

'Is that the Tilley lamp you mentioned, Peggy?' I couldn't help asking.

'It is indeed, and do you know what this is for?' She pointed to something sticking out of the base of the lamp.

I shook my head.

'It's to pump up the lamp until it gives off its strongest light.'

'And it's the best light you ever had to read or sow or knit at night,' her mother added.

'So you don't need electricity?' I said.

Mother and daughter laughed again.

'Well, now, John-John,' said Peggy quietly, 'many hours were spent talking about that around the fire last winter.' Peggy looked at her mother and her mother looked back. We sipped our tea in silence for a while and I tucked into the buns.

'John-John,' said her mother, 'Peggy told me you're very fond of going to the pictures.'

'Oh, not only that, Mam, the best part is when he gets home and tells me all about the picture he's just seen, isn't that right, John-John?'

I began to feel uneasy. 'And what, now, was the very best picture you ever saw?' her mother asked.

I hesitated. 'Well,' I said carefully, 'I suppose *The Quiet Man* was the best one on in the Ritz.'

'Oh, I heard it was just great,' said Peggy's mother enthusiastically, 'but sure we had no chance at all to get in to see it.'

'Never mind, Mam. Sure John-John can tell us all about it, can't you, John-John?'

'Well,' I said reluctantly, speaking only to Peggy, 'it's about this American boxer – it's John Wayne in the picture – who accidentally killed a man in the ring and he returns to Ireland because he's inherited this farm. Then he meets this girl, Maureen O'Hara, and they fall in love and they want to get married but her brother, who's a great big bully, won't give her the dowry her parents left her, so there's this great big fight between John Wayne and her brother.'

I started describing how the fight began and was really getting into the swing of it when I heard the crunch of boots on gravel. Then Michael Hannon was quietly opening the half-door behind us. I stopped short, suddenly feeling shy, but as if he was immediately aware of the situation, he said, 'No, go on! I heard a bit of it as I was coming in the door.' He sat down quietly near the door, well away from us.

I continued, still speaking only to Peggy. That was the easiest way for me. 'Then,' I said, getting back into the swing of it, 'Maureen O'Hara's brother gives John Wayne this terrific punch and we think he's finished but it only makes him mad and gives the brother a massive punch on the jaw that knocks him out through the door.'

I went on to finish the whole fight scene, forgetting all about my audience and really giving it my all, as if I was in the fight myself. Suddenly I stopped, aware of Michael Hannon's soft laughter from the chair inside the door. He was shaking his head.

'Well, there's no doubt about it now at all, John-John. You're a biteen of a storyteller, all right. Isn't he, now?' he said, looking at the others.

I knew he meant it. I felt great. Mrs Hannon was laughing too, just in appreciation.

'Well, you can't stop now, John-John,' said Peggy. 'Tell them about Abbott and Costello.'

'Oh, I don't know, Peggy,' I started.

'Oh, go on!' coaxed her mother and she had a big encouraging smile on her face.

'Good man!' said her father, adding to the encouragement.

'Well,' I started, 'Abbott and Costello are staying in this posh hotel.' I went through the whole story and they laughed at every incident, Mrs Hannon shaking her head. Michael Hannon was laughing into his hand, clutching his temples with a thumb and forefinger. Mrs Hannon clapped her hands at the best parts and threw her head back as she laughed. Then Peggy was looking at the clock on the wall. It was nearly eight o'clock.

'Lord, Mam, we have to go. It'll be near nine before we get back.'

We all rose together. Michael Hannon's eyes were still creased in laughter. He extended his hand. 'Well, John-John, we'll have to get you back here again soon to give us more stories, won't we?' he said to the others.

'Oh, we will indeed,' said Peggy's mother warmly and she squeezed my shoulder.

'Now, Peggy,' said her father, suddenly looking serious, 'we've had news from young Michael, from

California. You can read it yourself.' He gave the envelope to Peggy and she sat down again, looking anxious as she began to read. But almost immediately her face began to open up in a great big smile of joy. She jumped to her feet and grasped a parent in each arm. 'Oh, that's the greatest news I've heard in a long, long time,' she said, and there were tears in her eyes.

They were all silent, just standing there together.

'Peggy,' said her mother quietly eventually, 'won't you stay a while longer? Martin Brennan said he'd call in later.'

'No, Mam, I can't.' Peggy suddenly seemed restless. I got the impression that she didn't want to see this Martin, whoever he was. Her father made no comment.

We were quiet on the road home. It was getting cool, so we stopped at the same tree while Peggy put on her cardigan and I put on my jumper. Behind us the sky was a deep, burning crimson and the trees were turning black. The beautiful little steeple of the convent was perfectly drawn against the sky and a curlew called across the bog.

'So,' I said carefully, 'you had good news from America, Peggy?'

She came back from her dream of the convent and gazed at me, smiling faintly. 'Yes, we had. The money we were hoping for is on the way from my brother Michael out in California. It's more than enough to get the electricity connected, not just for us, but for the neighbours as well. Of course, they'll pay it back when they can.'

In spite of what she had said, she looked sad and dreamy.

'Well, that's good news, isn't it?'

She smiled. 'Of course it is! I was just thinking of my brother Michael. He was hoping to come home this year to marry a grand girl who lives just down the road. It'll be next year now.'

'Why?'

'Michael started off as a labourer on a building site just a few years back. Now he has his own company and he employs a whole team of men. But he owes a lot of money too. He's dying to get home. He was a grand fiddle-player and now all he does is work, work, work.'

'Peggy, if all your neighbours have farms, how come they have no money?'

'I wouldn't call them farms, John-John. That group of neighbours around us is like a little village that my grandfather called a *clachán*. There's not much good land around us. It's for grazing and making hay. The rest is poor land and bog. The way it works is that each family gets an equal share of all three kinds of land. '

'But I saw plenty of turf and hay in the haggard.'

'That's true. And we have three cows, a few cattle, a few pigs, lots of chickens. The truth is, we have plenty to eat, we're warm all winter and we owe no money.'

'But how do you get money?'

'Dadda sells turf in town. Michael, when he was home, grew carrots and sold them in the square in town at the market on Saturdays. Mam takes baskets of eggs round the shops and her salt butter is famous. Of course, in an emergency, Dadda would sell off one of the cattle.'

We cycled on in silence. The sun was gone but the sky was still bright. The air was full of the smell of hay.

'Why does Johnny Madden want the electricity so badly?' Immediately I felt sorry that I had mentioned his name in case it spoiled our mood.

But Peggy was matter-of-fact. 'Johnny has a lot of cows. And he has contracts now with the creamery. He's planning to set up a modern milking parlour.'

'So he's on his way to becoming a big farmer?'

'Maybe he is,' she murmured.

I glanced at her. It was difficult to read her face. We cycled on. I could see the lights ahead in town.

'I know you're curious about this Martin Brennan that Mam mentioned.'

I glanced at her. 'Who is he, Peggy?'

'He's a lad I've known all my life. Mam wants to see me married. I like him and he likes me. But I don't want to marry him.'

I didn't know what to say to that.

'Well,' she said quietly, 'were you glad you came out to our house?'

'Peggy, I really, really like your mam and dadda. They're just great!'

'They're the best parents in the world and I wouldn't want to live anywhere else.' She smiled broadly.

I felt happy and rich as we cycled into our street.

We were walking our bikes through the archway into our yard when I heard the shouting. We stood with our bikes in the gloom, listening. The voices of my mother and father were harsh and ugly with hate. I dreaded the atmosphere in the house, the threat of violence hanging over us.

Peggy looked at me. 'I'll go up to the girls,' she said.

I nodded. I knew she would look after them. My two brothers, I knew, would stay up in the attic and wait for things to blow over.

'Peggy,' I said, with sudden determination, 'I'm going over to Bradys'.'

She gazed at me and nodded. We left the bikes against the wall. I went back out through the wicket gate and crossed the street to Bradys'.

Bradys' kitchen was down in the basement, like most of the houses on that side of the street. Tommy was sprawled out on the floor, lining up his lead soldiers.

'Hey, where have you been? Where did you go after Mass?'

I told him about the trip out to Peggy's house. Mrs Brady came in. She looked at me in some surprise. 'Hello, John-John,' she said.

'Hello, Mrs Brady.' We stood gazing at each other for some moments. 'Mrs Brady, can I stay here tonight?'

There was a momentary pause. 'Well, of course you can, *a grá*. There's two beds up in Tommy's room.'

Tommy stared at me with his mouth open, then looked at his mother.

'Tommy,' said his mother, with that quiet authority she had, 'you take John-John up and show him where everything is.'

'Okay,' he said immediately. He scrambled to his feet and we ran together up the stairs, our feet making pounding sounds on the thin lino.

To his credit, Tommy asked me no questions. He chattered on into the pale midsummer night until he fell asleep in mid-sentence.

One for Sorrow, Two for Joy

~

1954

I was looking out the open attic window that beautiful morning, when a magpie landed in our yard. He strutted across the gravel as if he owned the place. I was ready to go for my catapult when he took off. I felt uneasy. One magpie was bad luck. Peggy had said so.

We were cycling out to her house that July when two magpies flew from left to right across our path.

'Oh,' said Peggy, 'two magpies, flying left to right. That's good luck. Did you know that?' But she was smiling, as if it was a joke.

'What does it mean, Peggy?'

'Well, there's an old tradition that if you start out on a journey and see a single magpie, you should turn back home, but it's only a *piseog.*'

I knew she meant *superstition.*

'And if you meet two, it's a good sign?'

'So they say. There's an old rhyme about them that begins: "One for sorrow, two for joy . . ."'

'Did people really turn back if they saw one?'

Peggy laughed. 'They didn't have to. They could *salute* the magpie and that broke the spell.'

'Is that it?'

'No, the rhyme goes on, right up to seven magpies. They all mean different things.'

I waited at the window in case he came back. I was going to go for my catapult when I heard someone coming in through the archway with hollow, echoing steps. A large man in a dark blue uniform walked a bike into the sunshine of the yard. My heart dropped. It was Garda Sergeant Kelly. That was the magpie's message! My stomach churned and I broke out into a sweat. Sergeant Kelly was here with a summons because of the damage we did in Broderick's yard.

The sergeant seemed in no hurry. He lifted his boot onto the fork of the parked bike and removed the left bicycle clip from his trouser leg. He did the same to remove the right one. Then suddenly he was looking straight up at me. He looked very serious and I quaked with fright. He pulled down the visor of his cap and crossed the yard below, disappearing in through the kitchen door. I waited in agony.

I heard his voice, surprisingly soft, carried up from the open kitchen window. He was talking to my mother. Then I heard the slam of the spring door into the bar and my father's voice. He was coming into the kitchen. I knew I was really in for it this time.

I heard my mother's voice on the stairs as she called something back down to the sergeant. Was she coming for me?

I was surprised to hear her footsteps stop on the landing below the attic stairs. Then there was a knock on a door and my mother's voice calling softly: 'Peggy.'

'Yes, ma'am.' I heard Peggy's reply clearly and I heard the door of her room opening below.

'Could you come down to the kitchen a moment, Peggy?'

There was no reply to this and I heard their footsteps going down the stairs. There was something quietly urgent about the whole thing. The kitchen door below closed and there was a murmur of voices. The deeper tones of the sergeant continued in a quiet monotone.

Suddenly there was a piercing shriek, like an animal cry, that made the hair stand on my head. I was frozen to the spot, straining to hear every sound.

The kitchen door opened and footsteps hurried up the stairs. From the landing my mother called up, 'John-John!'

I went racing down the attic stairs.

'Was that Peggy I heard?'

'It was.' She stared hard at me. 'Now listen, I want you to go up to Tommy Lenehan's and ask him to bring the taxi straight away.'

I stood my ground, mouth gaping. 'What happened?'

For a moment I thought she was going to rebuke me but she looked at me hard instead. She was practical and she knew that I would have to explain to Tommy why we needed him urgently.

'Peggy's brother Michael had an accident. A tractor turned over on him.'

'Is he dead?'

'He is. Tell Tommy I want him to take Peggy out home to her parents and then to bring them all in to the hospital.'

'Right,' I said. I went down the stairs in leaps and bounds but halted at the bottom. Peggy's anguished keening behind the door descended to a long groan that tore into me.

I ran the whole way up Connaught Street and then down O'Connell Street.

Michael was home at last from California. He had bought a good farm and a brand-new tractor. Peggy had talked for weeks of the forthcoming wedding.

I was wheezing hard as I ran in the door of Lenehan's pub-grocery. Tommy was finishing serving a customer in the grocery part and they were chatting as if there was all the time in the world. But Tommy kept glancing at me and the customer took the hint. I had got my breath back and I explained as clearly as I could what was wanted. Tommy was quiet and deliberate in his movements but his mind worked fast.

'Peggy that works for ye is Peggy Hannon, right?'

'That's right.'

'And her father is Michael Hannon from out there beyond Summerhill?'

'Yes.'

'Right, I know where to go now.' He started closing up, quickly, but he was unhurried. 'Wait there a minute,' he called. He was back in a thrice, minus his shop coat and wearing a jacket, tie and hat. We got in the taxi round in the yard and drove to our house.

My mother led Peggy from the kitchen, murmuring something to her. Peggy's face was white and puffy, her eyes all red. She kept her head down, looking at no one. My mother helped her into the car. Peggy slumped on the back seat, her head sagging on her chest. I stood by the kitchen door, staring at the white image of her face behind the glass. I felt completely helpless. I wished with all my heart that I could share her pain. She stirred and looked at me, a mysterious, sad smile in her eyes. Something passed between us. My father brushed past me, coming out the kitchen door with a suitcase. He handed it wordlessly to Tommy. Tommy nodded at him and immediately took the suitcase round to the boot, looking glad to have something to do.

I waved the tiniest wave as the car started moving out of the yard, the tyres scattering gravel. I saw Peggy's hand briefly at the window.

The pub and the bakery were closed the day my parents went to the funeral. It was more than a week before Peggy came back, a pale ghost of herself. She moved about the house in a kind of daze and I didn't ask her anything.

I came home from school one evening, shortly after her return, to find the archway gates closed and the wicket gate locked. Every instinct told me that this was trouble. The magpie was back in the yard that morning.

There was no choice but to go in through the bar. My father was standing behind the counter. He crooked a finger at me. The look on his face confirmed the magpie's message. I stood still, waiting.

'Go down to the bake-house and wait for me,' was all he said.

The bake-house was a shed at the bottom of the yard, beside the stables. The door was unlocked. I went in and waited. It was a hot day outside, but inside, standing on the concrete floor, it felt cold. Old machinery stood on benches, everything covered in dust. A cobwebbed window high in the end wall provided a dim light. On the wall, just inside the door, was a damp-stained framed poster with warnings about the dangers of electricity. There was a drawing on it of a man lying on the floor, with instructions about what to do in the case of electric shock. It was only then I saw the stick lying on the dusty bench beneath the poster. It was the kind of stick a calf-jobber might cut from a hedge to drive cattle. I knew what it was for. I heard my father's footsteps on the gravel outside. He came in quietly and bolted the door.

'Why did you do it?' he sort of murmured, giving me hardly a glance. I stood there, not knowing what to say.

'Why did you do it?' he said again, in exactly the same way. It sounded impersonal.

'Myself and Tommy didn't–'

The whack across my face was like being slammed with a wooden shovel. The whole right side of my face went numb. I thought my nose was gone and my ear was like a piece of ringing wood. Something was wrong with my teeth.

'Why did you do it?' he murmured again, as if he couldn't get the words out through his teeth. I felt a ferocious, searing pain across my right knee before it too went numb. I saw that he had the stick in his hand. It came down with vicious force across my shoulders, my arms, my back and the backs of my legs. I began to feel like pulp because everything was going numb.

'Why did you do it?' he kept murmuring, over and over, each time he brought the stick down. It seemed to go on for a long time and then it stopped. He calmly put the stick back on the dusty bench and went out, leaving the door ajar.

I noticed some blood on a jagged bit of the stick. I looked down. I remembered something catching in the leg of my trousers. There was a small triangular tear in the trouser leg just below the right knee. There was a little blood on it and it was already sticking the material to a cut inside. What I found nearly impossible to believe was that my own father had done this. That was the real shock.

I stood there, unable to think, until I began to feel cold. Then I started shivering uncontrollably. I knew I had to get to the bathroom. I tottered out the door and up the stony yard.

I met no one on the stairs, though I could hear Peggy moving around in the kitchen. In the bathroom, I found it almost too painful to sit down. I never knew it was possible to feel so wretched. I stayed there a long time, turning over all that had happened.

It all started when the Mullins gang visited our territory around Connaught Street. Tommy and I had met them when we were exploring the Leinster side, because my father had just got the keys to our new house over in Mardyke Street. Tommy had halted in front of the locked steel gates on Connaught Street that led into Broderick's yard. He knew that the Mullins gang would want to explore the forbidden territory of Broderick's new, half-built bakery. It would be like raiding an orchard.

'Is there no other way in?' demanded Mullins.

Tommy looked at me. Our yard backed onto Broderick's.

'We can't go through our yard if me fader is there,' I said, quashing a very uneasy feeling. I had to be careful. Losing face would kill off any possibility of joining the Mullins gang when we moved to Mardyke Street.

My heart sank when we found the bar locked up. My father was probably over at the new house. We piled through our wicket gate, down to the sheds at the end of the yard. I knew every foothold that took us up onto the roof. We lay there flat, like Indians, scouting every corner of the huge yard on the other side. There was no one around. We swung down, one by one, Tommy and I heading up towards the gates to make sure the coast was clear. We were about to go into the archway when we heard crashing sounds behind us. I couldn't believe what I was seeing. Mullins and his gang were jumping up and down on stacks of corrugated asbestos sheeting that were clearly intended for the new roof. One of the gang, Farrell, was smashing stacked panes of glass with a big piece of timber.

'Someone's coming!' shouted Tommy and we started to run. In panic, he stumbled into me, bringing us both down onto sharp rubble. As we scrambled up, we heard the key turning in the lock of the steel gates, echoing in the archway. I saw the last of the gang swing up onto our roof as we ran. Tommy was up first, throwing himself flat to look back. I was still climbing when we heard the shout behind. I didn't dare look, knowing it must be Benny Fox, the caretaker.

Peggy had come upstairs. I heard her moving from one bedroom to another. Then she knocked on the bathroom door.

'John-John, are you all right?'

'I'll be out in a minute, Peggy.'

Peggy must have heard the way I came down the stairs. She opened the kitchen door as I reached the bottom.

'Oh my God,' she cried when she saw me. She came towards me, her face white and her eyes enormous. She guided me slowly into the kitchen.

'Peggy,' I said, 'I can't sit down. It hurts too much.'

Peggy shook her head and tears rolled down her cheeks. She got a cushion and silently helped to ease me down on a chair. She sat and gazed at me silently, scanning me from head to toe.

'Tell me what happened,' she said.

I started at the beginning and told her everything. She asked questions once or twice. It took quite a while. She sat, pondering silently, when I finished.

'You should be taken straight away to a doctor or the hospital.' She looked at me but I had nothing to say. She got up. 'I'm going to talk to your mother.'

I sat like a zombie, listening to their faint voices, somewhere upstairs. Eventually, two sets of footsteps came down the stairs.

I saw my mother's swollen face as soon as she came in. The finger marks were red welts on the left side of her face. I felt nothing. I already knew. She stood and stared at me. Her manner was strangely distant. She spoke to me as if I were a stranger:

'Is anything broken?'

I shook my head.

'Lift your shoulders and put out your arms.' I did so. She came closer.

'Open and close your mouth.' I did as I was told. I stood up when I was told. She turned to Peggy.

'He'll be all right. He doesn't need to go to hospital.'

Peggy looked down and said nothing. We heard the kitchen door closing. We sat there silently for a while. Peggy looked at me with the kindness and understanding I knew so well.

'She's just too ashamed to take you to the doctor.'

I knew that. I also knew that Peggy couldn't take me without her permission. Peggy was thinking hard. She got to her feet and started putting on her cardigan.

'I'll be back in about half an hour. I'll get you something to eat then.'

I nodded and she was gone. I must have dozed off, because she seemed to return straight away.

'Do you want to eat now, or can you wait?'

'I can't eat anything, Peggy.'

'Would you be able to walk down as far as Doyle's shop?'

I nodded. 'If we go slowly. Why?'

'Larry will be there in about half an hour. He'll have a look at you.'

Dermot Doyle was in fact closing up but he saw us coming. He was serious for once. 'The young lad can go straight in the back room and wait,' he said, looking at me.

They sat me down and talked quietly outside until Larry came. He joined the murmured conversation, then came into me. He looked at me gravely as he closed the door. 'Show me all the bits that hurt,' he said. I went through each one. He listened mostly, his eyes scanning me all the time. 'All right,' he said at last. 'We'll do something very simple.'

But he sat, silently relaxed, as if he was miles away. He got to his feet slowly. 'Now, sit forward on the bench so I can reach your back.'

I shuffled forward painfully. The hand pressed gently on the base of my spine. After a while, it began to feel like a warm pad. I felt so relaxed that he reached up his left hand onto my chest to keep me upright. The heat gradually became intense and began to move up my spine, through the neck and into the head. It was as if life was flowing back into me. In spite of the heat, there was no discomfort.

'We're going to change position now,' he murmured. 'Sit back against the wall.'

He put his hand on my chest then moved it down so that it covered the bottom of the breastbone and the top of the stomach. We went through the whole process again. This time though, it felt as if something was draining out of that part of my body. I began to feel a strange peace.

Larry sighed and sat back on his chair, his face chalk-white as before. He closed his eyes, as if in exhausted sleep. We sat like that for perhaps ten minutes. When he opened his eyes, he was his old, smiling self.

'Right, you should be all right now.' Without another word, he went out into the shop and there was a murmured conversation before Peggy came in to collect me.

Back in our kitchen, I said, 'Why are my mother and father like that?'

Peggy looked at me as if deciding something.

'Whatever happens, it's very important for you to forgive your parents.'

'I will *never–*' I started angrily.

She raised her hand for silence. 'I know that it's not possible now. But just remember what I'm going to tell you. Forgive them for *your* sake. For *your* sake.' She looked at me closely, as if to see if the words had got through.

I didn't know what to say. We sat in silence. 'Peggy, what's that whole rhyme about magpies?'

She looked at me and laughed. I hadn't seen her laugh since her return. She took my hands in hers. 'Well now, John-John,' she said, 'as I told you, that's just a *piseog*. But why do you ask?'

I told her about the two occasions when the magpie had landed in the yard. She went on smiling but she seemed more thoughtful, looking down at our hands.

'All right,' she said at length, 'this is the rhyme: One for sorrow/ Two for joy/ Three to get married/ And four to die/ Five for silver/Six for Gold/ Seven for a secret never to be told.'

'What does it mean?'

She laughed. 'You mustn't think I know everything!' She shook my hands merrily, as if they were reins.

'Do you mean, Peggy,' I asked seriously, 'that it means nothing at all? I mean, seeing a single magpie?'

Peggy became thoughtful. 'I don't know, John-John. I don't know. But on the day Michael died, Dadda told him not to go out on the tractor, because a magpie had stood just outside our front door in the early morning. And Michael just laughed.'

Horse at Fogbound Bridge

~

1954

Fog hid the end of the bridge. A deep, unearthly sound erupted from the water below. The unseen Guinness barge was a monster warning all in its path. Then its squat outline emerged through the muffled silence to dock with cotton-wool contact against the foot of the Guinness warehouse.

'Tie her up!' shouted a voice, hoarse and hollow in the swirling air. A man sat unmoving at the back, coat collar turned up, peaked cap pulled down. A pipe stuck out from below a great black moustache. Little puffs of smoke jerked up in time with his bellowed instructions. I could only see the flat caps and backs of the two men below, silently obeying the voice that spoke.

A heavy clip-clop below and the black Clydesdale emerged, the drayman standing on the dray, shaking the reins. Immediately I noted the horse's sunken rump and the telltale outline of ribs. He trotted with a shortened, awkward gait. There was definitely lameness in the right front leg. From the way the hoof made contact, I guessed it was an injured heel or sole. They arrived at the barge just as a gangplank was slammed down from boat to dock. One of the men was already placing a porter barrel at the top end of the plank as the drayman threw down a big, square, stuffed sack at the bottom end to receive it. The drayman caught the rolling barrel as it hit the sack, and in one swift movement he lifted it to stand on the back of the dray cart. The horse, meanwhile, had his nose stuck deep into his nosebag. Suddenly he sneezed and a small cloud of dust rose around his head. He paused as if confused, then started a deep dry cough that shook his body. The drayman was part of the mechanical process of shifting the barrels. He paid no attention to the horse. The next barrel cannoned into the first with a hollow sound. The drayman and the two bargemen worked in silence, moving like machines, watched in silence by the man with the pipe. All three had stripped to their waistcoats, sleeves rolled up. The tops of their flat caps moved like bobbins. They worked swiftly but without hurry. One dragged the barrels across the deck with a scraping sound. The other received them, swinging them onto the top of the gangplank with a thumping, echoing sound. Under the drayman's cap a cigarette hung loosely down, an angled length of ash refusing to fall, even as he swung up the barrels.

'Back up!' he snarled to the horse. The horse hesitantly backed up two big steps, dragging his nosebag along the ground. Without pause, the barrels continued to cannon into each other, filling up the middle section of the dray cart. 'Back up!' he snarled again, and the end near the horse's tail began to fill up. As the last barrel went rolling down, the man with the pipe and moustache stirred himself.

'Gangplank!' he shouted, as he moved levers and gripped the wheel. The gangplank was pulled aboard and the barge glided out on the water, heading for the nearside arch of the bridge. I watched until it slid out of sight below me. I was just in time to see the Guinness dray move swiftly along the dock, the horse turning right to skirt the base of the castle, the clip-clopping trot echoing an uneven, out-of-sync rhythm. It faded up the foggy hill with a shifting jingle of harness. The dray would be in Connaught Street by midmorning.

'Hey,' said Mickey, as we left the barbershop, 'they're just outside your pub.'

The horse stood completely still, his head hung low. By contrast, drayman Mike Tracy moved with mechanical swiftness, offloading the barrels into our archway. As we approached, the huge figure of Paddy Hoctor stepped out from his butcher shop and walked right up to the horse.

'Jayz, that's a fierce cough that horse has,' he bellowed accusingly to the drayman.

'So what?' the drayman retorted. He halted suddenly, wiping the back of his hand across his nose. 'Sure, he's only fit for the knackers.'

'What did you say?' said Paddy Hoctor. His voice was

dangerously quiet. He stepped right up to Tracy, his face inches from the drayman's. He towered above him, a good head taller.

Tracy was bad news, barred from several pubs. Only weeks before, I had seen him emerge grinning from the courthouse across from my mother's shop. He had a great bruise around one eye and various cuts on his face. He was greeted like a hero by a bunch of characters like himself. A small group of bargemen stood nearby. They kept glancing over at Tracy. Not for the first time, Tracy had been up before the district court for vicious, drunken brawling. Justice Michael Carney had bound Tracy and a bargeman to the peace. He warned Tracy that he would jail him if he came before him again. Tracy somehow managed to keep his job at Guinness. It was all in the *Westmeath Independent* a few days later.

A battered lorry came roaring up the street and halted with a squeal of brakes behind the dray. The legs of two dead horses stuck up from the back and there was an overpowering, choking stench. The driver leaned out the window, a Woodbine dangling from his lips.

'I'll be round again this day next week. Will this lad be ready?' he called, indicating the horse.

'He'll be ready,' shouted Tracy.

The driver waved and with a crashing of gears the lorry laboured up the street.

'See what I mean?' Tracy snarled.

Paddy Hoctor stared down at him for a moment then walked over to the horse. He patted the beast gently on the neck, then took his muzzle firmly in his two great hands. As carefully as he could, he prised it open to reveal the horse's long, yellow teeth. The horse backed up a few steps but he wasn't frightened.

'He's twenty-four, if that's what you want to know,' said Tracy.

Paddy turned slowly and looked at him. 'Is this how Guinness looks after its horses?'

'He doesn't belong to Guinness. He belongs to me. They're selling off the horses.'

Paddy nodded. We all knew that Guinness was soon to be delivered by lorry. And that the bargemen were to be no more because the canals were going to be closed.

'So he's yours?'

'He is.'

Paddy became thoughtful. 'I'll buy him from you.'

'You'll what?'

'I'll buy him from you.'

Tracy seemed dumbfounded. He spat out the smoking butt onto the footpath. He took a thin paper packet of Woodbines, all bent and crushed, out of his trousers pocket and lit one. He seemed to be giving himself time to think.

'How much will you give me?'

'How much do you want?'

'You'll give me a tenner for him anyway.'

Paddy Hoctor snorted. 'You'll be so lucky. I'll give you five.'

Tracy took the cigarette out of his mouth and spat on the footpath. 'He won't go for that.' He reached up and started taking the next barrel off the dray. But I noticed that there was a certain deliberation in his movements, as if he had lost his rhythm.

'So be it,' said Paddy Hoctor. 'Let him go to the knackers.' He walked away and we watched him step back into his shop.

It seemed to me that Tracy had ever so slightly slowed down. He pulled off his cap and wiped the sweat off the top of his head with it. 'Have ye nothing to do?' he snarled at us.

We backed away but stopped again up at Hoctor's Butchers. Tracy continued to offload the barrels. When the last one was dragged off the dray and stacked inside the archway, Tracy slowly emerged and stood staring at the horse. He glared at us but we were already crossing the street to meet Tommy coming out of Brady's.

'Hey, what's going on? Is that the horse you were telling Mrs Webb about?'

'That's him,' I said.

'Gawd, he looks knackered,' said Tommy.

We stared in silence as Tracy threw down his butt, walked up the street and stepped into Hoctor's Butchers. The voices inside the shop were loud but we couldn't make out a thing. Then the two men were standing in the street.

'Have we a bargain?' demanded Paddy Hoctor.

'We have,' said Tracy.

Paddy Hoctor spat on his right hand and held it out. Tracy did likewise and brought his hand down on Paddy's with a resounding smack.

'All the harness belongs to Guinness,' said Tracy.

'What I'll bring here tomorrow is just the horse on a halter.'

'That'll do.' Paddy Hoctor stepped back into his shop. The show was over.

Tracy climbed on the dray, shook the reins and departed up the street.

'I don't get it,' said Tommy, scratching his head. He turned to me. 'Mrs Webb stops you in the street, says it's a disgrace the condition that horse is in and she's ready to tackle Mike Tracy there and then.'

'And that's when yours truly strongly advised her to have nothing to do with Tracy because he's real trouble. I pleaded with her to leave it to me.'

'Because you, of course,' said Tommy cynically, 'had this great big plan.'

'I had no plan at all. But I told Mickey about it.'

Mickey smirked. 'And Mickey,' said Mickey, 'told his fader, who had a word with Paddy Hoctor.'

'Yeah,' I said, 'they had a few pints together in our pub last night.'

Mike Tracy walked the horse in through our archway next morning and down to the stable that had been got ready for him. That was the arrangement. I was still spreading straw when the horse was walked in. Tracy barely glanced at me. He undid the head collar without a word and was about to leave.

'What's his name?' I asked.

'The horse? No name. He's just *the horse.*' He turned and left.

In the kitchen, Peggy was moving the big steaming iron

kettle to the side of the range. I was hardly in the door when my father came from the bar carrying a galvanised bucket.

'John, don't go anywhere. I have a job for you.' He placed the bucket in the middle of the floor.

Peggy immediately brought over the steaming kettle but paused to say, 'Mrs Webb sent in some bottles of stuff and some kind of food for the horse.'

I noticed that Peggy never addressed my father as 'boss' the way the other girls did.

My father took the kettle from her and put it on the floor beside the bucket. 'Where is it?' he said.

Peggy handed him a tattered old bag that clinked with bottles. He took them out and frowned at them. I was tempted to laugh. I recognised Mrs Webb's old meadowsweet and white-willow bark home cures. She believed all older horses suffered from arthritis. My father read her instructions on the labels and tipped in small quantities from each bottle. I saw that the bucket was three-quarters full of wheat bran. There was also a package of chopped carrots and apples. These he tipped in too, looking uncertain about the whole thing. Steaming water was poured in and he stirred the mixture into a wet mash.

'Now,' he said to me, 'take this down to the horse and watch how he eats it. And I want you to stay there until teatime and watch how that horse behaves. Right, off you go.'

Teatime, I thought in horror. That was hours away! I looked at Peggy.

'Here,' my father said, taking a small paper bag out of

his pocket and handing it to me. Inside were Emerald chocolate toffees, my favourites! 'That should keep you going.' He went on stirring the mix.

I looked at Peggy, standing behind him. She smiled and winked at me. Did she know something about my father that I didn't know?

The horse moved listlessly and sniffed at the bucket. Slowly he found his appetite and began to eat, sometimes slurping the mix. He was clearly enjoying it. When he finished, he looked at me as if to say, 'Is there any more?'

I left the bucket outside and got a stool to sit and watch. Gradually the horse's head dropped and soon he was asleep. Half an hour later I was almost asleep myself. Suddenly restless, I jumped to my feet, startling the horse. I was immediately sorry and went over to pet him. Then it occurred to me to feel under his jaw to see if there were any telltale swellings there. Finding nothing there, I slowly began to do the same with his massive jaws. I did it very gently, the way Mrs Webb would. I laughed when I saw that the horse had closed his eyes, as if he was enjoying attention. Suddenly his eyelids opened and I was looking into old eyes that were full of sorrow. Something jumped in my chest. For the first time, I felt I understood something about Mrs Webb.

A few days later, Mrs Webb arrived in our archway just as I came out of the stables. She waved cheerfully down to me then turned to face my father as he came out the kitchen door. He had his charming smile in place. They stood apart as they spoke, eyeing each other up.

Mrs Webb turned as I approached. 'Hello, John-John,' she sang out cheerfully.

'Hello, Mrs Webb.'

'And how is your patient this morning?'

'I think he's comfortable. I've put down loads of straw because of that sore front leg.'

'Oh, good man, just the thing,' she said enthusiastically. She turned to my father. I saw an instant change in her manner. With me she showed a kind of friendliness that seemed to reach out and touch me. Facing my father, she seemed to retreat behind her eyes. 'So yes,' she said to him, 'I should really appreciate it if the horse could stay with you for the week, to give him a good rest.' She spoke to him as if from a distance. She sounded *so* posh.

'Oh sure that will be no trouble, no trouble at all,' my father said with emphasis. I had the strange impression that something in him bowed to her. Then he glanced at me and I didn't see the lord and master I knew. I looked away, pretending I hadn't noticed. I knew all about his ferocious pride.

'Shall we go down and have a look at the poor chap?' said Mrs Webb, all businesslike.

We walked down the yard in a constrained silence.

As soon as we walked in the door, Mrs Webb paused and gazed around at our newly built stables. 'My,' she exclaimed, 'this is a really good set-up.' She gazed at the six new looseboxes in turn and touched the iron restraint frames above the half doors.

The new stables, built after the old ones burnt down the year before, had drawn nothing but praise from the farmers on fair days. My father had planned the whole layout.

A horse's head, hay still clamped in his jaws, suddenly stuck itself out from the last loosebox.

'Oh my, oh my,' exclaimed Mrs Webb and rushed over to touch his muzzle. Mike Tracy's horse blinked, as if in surprise, the hay fixed in his unmoving jaws. 'Oh,' she said to my father, 'he already looks *so* much better.'

'I gave him warm bran mash for the last two days,' said my father modestly, 'then only hay and water.'

'Good, really good,' said Mrs Webb approvingly as she stroked the horse's neck. 'No oats, I hope?'

'Oh, God no,' said my father, as if it was the last thing on earth he would do.

'Mrs Webb,' I said hesitantly, glancing at my father.

'Yes, John-John,' she said, suddenly switching her attention from the horse.

'He was backing up against the wall and rubbing his rump against it. Then he looked at his flank and pawed the floor a few times.'

'And what do you think that means?' she asked brightly.

'Could it be colic, do you think?'

'It could indeed.' She frowned. 'That's what worries me.'

We all gazed at the little dry piles of manure on the straw.

'Well,' said my father, 'the bran mash should help out there.' He looked from one to the other of us. He seemed surprised that I had spoken so easily with Mrs Webb.

'Indeed,' replied Mrs Webb. She nodded in approval.

'Well,' said my father, clearing his throat and glancing at me with a strange blank look, 'John here tells me that the horse spent most of his first day leaning against the wall. That could mean laminitis.' He stared at me this time. He was well aware – as was I – that he was departing from his usual way of dealing with me.

Mrs Webb gazed at him searchingly. Horse talk seemed to be providing a common language. 'Yes, it could. It could also mean that his general condition is very poor. Shall we take a look at his foot?' She didn't move, clearly expecting my father to lift the horse's great heavy hoof.

My father was in his good suit. He looked at me.

'I tried lifting his foot yesterday and he wouldn't let me,' I said to Mrs Webb.

'Listen, John,' my father said, 'move him over against the wall.'

They watched in silence while I grasped the head collar and pushed my fist hard into his flank. Slowly, hesitantly, he stepped sideways until he was against the wall.

'Try him now,' said my father, taking charge.

I ran my hand slowly down over the fetlock joint and grasped the heavy white feathering above the great hoof. 'C'mon, boy,' I urged, gradually applying the pressure to lift. I was acutely aware of being watched, and of the silence. Something lurched heavily above me and slowly the horse allowed me to lift his foot. I held it on my knee the way blacksmiths did.

I was surprised to hear Mrs Webb laughing. 'Oh, look,' she said, 'he's leaning against the wall to help you, John-John. Isn't he clever?' She moved in swiftly to give the horse a quick affectionate rub on the neck. Immediately she bent to examine the upturned hoof. 'Now, just be particularly vigilant for one moment, John-John, while I touch his hoof.' She gently placed a finger on the sole of the hoof, frowning and looking worried. 'You can let his foot down now, John-John. It's as I thought,' she said to my father, 'definitely laminitis.'

My father nodded sagely. A slight smile was fading from his face.

We spent about an hour with the horse. It was decided that Mrs Webb would return the following day with special padded boots for the horse's front feet. In the meantime, my father instructed me to keep the straw bedding good and deep.

It was getting dark as I came out of the stables. Our house was black against a cold red sky except for the light that showed in the little bathroom window over the archway. I thought I heard singing. It was quiet, dreamy singing, in a man's baritone voice. Shadows moved behind the bathroom window and I realised that it was my father. It was one of his old favourites, 'Danny Boy'. I listened, standing in the cold, the horse snuffling and moving about behind me. Then it struck me. The horse would no longer be just *the horse.* He would be Danny Boy.

Brothers

1954

We had got off early from school. I was just about to turn in at our archway when I stopped dead. The figure coming up the foggy street had something in front of him that made a peculiar, rumbling noise. It was my older brother, pushing a truck with a porter barrel on it. He stopped before me, standing the truck on end, and I stared. His face was white, the left side swollen with a great red welt.

'What happened?' I said. 'Did he do that?' I meant my father.

'Yeah,' he breathed. He looked as if he had been hollowed out. I could see him pushing that barrel up from the docks into the square, along Barrack Street and the whole way up Pearse Street hill. He would have met all the lads coming home from school and probably the girls from St Peter's.

'What about the match you were supposed to be playing?'

My brother was captain of the team. He shrugged hopelessly.

'He wanted an extra barrel of porter for the fair tomorrow. I told him I had a match to play. That's when I got this.' He pointed vaguely at his face. His voice was dull.

The bar door opened. My father stared at us then crooked a finger at me. 'John, come here. I want you.' He went in. I followed and my brother pushed the truck down the yard.

'The two of you,' my father said, 'will be working with Ted below in the bakehouse, bottling stout. You can wheel the barrels down. Right, off you go.'

I went into the kitchen to dump my schoolbag. I had hardly enough time to say hello to Peggy. She was quiet and serious but she had a cup of tea and a bun ready for me. She looked me up and down. 'You need to get into your old clothes, John-John,'

Immediately I remembered the reddish-brown dust that came off the barrels, leaving stains that were very hard to remove. The tea and bun went down in a thrice, then I was running up to the attic. I changed quickly and was down again and out in the yard before my father came out from the bar. He looked down the yard once and went back in.

The barrels were stacked in the archway. As I rolled down the first barrel, I could hear the regular sound of the corking machine below in the bakehouse. Ted's high tenor voice rose above the sound and my brother replied in a low murmur. Ted had worked on the farm until my father sold it. Now he was a general handyman and helped in the bar. Peggy came out with a basket of washing and started hanging things up in the open shed between the stables and the house.

As I rolled down the second barrel, I heard an angry yell from my brother: 'Hey, what are you doing?'

I stood the barrel, ran down and burst in the door. My brother was grappling fiercely with Ted, who had him by the collar.

'Let me go!' my brother screamed. There were tears in that cry.

'Let him go!' I yelled. I grabbed a bottle of stout off the bench and threw it at Ted. He ducked and the bottle smashed into splinters high on the wall behind, splattering foam and stout on everything.

'Let him go!' shouted a voice behind me. I turned to see Peggy's white face and furious eyes.

My brother wrenched himself away at that moment, pulling Ted almost on top of us.

'Get away!' shouted Peggy and swung the yard brush she was gripping.

Ted collapsed backwards with a horrible gurgling sound, clutching his groin. Peggy grabbed me and pushed me hard after my brother out into the yard. I heard the bakehouse door slamming and then Peggy was shooting the bolt. She turned the huge old key in the lock for good measure. She marched us silently up to the house, her face a grim mask. We had hardly got to the kitchen door before Ted started hammering on the bakehouse door.

'Peggy!' The shouts were muffled. 'Let me out!'

Peggy stared grimly back at the door for a moment before ushering us inside.

'Peggy,' I began.

'Listen, John-John, I want you to take your brother up to your room and wait until I call you. I need time to think.' Her look told me there was no arguing.

We went silently up the stairs and sat on our beds in the attic.

'What happened?' I said.

He shrugged listlessly and moved his head from side to side as if he had a stiff neck. 'He asked me what happened to my face. He put his arm around me, pretending to feel sorry for me.' He broke off, his face a white grimace of anger and shame. He never looked at me but I saw the traces of tears. I went on staring at him. There was nothing I could say.

We heard the bar door below slamming with its hollow, windy sound, then the kitchen door. There was no mistaking my father's voice and Peggy's quiet murmur. There was a pause in which we could hear the distant banging on the bakehouse door. We waited to hear my father's footsteps crunching on the gravel of the yard. Instead, the kitchen door banged and we heard his heavy step coming up the stairs. We looked at each other as the steps came up the attic stairs. Then he was standing in the room. He nodded to me. 'You go down to the kitchen,' he said and turned his attention to my brother.

I got off the bed and started down the stairs. Behind

me I heard his first question: 'Tell me what happened.'

Peggy stood in front of the range. Her hands were clasped and her face was white. 'He came in from the bar when he heard the racket. I had to tell him.'

'Peggy, he'll kill Ted!'

She nodded in agreement, her eyes full of dread. Suddenly she galvanised herself. 'Listen, John-John; go down to your mother straight away and tell her what happened. Take my bike.'

I shot through the archway and zoomed down Connaught Street, as if escaping the sound of Ted's banging.

My mother listened with fixed attention, her mouth slightly open. 'Go down,' she said before I'd finished, 'and tell Sergeant Kelly we need him up in Connaught Street this minute. Go!'

I freewheeled dangerously down the hill and threw the bike on the barracks' steps. Sergeant Kelly looked up from the newspaper on the desk. I gasped out my story. He never said a word, nor did he move until I'd finished. He turned his head to the two guards talking over near the fireplace. 'Mick, Tom, on your bikes now! Bit of trouble up in Connaught Street. Follow this lad up and I'll be along shortly.' He scooped his bicycle clips off the desk as if there was all the time in the world.

I ran out, grabbed the bike and started back up the hill, standing on the pedals. I was surprised to see the two guards on their bikes not far behind. I waited for them outside the archway then freewheeled down the yard to the bakehouse. They dropped their bikes beside mine and burst in the bakehouse door. We had heard the crashing sounds and yells of pain as soon as we entered the yard. I saw the two guards rush at my father and there was a lot of shouting and something heavy crashed to the floor. Unexpectedly, Ted staggered out, blood all down his shirt front from his nose. The whole side of his face was red and swollen. He glanced at me and sort of half-trotted up the yard then lapsed into a fast, limping walk out through the archway. He turned right and disappeared. One of the guards yelled in pain and crashed to the floor, bringing a heavy bench down on top of himself. The other guard was holding on to my father's arm and shouting when Sergeant Kelly came in through the archway and freewheeled down. He dismounted calmly and walked in, half closing the door behind him. He said something calmly to my father who shouted something back. There was something of a silent scuffle then and next thing I knew, my father was pinioned on the floor. One of the guards came and shut the door. Suddenly all seemed calm and quiet.

I went into the kitchen, where Peggy had been watching from the window.

'Is he still up in the attic?' I said.

Peggy nodded. She was pale and distracted. 'Here,' she said, 'take this up to him.' She handed me the big steaming mug of tea and a plate with two buns.

I sat in silence while my brother drank the tea. He ate the buns very slowly and thoughtfully.

'Do you still think I'm his favourite?' I asked quietly. We both knew I was talking about my father.

He took a long time to answer. 'You'll always be the favourite,' he said without emotion, as if it was gospel.

'What about the thrashing I got over what happened in Broderick's yard?'

'You deserved that,' he said hollowly. He seemed strangely removed from everything he said.

We were silent then, both thinking.

'Why do you think,' I said, 'he was beating the shit out of Ted down in the bakehouse?'

He stared back at me, as if he didn't know the answer, so I supplied it: 'It was because of what Ted did to you.'

He looked as if he was trying to absorb this idea, then he shook his head. 'If Ted injured one of the horses in the stables on a fair day – even by accident – he'd beat the shit out of him anyway.'

There was no need to say anything. It was clear what he meant. We were his property, exactly as the horses were. It was the wrong time to say it, but I knew that my brother was my mother's favourite, for all kinds of reasons. We sat on beds, facing each other, but the space between us might have been a wide river. We would be forever on opposite banks. In a way that surprised me, I fully appreciated his situation at the moment. Apart from what had happened with Ted, the fact that he, the captain, the best footballer in the school, had not turned up for this important match, would be disastrous for him. He was popular and reliable. To have to explain the next day, without revealing what went on in our family, would be agony for him. He hated telling lies. All this I understood perfectly. And deep within me I felt a sorrow that we could never be brothers in any real sense.

A few days later I hesitated just inside the kitchen door. My mother and Peggy were standing opposite each other, deep in serious conversation. My mother glanced over but then ignored me. I quietly sat at the table.

'So what did the doctor say?' my mother asked.

Peggy fetched a deep sigh. 'Well, at least it's not rheumatoid arthritis, which is what we thought it was. But it *is* arthritis.'

'And it came on suddenly?' my mother said.

'Oh,' said Peggy with another sigh 'she was baking as usual and she dropped the griddle and all the cakes across the floor..'

'She couldn't hold it, you mean?'

'Well, that's just it. It's affected her hands and her wrists –' Peggy broke off to wipe away a tear.

We were all still and silent. The clock on the wall seemed louder than usual.

'When will you need to leave?' my mother asked gently.

Peggy leaving! I felt something jump in my chest. The thought blocked out the rest of the conversation. I came out of a dream when I heard my mother say, 'Don't worry, Peggy, I'll get John-John to run down and get it for you.' She was taking a folded letter from Peggy.

'John-John,' she said, handing the letter to me in turn, 'can you hand this in to Mrs Melvin. She'll tell you when to go back and collect it.'

One for Sorrow, Two for Joy

I ran down to Melvin's chemist and Mrs Melvin told me to come back in fifteen minutes. I ran back, wheezing as I entered the kitchen. Peggy was by herself. Her unsmiling gaze stopped the questions flying around in my head. Carefully I said, 'Are you going home to take care of your mother, Peggy?'

She looked at me as the smile returned to her eyes. She reached out and gently took my chin in her hand, gazing into my face. 'I won't be too long, John-John. While I'm away, you're to look after your brother. Promise me you will.'

I nodded, not sure I could control the waterworks behind my eyes.

'He's moping around up in the attic. You might try and get him out of himself.'

My brother hardly reacted as I came in the door. He was sitting on his bed, reading. All he ever read were the Biggles books. I sat on my bed and gazed around. He went on reading as if I wasn't there.

'Hey,' I said, 'do you want to kick the ball around in the yard?'

He looked up and gazed at me lifelessly. He knew I had no great interest in football. 'Maybe,' he murmured with a shrug. But he went back to his book.

I waited for a bit. Then I got a book and sat on my bed. It wasn't long before he was yawning.

'Will we go down in the yard?' he said.

'Yeah, okay.'

The ball thumped around the yard and we never spoke. Now and then it slammed hollowly against the bakehouse door, reminding me of Ted's banging. The ball and the activity seemed to be bringing my brother back to life. The repetition was beginning to bore me. My brother grabbed the last ball but kept it under his arm.

'Listen,' he said, 'I think I'll go down to Larry Murphy's and see if he wants to come out.'

I nodded. I'd had enough of football anyway. Larry was on his team. My brother sauntered out through the archway and I went back up to the attic.

Tommy Lenehan's taxi came just before teatime to take Peggy home. He put her case in the boot then spent some time fastening her bike to the back of the car. My mother was at the kitchen door to see her off and I stood in the yard. She gave me a long, hard hug, got in the car and it went out through the archway, crunching across the gravel. I went back up to the attic. I picked up the book I'd left on my bed. I didn't want to think about anything.

Anger

1954

I don't remember how the fight started. But it was the week we moved into the huge old house in Mardyke Street, opposite the Royal Hotel. There were two enclosed yards behind, with several sheds, and my older brother and I were in one of these sheds that summer's day. I know it had something to do with my brother's announcing a territorial claim over that particular shed. That didn't matter to me. What mattered to me was something that I once again recognised in my brother, and which no one else seemed to see: his complete and dedicated selfishness. It wasn't easy to see this. He was a charming and very popular boy – the best footballer in the school. He was also my mother's favourite, who could do no wrong.

This wasn't a case of simple jealousy, although jealousy was present. It was more complex than that. He belonged to my mother's side of the family, in every way – in looks, in character, in temperament. Even in basic attitudes, he mirrored my mother and her three sisters – who all lived nearby – and their children, our cousins, who ganged up on my younger sister and me, who belonged to 'the other side'.

I was ten years old at the time; my brother was twelve. We were both big for our age, although he was bigger than I was.

I realised I was in a real fight when I received a stinging blow to the side of the head. The pain and the violence astonished me, but suddenly anger welled up in me such as I had never known, and I threw myself at my brother, with a ferocity that must have surprised him. It was a primordial anger, which rendered me impervious to pain, and indifferent to danger.

Tins of paint came crashing down from shelves; stacks of old glazing my father was keeping for something smashed. Locked together, we crashed to the floor, rolling and snorting, wet, sticky paint oozing through the back of my shirt, splinters of glass biting into my knees and elbows and arms and back. I merely noticed, felt nothing.

I was vaguely aware of a door opening, then suddenly being suspended in mid-air. There was my father's face above me, grim and terrible. He was a large and violent man, but I looked him straight in the face, completely unafraid. He held us both by the scruffs of our necks, like a pair of young pups. He put me down – none too gently – raised a large finger slowly, in his deadly manner, and fixed those eyes on me. 'You stay here,' he said.

One for Sorrow, Two for Joy

*

It seemed like forever since my father had carried my brother out the shed door. I sat, perfectly still, on an upturned paint tin. My mind was empty. I had no feelings left. Blood was caked on my face, and almost everywhere else on my body. Viscous paint was wet and cold on my back. I hadn't bothered to remove the two splinters of glass from the palm of my right hand. I just kept staring at them, as if the hand were some kind of inanimate object. I was getting colder and colder but I would not move. I heard footsteps coming. I knew it was my mother, but I didn't look around. I didn't need to. I knew she was staring at me steadily, as if assessing my state.

I had heard people say how beautiful she had been when she was young. I turned and stared back. The slightly aquiline features came from her mother. I always thought the nose too long, and when she looked at me like that, it was as if it was down along that nose. Something was going on behind her eyes.

'You'd better come in now, or your dinner will get cold.'

I listened intently to what she said. Inside the words were other words, which said, 'You'd better do as I say, or you'll be sorry!'

I knew that look. That's how she looked at my father. It meant, *Men have to be managed, and I know just how to manage them*. It infuriated him. She was looking at me with that look now, as if I were some dangerous, unpredictable animal in a cage.

I knew what was going on. I shook my head and turned away from her.

There was a momentary silence, and I heard her quick steps walking away. She turned at the door.

'There'll be nothing else to eat tonight.' And she went in.

It was getting dark when I heard Peggy come out. I hadn't moved. I never saw her without her apron. Her steps approached evenly and calmly, like everything else about her. She never raised her voice or got excited. She had a low, steady voice, which was husky and strong. She stood behind me in silence a moment, smelling as always of apples and flour and cooking.

'I made some soup for you, John-John,' she said.

She didn't touch me or try to persuade me, or manipulate me, or shame me. It was a flat statement, allowing me free choice. Peggy always played fair. She was just and she was kind, without a trace of sentimentality. She was the one consistent human being I knew. I rose, and without a word, followed her into the kitchen.

A few days later, Tommy Brady's father, Jack, tapped on the bar window. We were closed, getting ready to reopen the new premises for business. I let him in.

'How's young John-John?' he cried in his hearty manner, tousling my hair. 'Is your father in?'

'I'll get him,' I said, feeling cross. I hated having my hair tousled.

'Jim!' he exclaimed, as soon as my father came in.

I saw my father's face light up.

My father was a very proud, often arrogant, frequently

violent man. But anyone who could make him laugh could hold his attention for hours. And Jack could make him laugh.

'Just dropped in for a chat, Jim; big election coming up.'

But Jack didn't talk about the election. He started into local rumours and the funny stories that went with them. My father laughed until tears ran down his face.

Peggy had told me that Jack had started out in local politics but that now he was very important in the election campaigns run by the Fianna Fáil party.

I worked very quietly so that they would forget I was there. Arched mirrors, set in dark wood, covered the entire wall behind the counter where I was cleaning. Glass shelves traversed them, crowded with spirit bottles covered in dust. I was to take down each one, dust it off and polish the mirrors behind. Jack Brady and my father were perfectly framed in the large central mirror. They sat near the stove.

Suddenly, Jack dropped his voice but I could still hear every word.

'I just dropped by really, Jim, because I heard about that business of the two guards wanting to take you to court.'

'Oh, right,' said my father, sobering immediately.

'Now, Jim, I've had a word with Sergeant Kelly. You and I have been friends and neighbours a long time, haven't we?'

'Oh, we have,' said my father, clearly not sure where this was leading.

'Now, Jim, there is no way on earth that these young guards – not even from the town, either of them – are going to take a respectable businessman like yourself to court. They want to disgrace you!'

'I know they do,' my father said.

'Now, we're men of the world, Jim. This is not going to happen. I was on the phone today to the minister of justice.'

'Is it that serious?'

'Believe me, Jim; these two young smart-arses are out to get you.'

'What do you suggest?'

'There's a vacancy in a garda station in a small village above in Donegal. That would suit Garda Callaghan very well.'

There was silence from the bench where they were sitting. I looked in the mirror. Something had been suggested. My father was working it out.

'Does he want to go there?'

'It's the last thing in the world he wants! He thinks he's due for promotion. Ambitious young lad, you might say.'

There was another pause. I made not a sound.

'Do you think that will keep him quiet?'

'It certainly would, normally. The problem is the other lad, Garda O'Meara.'

'What about him?'

'He's stubborn as a mule, and worse, he's thick as two planks. He's persuading the other lad to hold out, no matter what.'

'What's to be done?'

'There's another garda station in a small place near Mullingar. They need a sergeant and O'Meara has been offered the promotion.'

'Will he take it?'

'He's already accepted.'

I called to Tommy Brady's house the following morning. We always walked up to school together.

'Will we call in for Kevin?' I said. This was Garda Callaghan's son. He hadn't been to school all week.

'Oh, he won't be there,' said Tommy.

'What do you mean?'

'I heard his father was being moved to some place in Donegal,' he said with studied casualness. He wore the same 'Honest Joe' expression that was typical of his father. He even looked me straight in the eye in the same manner. Suddenly I wanted to punch him hard in the head.

'Tommy!' his mother called from upstairs. 'You forgot your copybook!'

Immediately my attitude changed. I liked Mrs Brady. She was a fine person.

As we passed Callaghans' house, the last one on Connaught Street before the Battery Bridge, I noticed that all the curtains were drawn.

'You're very quiet this evening,' Peggy said.

'I was thinking about Kevin Callaghan. After my brother, he was probably the best footballer in the school.'

Peggy was peeling apples, taking her time. Six baking

tins, the pastry already in them, were lined up on the table.

'Yes,' she said with a sigh, 'I heard about that.'

'Why did they do it, Peggy?' I said, suddenly angry.

Peggy gazed back at me without answering. I saw only kindness and understanding in that look. I watched her rolling out the pastry. There was only the thumping sound of the rolling pin and the ticking clock on the wall. They had comforted and reassured me many times before back in Connaught Street.

'Well,' I said, 'it's good that Jack Brady heard what the guards were trying to do.'

She looked at me and smiled. 'He didn't just hear about it. Your mother had a word with Mrs Brady.'

It took me a moment or two to get it. My mother had once again arranged things without informing my father. It would have infuriated him had he found out. Peggy was gazing at me, smiling, and her hands, arms and shoulders went on rolling out the pastry. 'That's what women have to do,' she said.

Summer and Smoke

∼

1955

Wood smoke wafted through Steffi's crowd. The bonfire behind them danced with their shadows and lit up the darkening trunks of the trees.

'What do girls talk about so much anyway?' said Tommy.

'Don't know,' I murmured. Why had Steffi asked me to wait?

Up at the bridge, the regatta was officially ending. A loudspeaker boomed and echoed across the water and a great cheer went up. It resounded off the castle walls and the steeples of St Peter's, pink in the last of the sun.

Suddenly Steffi was striding towards us.

'Hey, Tommy, how are you?' Without waiting for a reply she said, 'I see Daddy's coming.'

'Where is he?'

She pointed up towards the yacht club. 'That's our new boat,' she said.

'Jeez,' said Tommy.

The lights from the yacht club picked out the brass fittings and the sleek, varnished lines of the cabin cruiser moored alongside. Steffi's father was in the wheelhouse, starting the engine and waving to a small group on the wooden jetty. He was dressed for the occasion, in a blazer and cap with a visor. He saw us coming and waved us on. I looked back. Tommy waved and walked away.

'Daddy, I've asked John-John to come as we're going to see the islands.'

See the islands? This was new to me. What was going on?

'Okay,' he called cheerfully. 'How's John? Climb aboard!'

As soon as the man on the jetty released the guy rope, amid final shouts and waves, we were off. The powerful engine hummed behind us, thrusting us forward. The prow rose proudly, silently cleaving the liquid darkness of the water, rolling the waves smoothly aside to become foamy wash behind us.

'Oh, I love this time of evening,' said Steffi. She spoke to the gathering shadows, or to herself.

I listened intently. The waves washed left and right, ever diminishing until they lapped and gurgled as they shook the reeds on the shore.

The noise behind was fading, picked up suddenly with an energetic roll of drums. The loudspeakers boomed and echoed distantly, followed by fainter cheers and clapping, before Sid Shine's band swung into *Beale Street Blues*, the brass piercing the velvet gloom.

We passed under the railway bridge, heading up to Lough Ree. Away from the town, the sky was a great pale bowl, flushed scarlet to the west. Steffi and I stood in the prow, riding the waves.

'Isn't this great?' she shouted, but the wind snatched her voice away.

'Yeah, it's great,' I shouted back. I looked over my shoulder.

Her father was waving us back to the wheelhouse. 'Would you like to take the wheel?' he shouted to me. He stepped aside and held it until I had it gripped in both hands, feeling lightheaded. He stood behind me. I smelt the whiskey on his breath. But his eyes glowed with warmth. He created a feeling of adventure and he had the knack of including everyone around him.

'Imagine how the Vikings must have felt, coming up into this lake for the first time,' said Dr Nolan.

Immediately I felt the excitement of it. We were ferocious Viking warriors now, no longer braving the ice-floes of the northern seas but discovering a land of milk and honey and golden sunsets. I experienced the arrogant pride as our prow cut through the waves, imagining the scaly dragon's head and neck curving high above it, terrifying all who saw it.

'Yes,' said Steffi quietly, 'but what about the monks on Inchcleraun?'

Instantly I was a monk on the leafy island, watching in terror as the dragon's head glided silently towards us, its evil eye fixed on our peaceful community. I could see the monks running in fright; hear the bell clanging the alarm in the *clogás*, the smell of bread still fresh on the air from Brother Fintan's bake-house. How would I behave in the bloody slaughter to follow?

We were going past the first of the islands. A ruined *clogás* rose above the trees.

'How many islands are there?' I asked, feeling I had to say something.

'I don't know the exact number,' said Dr Nolan, 'but families still live on six of them.'

We passed several islands in silence. I could see the monastic ruins of Inchcleraun in the distance. We headed directly towards a wooded island. Branches overhung the water of a little inlet, at the end of which I saw a wooden boathouse with a jetty running out from it.

'And this is ours,' said Steffi quietly.

'I didn't know you owned an island,' I said.

'We don't exactly, at least not yet.' Her father met her gaze and she said no more.

Dr Nolan cut the motor and we glided silently in through the open doors. Steffi stood in the bow, expertly handling a boathook to soften the collision with the tyres hanging on the concrete dock wall at the end. Concrete docks lined three sides of the boathouse, with steps up in the nearside corner. We jumped out and secured the boat fore and aft. The wooden walls ticked as they cooled from the heat of the day, and a breeze hummed under the tin roof. The place smelt strongly of oil and petrol. Dr Nolan switched on a light and our feet echoed in the empty space. We heard the sound of a motorboat approaching. Dr Nolan looked at his watch.

'That'll be Michael,' he said.

'Are we going back with him, Daddy?' said Steffi.

Her father thought for a moment. 'Look, Michael and I have to meet the owners over in Glasson. We'll be back to collect you both in about an hour.'

'Is that okay, John-John?' said Steffi.

'Sure,' I said, wondering how I could explain it to Peggy when I got home.

The motorboat docked at the jetty outside. The man who walked towards us into the electric light was Michael, the solicitor, Molly Shine's nephew, really her son. He stood and waved. 'How's Steffi?' He merely looked at me and nodded.

Without another word, the two men went down the jetty, got in the boat, and we watched it drone across the lake to the far shore. The sound faded into the rich cooing of wood pigeons in the tree overhanging the boathouse. A pale moon was rising from behind the building. I was puzzled by a dark spot in the sky beside it.

'Hey, look,' I said, pointing upwards.

'What is it?'

'I'd say it's a hawk.'

'Jeez,' said Steffi, 'he's not moving. What's he doing?'

The wings were moving so rapidly, they kept him in one place. He looked like he was hanging in the sky, his head completely still.

'I'd say he's waiting for his supper to make a move in the grass down there – a mouse or a water rat.'

'Ugh!' said Steffi, making a face.

A great flapping of wings startled us and two wood pigeons dropped from the tree overhanging the boathouse. Immediately they started their strutting, pecking at unseen things on the concrete apron outside.

'Hey, look at that,' said Steffi, laughing.

The male pigeon was strutting around the female, dragging his fanned tail along the ground. The female went on pecking, ignoring him.

'What a show-off!' I laughed nervously. I had watched too many pigeon mating games not to know what was going to happen next. It would be too embarrassing to watch it with Steffi there. We were laughing our heads off as they locked beaks in their kissing routine when something dropped from the sky. Steffi shrieked and the pigeons instantly took off in fright. But they were too late. The hawk sunk his barbed claws deep in the female's back when she was about six feet up in the air. Then I saw that it was a kestrel, not a hawk.

He landed his cargo skilfully on the ground. The pigeon's body had gone completely still, wings half open, stunned or dead. The kestrel placed one claw on the ground and kept the other deep in the pigeon's back. The vicious, hooked beak descended and ripped flesh from the body.

'Oh, John-John, *do* something!' cried Steffi, grabbing me by the arm. I bent and picked up a dry, broken branch and advanced, still numbed by the swiftness of the kill. The kestrel ignored us, his back almost fully turned. The crackling twigs alerted him. He went completely still, his head swivelling almost full circle, stopping me dead with a stare. He had the cold, killer's eyes of a Viking, completely unafraid. Suddenly, I had no idea what to do. I dropped the dry branch and reached for a large stone. As I pulled back my shoulder, ready to launch it, the kestrel took off in a flutter of wings.

'Oh God,' groaned Steffi. She walked carefully up to the remains of the pigeon. Her face puckered up in disgust at the mess of scattered feathers, entrails and gore.

'Oh Lord,' she said, clutching her throat. 'Let's sit down.'

We sat down on the jetty, our bare feet dangling over the water. Steffi hung her head, deep in thought. She studied her knees, summer-brown, with an old scar on the left one. Suddenly, with a deep sigh, she straightened up, raised her arms above her head and started redoing the ribbon that held her hair in place. The movement lifted her whole torso, arching her back the way a swan stands up in the water.

On a rise behind the boathouse, a small wooden house with a veranda was just about visible. 'Is that the house you'll be staying in when you come here?' I asked.

Steffi had been staring steadily out across the water. It was strange to hear the distant jazz at the regatta, like sounds from another world.

'We'll probably never come here now,' she said quietly.

'Why would you not?'

We were sitting close together. She swivelled on her

seat and gripped my hand fiercely. A grimace of pain seemed to grip her face and tears hung in her eyelashes.

'I love this place, John-John. I never, ever want to leave it!' She gazed longingly into my face. I gripped her hand. I had no idea what to do or say.

'What's the matter, Steffi?'

She turned away, taking her hand out of mine. I felt helpless, wondering if I had said the right thing. I wanted to put my arm around her, but something told me it would not be the right thing to do. She was staring out across the water again. But why would she talk about leaving this place? I looked at her. She was tearful and downcast, her whole body slumped. She took a deep, sobbing breath.

'It's just that Daddy and Mammy had a terrible row last night.' She looked at me closely, as if to check on my reaction. I was tempted to laugh, but I put my mask firmly in place. I had a vision of the good-humoured doctor and his cultivated wife having a row. Immediately I heard my own parents above on the landing, their voices loud and harsh, ugly with hate. I heard a loud smacking sound, a scream and a body tumbling down the stairs. I pulled a shutter sharply across my mind, closing off the vision.

'Was it the first time?'

She slowly shook her head. I waited.

'It's been going on ever since Michael started coming to our house.'

'I don't understand.'

Slowly, the story came out. As far back as Steffi could

remember the same group of old friends had come to their house every Wednesday to play bridge. They had all known each other forever. They did everything together, went everywhere together. Then Michael was invited to their Wednesday evenings. 'That's when all this started happening.'

'How do you mean?'

She paused, as if trying to find the starting point. 'First, Daddy got involved in buying this racehorse with Michael and Mrs Webb's son, Nigel.' She stopped, stuck again.

I felt the need to help her. 'Was the horse a bad buy, or what?'

She shook her head, frowning at something. 'No, he wasn't. From the beginning he just won and won and won.'

'Sounds like a good investment,' I said, with what I hoped was a cheerful note.

She turned on me angrily. 'It was the *worst*, the very worst thing that could have happened.'

'Why?' She shook her head and made a sound with her lips.

'Well, that's when the rows started!'

'What were they about?'

'They were always about money.'

'Okay.'

There was another long pause while she considered the lake. In the distance, Sid Shine's band was getting 'In the Mood', pumping a steady rhythm into the night.

'You know Patricia Egan, who hangs around with us?'

'Sure. She's often in our house with Mari.'

Everything in Steffi had slowed down. 'Well, she went on and on about this new boat until I felt I had to invite her to go on a trip.'

'So?'

'Daddy took a whole bunch of us down to Lough Derg, to see Portumna Castle, Dromineer, Inis Cealtra – all those places.'

'Well, how did it go?'

Steffi didn't answer. She looked angry. She turned to me. 'I *hate* having to pretend. I just *hate* it.'

'I don't understand. What did you have to pretend about?'

She thought about that and seemed to calm down. 'Look, John-John, they think we're very well off or something and I'm caught up in all that.'

'What's going on, Steffi?'

She gave me a haunted look.

'The racehorse was sold, weeks ago. Now the boat has to be sold.'

'Did your father tell you that?'

'No. I got it out of Pauline but she wouldn't tell me anything else.'

Pauline was their housekeeper, Peggy's friend. There was a splash in the reeds. I tried to make out from the sound if it was a fish or water hen.

'John-John, promise me something.'

'Sure; anything.'

She let out a deep sigh and looked away. 'I hate what's happening.' She paused to examine my face. 'Promise that you will never mention what I'm telling you to a soul.'

'I promise.'

She gazed at me then gave me a quick impulsive hug. We sat in silence, listening to the sounds, looking across the darkening lake. I could see her reluctance to say more. She was looking down, rubbing each finger of her right hand in turn, as if counting them.

'Steffi, you don't have to tell me anything you don't want to.'

Faint lights from the Hodson Bay Hotel became visible every so often behind the stirring trees on the far shore. From somewhere behind it came the hoarse hooting of a train steaming northwards to Roscommon.

'It's just that I've never talked like this about my parents before.'

'I know.'

She stopped rubbing her fingers and became still. 'The worst thing, I think – for Daddy anyway – was when the friends stopped coming to play bridge.'

'Why was that?'

I thought she wasn't going to answer.

'I asked Pauline once why Daddy was never there to see patients any more. I knew he went all over the country to races. Then he bought the boat. Now he's talking about buying this island.'

'You mean; you asked Pauline where the money was coming from?'

She hesitated then nodded reluctantly. 'I had to drag it out of her. She said something about Daddy and the friends betting on the horse then she shut up and wouldn't say another word.'

'She was probably afraid of getting into trouble, or even losing her job.'

'She'll be losing her job anyway.'

'What do you mean?'

'John-John, we're moving to Dublin.'

She looked at me directly now. I felt as if I had received a tremendous blow somewhere between the chest and stomach. Steffi leaving – I couldn't understand it. A curlew called from somewhere far away. I made a great effort to sound normal.

'So, you'll be going to school in Dublin, then?'

'Yes, I'll be going to Mammy's old boarding school.'

'When?'

'September.'

It seemed there was nothing more to say. It was as if life had run out of meaning. There we sat on a darkening jetty, our bare feet dangling above the water, drawn together yet pulled apart.

Suddenly she was staring at me.

'What?'

'I meant to ask you earlier – what happened to the side of your face?'

It felt enormous and it was throbbing, though in the mirror that morning it had looked all right.

'Oh, nothing,' I said lightly. 'Just had an argument with a wall.'

She went on staring. 'What really happened?'

I found everything in me hesitating. I felt the same

shame my mother must have felt.

'Was it your father who did that?'

I looked at her, shocked by her directness. Would Peggy have talked to Pauline?

'What have you heard?'

'Look, John-John, I've heard things. That's all.'

It was somehow an unexpected blow that she knew. We were both thoughtful.

She took my hand. 'You don't have to tell me anything,' she said evenly. It left me with a choice.

'Well,' I said, feeling that a long time had passed, 'it was for something that wasn't even my fault.'

I started telling her the whole story of the beating. She looked at me all the while, wide-eyed and serious, as if watching the words come out of my mouth. When I finished, she looked away, clearly shocked to the core.

'That's . . . awful. I had no idea it was as bad as that.'

She reached over slowly and took my hand. She held it tightly, looking down into the water.

A distant sound grew into the drone of a motorboat and we saw the prow cutting through the water towards us. The sky above was still bright, the world below full of shadows.

'Hey,' called Michael, 'you're still here.'

They tied up the boat and her father said, 'Were we a long time?'

'Not too long,' said Steffi.

The two men moved towards the boathouse.

'What happened here?' said Dr Nolan, looking down at the mess of feathers. Steffi looked at me as if she had a bad taste in her mouth. I explained as briefly as I could what had happened.

'Yes,' said her father mildly, 'nature can be cruel.' But he seemed to be thinking of something else. Michael barely glanced at the feathers. He went straight into the boathouse.

Coming back under the railway bridge was like re-entering a forgotten world, where the celebrations still continued. All the lights were on in the yacht club and a hubbub of talk and laughter rose from the shadows among the trees along the riverbank. Steffi's father and Michael were silent the whole way and so were we. We tied up the boat near the bridge and walked home. Steffi and I walked ahead. Her father and Michael's conversation was a low murmur that we couldn't make out.

'So, when will you be going to Dublin?' I said.

'I'll be starting school the first week in September. We're moving some time in August.'

Our feet made dry, scuffling sounds in the deserted canyons of the streets. Two tipsy men walked ahead of us, their voices echoing back along the walls.

'Will you write to me, John-John?'

'I'll write to you, Steffi.'

We stood outside her door, facing each other. I took both her hands in mine. I didn't know what to say. She squeezed my hands hard, then turned to go in. In a daze, I automatically crossed the street and put out my hand to open our wicket gate. With a shock, I realised that we no longer lived here. The windows above were blank, the gates closed against me. The house had been sold, but no one had moved in. Connaught Street was no longer my home.

Steffi was still standing there, holding the half-open door. She gazed at me steadily, slowly raised her hand and seemed to melt into the shadows.

Foy's Toyshop

~

1955

As I walked up Church Street, I saw Tommy staring into Foy's window. Church bells were ringing. Cotton-wool snow floated gently from a black-velvet sky, carpeting the footpaths in a soft, crunching cover. Muffled men in hats and warmly wrapped women grasped the iron rail before carefully stepping down into the steep Friary Lane, glazed with ice and pocked with broken snow. Cars and bicycles swished slowly up and down Church Street, throwing slush aside like discreet snow ploughs.

Foy's Toyshop was near the top of Friary Lane. The two great plate-glass windows came down to within inches of the footpath. Immediately inside, a smiling life-sized cowboy in checked shirt, leather waistcoat, boots, spurs, hat and chaps pointed a pair of six-guns at all who passed or stared in.

'Hey,' said Tommy immediately, pointing at the cowboy, 'remember John Wayne and the Apaches in *Rio Grande*?'

'Sure do! This guy had better watch out.'

Coming right up behind the cowboy in the window was a hook-nosed Indian chief in fringed buckskin and magnificent feather headdress, his tomahawk raised with evil intent. But Tommy was on to it. Whipping out a pair of imaginary six-guns he shouted, 'Bam, bam, bam!' as he filled the murderous Indian full of lead. I was embarrassed. We had long outgrown cowboys and Indians but Tommy was oblivious to the amused looks we attracted from passersby.

The Indian chief continued to stalk his prey. A painted canoe hung on wires from the ceiling above.

Coming home from the Ritz years before I had said to Peggy, 'Why are cowboys good and Indians bad?'

She laughed but didn't answer straight away. 'Well, you see, the white man – the cowboys – took the Indians' land so the Indians were fighting back.'

'But why does that make them bad?'

She looked down at me and smiled. 'Now *that* is a different question altogether.'

And that seemed to be that. But I puzzled over it the whole way home. The thought brought me back to Foy's. Tommy was pointing at a massive cardboard star, suspended from a single wire and turning gently in the warm air of the shop.

'That's the thing I was telling you about,' he said, his voice rising in excitement. 'Let's go in.'

I gazed up at the star. It was painted silver, with sparkling frost. Electric light blazed from inside it through tiny pinholes, glinting on everything as the star turned.

'Can I help you, boys?' said a deep-voiced Santa, coming up behind us. We knew it was Mr Foy though.

'How much is the star?' asked Tommy, pointing up.

Mr Foy looked up. 'Well,' he said, 'that's not for sale, I'm afraid. It's just part of our Christmas decorations.' He looked at our disappointed faces. 'What do you want it for?'

'We're doing this play in St Peter's Hall,' I said.

'And we need a moving star,' said Tommy, 'to guide the Three Wise Men to Bethlehem.'

'A nativity play!' He frowned up at the star. 'How would you get it moving?'

'Tomsie McGee has yoked up this pulley thing on a wire,' I told him.

'And it works,' said Tommy.

'I see,' said Mr Foy thoughtfully. 'Just wait here a moment, would you?'

He was back in a thrice, carrying a stepladder. He steadied it against a shelf, climbed up and carefully dismantled the star, exposing a bare light bulb. Tommy meanwhile was eagerly exploring the shop.

'But, Mr Foy,' I said, 'how much does it cost?'

The benevolent Santa figure was slowly folding the brilliant star flat and handing it to me. 'If it helps to guide those Three Wise Men across the hazardous deserts to Bethlehem, consider it a gift from Foy's Toyshop,' he said.

'Hey, look what I found,' exclaimed Tommy, holding up a life-sized pink rubber doll.

Mr Foy raised his cotton-wool eyebrows almost to

his Santa hat but I knew what Tommy was about. We were responsible for getting the props we needed for the play. The rag dolls the girls had brought looked ridiculously small in the crib and the doll Tommy had found looked perfect. We explained all this to Mr Foy.

'Well now,' he said, holding out his hand for the doll, 'let me first show you what this little lady can do. You stand there,' he said to me, and to Tommy he said, 'and you stand over there.'

We took up our positions.

'Now,' Mr Foy said, looking at me, 'catch her under the arms!' and he threw the doll.

I caught the doll as directed and immediately I heard the loud gurgling laugh of a baby. It sounded so *real* and we all laughed. I turned it on its side as instructed and it cried pitifully. When I turned it face down, it howled.

We were still laughing when Mr Foy said to Tommy, 'When I throw it to you, catch it hard around the stomach, okay?'

Tommy deftly caught it and then looked sharply down at his trousers. The doll had peed all down one leg! The look on Tommy's face was so comical that we fell about the place laughing.

'Mr Foy,' I said when we'd recovered, 'it would be perfect but we could never afford it.'

'Well, in fact, you have no problem because this I would like you to also consider a gift from Foy's Toyshop to a worthy cause.'

We started to thank him profusely but he would have none of it and we left the shop feeling slightly embarrassed for some reason. Out in the street we stopped uncertainly. Tommy seemed gripped by a compulsion to linger around that magical shop window. We gazed in, Tommy clutching the large pink doll, oblivious of the looks of passersby.

'Hey, look at that!' Tommy pointed to the far left corner of the window, where a little red and green train zoomed around, shooting under bridges as the station master looked on from a little brick signal box. Signals dropped and lifted as the train emitted husky steam-whistle sounds, faint behind the plate-glass window.

'If you had the money,' I said, 'what would you go for?'

'If I *had* the money,' said Tommy, 'I'd go for that train.'

'What's so special about it?'

'What's so special? That,' said Tommy dramatically, 'is a Marx 666. I was looking at it before I found the doll.'

I knew I was supposed to be impressed. But I preferred real steam trains. 'So do you think you'll get the money for it?'

'Oh, I'll get the money all right,' said Tommy, with his special faraway, calculating look. I knew then that he meant to get it. Through persuasion, persistence or promises he would get some of it out of his mother. The rest he would gradually prise out of old aunties and uncles. When he really wanted something, he got it.

We wandered down Church street and across the

bridge, both of us immersed in thought. I found myself wondering why adults seemed to spend their entire lives thinking about and trying to make money. It made no sense. It was as if only money was real and magic didn't exist. All the same, I realised that there were things I wanted too, and only money could buy them. In the English comics we read, chaps in posh boarding schools talked about pocket money. *Pocket money* was a term never used in our family – or Tommy's or Mickey's – for the simple reason that we never got any.

Halfway across the bridge, Tommy halted. 'Hey,' he said, 'I'm going back to Foy's.'

'What for?'

'A real Marx 666 is supposed to have tenders, flatbed cars and boxcars.'

'What?'

'I'm going back to see if it has. Are you coming?'

'No, I thought we were going back to your house'

'Well, come on back with me if you're going home.'

'No, I'll go on up to Mickey's house.'

Tommy turned back and I trudged carefully through the snow on the bridge. Mardyke Street on the Leinster side was still foreign territory. Going up to Mickey's house on Connaught Street was like going home.

The well-dressed man approaching me across the square was already smiling in greeting. 'Well, well,' he said, 'and how's young John-John?'

'Timmy, how are you?' Timmy Dalton and my mother had been friends before I was born. My sister speculated that they had been sweethearts, which I found embarrassing. All the same, it wasn't possible to dislike Timmy. He was the popular and efficient manager of the sorting office behind the post office, where my uncle was postmaster.

'You're just the man I was thinking of,' said Timmy.

'Why is that?'

'Would you like a job?'

'What?'

'I mean a temporary job, over the Christmas holidays?'

'What kind of job?'

'Oh now, nothing much,' smiled Timmy, 'but you'd get paid!'

Paid? That meant money. Suddenly I was very interested. 'What would I have to do?'

'Well now, it doesn't require an Einstein. The sorting office is just bedlam this time of year, with paper, packaging and bits of string all over the place so we can't find anything. All you'd have to do is just keep the place tidy and put things back in their place.'

'When would I start?'

'Tomorrow morning, seven o'clock sharp.'

I gasped.

Timmy grinned. 'See you at seven,' he called as he walked away.

My mother was surprised but pleased that I was to be in paid employment. Peggy said she would set the alarm for half past six. I felt that I had been plucked out of a dream and placed firmly in a new adult game.

It was still dark as I crossed the square. One light, a yellow halo behind the fog, lit up the arched window in the stone façade of the post office. In the shifting shadows of the yard behind, men were already pushing around big trolleys with rumbling wheels. The sorting-office door opened onto a buzz of morning chatter in a warm, brightly lit room. Timmy Dalton saw me immediately and came over smiling.

'See this?' he said, pointing at the floor and around the benches. 'Your job is to clear all that up. Can you do that?'

I gazed around at the chaos of bundled brown paper, heaps of string and scattered sheets of paper. 'Sure,' I said uncertainly, gazing around in amazement. Postmen stood at the pigeonholes, sorting mail. One or two glanced over, their hands working automatically, carrying on conversations while they glanced or frowned at each envelope before slotting it into its rightful place.

'Where does it all go?'

'See these sacks. Stick it all in there and then I'll tell you what to do next. But look at each sheet of paper in case it's a receipt or something.' And off Timmy went.

By mid-morning, I had cleared the mess. Mailbags bulged and sheets of paper were neatly stacked. I had been watching Michael Walsh at the sorting desk. He was a tall, skinny fifth-year student from out Kiltoom. He kept scratching his head before asking the regular postmen about the addressed envelopes he was holding up close to his glasses. I could see that the busy postmen were getting somewhat impatient, and I knew all the streets that Michael clearly wasn't familiar with.

'Hey,' I said as Michael enquired about the street number for Mrs Theresa Murray, 'I know where *she* lives.' I went right up to Michael, looked at the address on the envelope and told him exactly where to find the house.

'Sure, let this lad help you,' said Peadar Devine the postman, 'since he knows the town.'

'Yes, John-John,' said Timmy, coming up, 'if you've finished, you can help Michael sort his lot out.'

I went to work with a will and between us the job got quickly done. Since I had finished my own job, I was then delegated to accompany Michael on his round. People I knew to see but had never spoken to chatted to us on the doorsteps. By the end of the morning, I realised that I really enjoyed working.

After lunch I was trudging the streets again with Michael, this time delivering the parcel post. We had a post-office bike with a big front basket, like a butcher's bike. I discovered that Michael was hoping to study engineering at Galway University.

'Why do you want to become an engineer?'

'Oh, I have a brother who's an engineer. He's working on a huge project in Canada, up near the Rockies.'

Immediately I imagined myself galloping a horse across a sunny, grassy plain towards massive mountains, blue in the distance. 'God, that sounds great!'

'Yeah, there's hundreds of men working on it. They live in these log cabins. They go riding in the foothills . . .

and the *money* they make!' Gone was the goofy Michael of the sorting office. A light was shining within him. I realised how far ahead of me he was. Years of study were already behind him. He had to be brilliant at maths. And university? Well, it seemed light years away.

'How would you get out there?'

'Oh, I'd fly,'

The world suddenly seemed to be opening up. I thought of flying off to all kinds of exotic places. I sailed down the Nile, sipping coffee on deck while Bedouins on camels and distant pyramids shimmered in the haze.

'So what do you want to be?' said Michael, interrupting my reverie.

'Oh, I was sort of thinking of becoming an architect,' I said. I knew it didn't sound very convincing.

'Right,' he said. That seemed to be the end of that.

Tommy Brady wanted to be in politics like his father. Mickey had only ever wanted to be a jockey. What I really wanted to be I was keeping secret for the moment because it would make me different. I wanted to be a writer. I knew that the day I saw a book lying open on the table in Dr Nolan's sitting room while I was waiting for Steffi. I started reading the long introduction about the writer, who was called Alexandre Dumas. I didn't realise that Dr Nolan was standing behind me.

'Would you like to borrow it?' he said, smiling.

'Yes *please!*' I saw the title on the cover only when he handed it to me. It was *The Count of Monte Cristo*.

But how does a writer get started? I looked at Michael, walking the post-office bike beside me up the street. He had the look of a man who was on his way.

'Do you know where this lady lives?' said Michael, stopping the bike to peer at one of the parcels.

'Oh, that's Miss Dolly Patterson. She lives right up the end of Connaught Street with her cat, Sylvester.'

'Sylvester? You're joking me!'

'Nope. Sylvester is a gentleman. You've got to show respect.'

Michael smirked. We walked on, both immersed in thought.

There was another reason I was keeping my ambition to be a writer secret. It was because of the doubt my mother had planted in my mind. I felt certain that Tommy and Mickey would succeed. I too wanted to succeed. But what my mother said made me feel that what I wanted most in life would doom me to failure and poverty.

She and I were coming home from a drama festival play in St Peter's Hall one night when I said, 'I'd love to be able to write a play like that.'

She looked at me curiously. 'Yes,' she said sadly, 'it would be lovely to be a writer. But you have to make a living too.'

The simple words destroyed a dream. My head was still full of the life of Dumas, his fame, his wealth, the reward for the pleasure of using his talent. I could think of no better way of life.

I listened to our footsteps in the dark, empty street. We were out of step and there was a question I had long wanted to ask. 'Would you like to have been a writer?'

'Oh, one time, maybe,' she said with a big sigh.

I had asked because of the book I had found in the attic of my mother's old house in Roscommon. It was a big old Edwardian house at the end of a long drive, surrounded by ancient trees and farmland. The trunk where I found the book was full of things from her childhood. Right on top of everything, wrapped in paper, was an old novel, in perfect condition. As I lifted it out, a folded sheet of paper fluttered to the floor. It was a note in faded blue ink that simply said: 'Be sure to send me your latest stories.' On the flyleaf of the book, in the same handwriting and faded ink was the inscription 'To Mary, wishing you a happy birthday – Sr Assumpta.'

Frost glistened on the roofs in Connaught Street as we arrived at our house.

My mother rooted in her bag for the key. 'The saddest day of my life,' she said, 'was when that house we were born in was sold.'

'Which house is it?' said Michael, pushing the bike.

'It's that one right up at the end.'

It was a house just like Steffi's. Miss Patterson and Sylvester came out to meet us. Sylvester sat calmly on the doorstep, surveying us. His sleek fur bulged slightly over the neat blue ribbon around his neck. In moments of surprise Miss Patterson's ample eyebrows tended to fly up to her hairline. It was happening now. 'Oh John-John, are you working for the post office now?'

Miss Patterson could be a bit dotty at times but I

didn't want Michael to think she always was. 'Oh no, Miss Patterson, it's just for the Christmas holidays.' I looked at Michael.

Michael handed over the parcel with a sort of respectful little bow. He understood. Allowances had to be made.

Miss Patterson seized on the parcel, frowning at the thing in her hands. It was a biscuit tin, I guessed, with something light inside. 'Oh Sylvester,' she cried 'the special lemon sponge we ordered has *arrived*.'

Sylvester mewed with pleasure. His tail went straight up and he rubbed himself luxuriously along the wall. He probably wasn't partial to lemon sponge but he clearly knew that he would surely benefit from Miss Patterson's ebullient mood.

Miss Patterson invited us to take tea with her and Sylvester but we declined, citing pressing deadlines. We went down Pearse Street, O'Connell Street, Bastion Street and Chapel Street. I had taken over wheeling the post bike and it was getting lighter all the time.

I couldn't help thinking again about Sister Assumpta. She was the mother superior of the convent where my mother and her sisters had spent their earliest years as virtual orphans while their mother went out to work. Their gambling, alcoholic father had lost everything and left them to work, and eventually die, down a South African mine. The book Sister Assumpta had given my mother for her birthday was *Little Women* by Louisa May Alcott. Sister Assumpta was her aunt, my grandmother's sister.

One for Sorrow, Two for Joy

*

Back at the sorting office, the kettle was permanently on for tea and there was always an open tin of biscuits on the table.

Timmy Dalton grinned when he saw me flopped down in front of a cup of tea. 'Well,' he said, 'how did you get on today?'

I gave him my report, starting with a detailed account of the encounter with Miss Patterson.

He laughed heartily, slapping his knee at the good parts. 'And how is the man of the house himself, Sylvester?'

I started into my account of Sylvester, which he clearly enjoyed. Timmy had the knack of giving the impression that he didn't want to leave your company, as if he had all the time in the world. Meanwhile, the busyness of the sorting office swirled around us.

As it turned out, I was needed for the three weeks I had off for the holidays. I was home by lunchtime on my last day and I flopped down on a chair in our kitchen.

'So, what are you going to do with all this money you've made?' said Peggy as she set the table.

'Oh, I might get something nice to wear.' I was saying nothing for the moment about the scarf and other items I had seen in Heaton's window.

'And didn't you like what you got for Christmas?' she said casually as she laid out the knives and forks.

Immediately I knew that the new penknife in the stocking I hung at the end of the iron bedstead had been from Peggy. 'Oh,' I said enthusiastically, 'the penknife was just what I wanted. One of the lads from our class said he got a properly made catapult in Foy's and it soon broke. And he said you can't fix them easily. But with a penknife you can always cut a fork from a bush and shape it with a penknife. Yeah, it was just what I wanted.'

'That's good,' said Peggy, smiling mysteriously. She knew well what I was doing.

I stared into Heaton's window, knowing what I wanted. I was talking myself into my next move.

Tommy Curley didn't move from the oil heater when the door opened. He stood there, hands behind his back, the tape measure draped around his neck. He moved slowly, putting on his shop face and rubbing his hands. Things were clearly quiet. 'Cold out there, I'd say,' he said. He was courteous, even distant.

'Oh, it's *freezing*,' I said.

Tommy gazed at me. 'Well, how's the riding gear going for you?'

'Grand.' The tape around his neck had measured me. I was twisted like a mannequin or told to turn while he and my father had talked about the weather, crops and the price of cattle.

'Well,' he said, 'how can I help you?' He didn't use my name because now I was a customer.

'There's one or two things in the window I'm interested in.' I'd heard my father say that many times and I used the same offhand manner. I clutched the money in my pocket, savouring its power.

'Okay,' said Tommy carefully. It felt like the opening move in a game. 'So let's see.'

We went out the shop door and stared in the window. I pointed at various items. Then we went back inside.

'Well now,' said Tommy, busy laying out scarves on the counter, 'these are all different prices.' He stood silently while I turned over each scarf in turn.

I knew very well what the prices were and I had a good idea what I wanted. The one I fancied felt coarse and heavy when I rubbed it between thumb and forefinger.

Tommy had been studying my face. 'Maybe you'd like to try it on over there at the mirror,' he suggested. He wasn't pushing anything.

We looked at it together in the tall mirror. Even in the dim light I knew it wasn't right.

As soon as I rubbed the second scarf between my fingers back at the counter, I knew it was for me. I was well aware of the price. But some instinct told me not to show my feelings. I had spent enough time around farmers on fair days to know that if you wanted something at the right price, you played the game. My father certainly did. I went through the motions of trying out the third scarf but then lingered with the one I wanted, as if I might be interested.

'That one now,' said Tommy quietly, 'is a bit pricier.'

I sighed and put it to one side. 'Maybe we could look at the gloves,' I said.

Tommy didn't move. 'I think it was the black leather ones you were interested in?'

'Yes,' I said, 'the soft ones.'

'Right, now they're a bit more on the expensive side,' he said carefully.

I nodded and looked aside, perhaps a bit sadly.

'But look,' said Tommy, 'since you're a new customer and this is your first purchase, if you wanted the two items, we'll see you right.'

I looked up hopefully and Tommy looked back.

'Just give me a minute,' he said and got a pad and pencil out of a drawer. He bent over, frowning and scribbling figures. 'Now, I think you'll like the sound of this better,' and he told me the new total.

'Ah,' I said doubtfully. I turned over the scarf regretfully, then I turned over the gloves. 'Maybe I'll just get the gloves.'

Tommy scratched the back of his neck. 'Look, just give me a minute,' and he went to work with the pencil again. He frowned over the paper then straightened to his full height. 'Right, now, the very best I can do is this,' and he handed me the piece of paper.

I looked at it as if the man was taking my very last penny but I nodded. 'Okay,' I said.

As I left Heaton's, on an impulse I decided to walk on up to Foy's. The electric train set was gone. Had Tommy bought it?

'Peggy,' I said 'I'm going across to Connaught Street to Tommy's house,'

'Okay, she said, glancing out the window.

Evening was closing in. I went back up to my new

attic room, far bigger than the one in Connaught Street. I tried on my purchases in front of the mirror. Then I was down the stairs, out the hall door and into the bright lights of Mardyke Street.

Connaught Street seemed dark and quiet. The person I wanted more than anyone else to meet was Steffi. But Steffi was gone. Instead I spotted Tommy and Mickey coming up the street.

'Hey,' said Tommy loudly, 'do you see what I see?'

'Hey,' said Mickey, 'I think it's John-John, in disguise.'

They came right up to me but stood back, as if to have a better look. Tommy reached out to touch my new scarf.

'Hey,' I protested, 'no touching. Only he with clean hands may touch, when invited.'

'Hoity-toity!' said Tommy. 'And look! I don't believe it – new leather *gloves*.'

I bunched my fist and held it close to his nose. 'Want to smell them at close quarters?' I said, offering to punch him on the jaw.

'What are you going to be when you grow up, John-John, a model? You'd look just right standing in Burgess's window, like this.' Tommy went completely stiff, his eyes staring blankly, in a typical mannequin's pose.

'So *when* are you going to grow up, Tommy? When you're eighty?'

'I know,' said Mickey, 'no more *John-John*. Let's call him *Style Man*.'

'Style Man, Style Man!' they chanted, backing out of reach of my leather-clad fists.

In fact, I didn't mind at all. *John-John* now sounded

babyish and *Style Man* placed me firmly in the adult world, where I felt I belonged.

'Hey, Tommy,' I said, 'I see the train is gone from Foy's window.'

'Of course,' said Tommy. 'I bought it.' He gazed at me with a smug look. 'Want to see it?'

'Sure.'

'I'm off for me tea, lads,' said Mickey. 'See yiz.'

Warm air, rich with baking smells, wafted up from Bradys' basement kitchen. Mrs Brady stood up from the oven, wiping her glasses with her apron. 'Well, John-John,' she said warmly, 'we haven't seen you for a while.' She took in the scarf and gloves but said nothing.

'Oh, I've been working, Mrs Brady.'

'Working?' she said in surprise.

'In the post office,' said Tommy darkly, 'organising all the postmen.'

'Well now, John-John,' she said, ignoring her son, 'what would you say to some nice fresh queen cakes and a cup of tea?'

'I would say *yes please*, Mrs Brady.'

She laughed and bent to the oven again.

'Look,' said Tommy. He had started the train and it went round and round in circles, as it had done in Foy's. Tommy seemed a bit bored with it.

'Why have you all the soldiers lined up?'

'Because,' said Tommy, 'this is a troop train. These lads are going off to war.'

'Which war is that?'

'It's the American Civil War. These lads are General Jackson's Confederates.'

I looked at the toy soldiers. 'They can't be Confederates because *they* wore grey. These lads are wearing blue.'

'I know that,' said Tommy indignantly, 'but I only have red or blue. They'd look daft as Confederates in red.'

'Tommy,' called his mother, 'don't forget the shoes.'

'Okay,' Tommy called back. He stopped the train and picked a pair of shoes from those lined up against the wall. He immediately started applying polish while I watched.

'What are you doing?' I asked.

Tommy gave me a glowering, resentful look. 'This was part of the deal for getting the train. I'm now the official boot-polisher round here.' Tommy threw down the first pair and reached for the second.

I looked at the scuffed toecaps of the first pair. 'Hey, you've missed the toes,' I said, pointing it out.

Tommy glanced at the shoes. 'Ah,' he said, 'Mr *Perfect*. What does it matter?'

Mrs Brady had come up quietly behind us. She stood with hands on hips. 'Tommy Brady,' she said deliberately, 'if a job is worth doing, it's worth doing well.'

'Okay, okay,' said Tommy, lifting the first pair of shoes again. I watched in silence. Tommy's face was getting red with the effort he was putting into the task.

'Tea time!' called Mrs Brady, pouring tea into a third cup. 'Tommy, wash your hands.'

'These are lovely,' I said, when silence followed the first sips and bites.

'They're our favourites,' said Mrs Brady. She seemed

to study her plate. 'And tell me,' she said, as if continuing a conversation, 'did you just go into the post office yourself and ask for a job?'

'Oh no,' I said and I told her all about meeting Timmy Dalton in the square.

She abandoned her tea and a half-eaten queen cake to listen, sitting erect, with her hands folded on her lap as I told her all about the post office job. Tommy meanwhile shoved in a second queen cake, then bent low over his cup to wash it down.

'Well now,' said Mrs Brady with a big smile when I had finished, 'isn't it grand at your age to earn your own money and have a taste of independence.' She turned towards Tommy, with her eyebrows raised humorously. 'And I'm sure that next year Tommy will want to join you and earn a bit himself?'

Tommy had sat slumped, completely still, his eyes shifting from me to Mrs Brady throughout the conversation. He shrugged and did something with his lips. 'Maybe' was all he would say. But everything else in him was saying 'no way'.

Mrs Brady laughed tolerantly. Tommy scowled.

I looked up at the clock. 'Oh, I told Peggy I'd be back before six.' I stood up. 'Thanks for the tea and the lovely buns, Mrs Brady. I have to go.'

Mrs Brady stood up too. 'Well, John-John, nice to see you again.'

'See you, Tommy,' I called as I started up the stairs.

'Yeah, see you,' he said.

*

Back in our kitchen, Peggy stood still while she inspected my new scarf and gloves. 'Yes,' she said slowly with a faint smile, 'very nice.' She turned to the sink. 'We haven't seen much of Tommy lately, have we?' she said casually as she filled the kettle, 'or Mickey.'

'No.'

We let that hang in the air.

She lifted the heavy kettle onto the range. Droplets of water spat and bubbled on the hot metal. 'Tell me, have you heard from Steffi at all?'

'Oh, I wrote one letter and she wrote back.'

'How's she getting on?'

'Fine. She's in first year at boarding school now, playing hockey and doing all sorts of new things.'

'Does she miss Connaught Street?'

'I suppose.' I didn't want to mention that she said she missed me. She was gone and it only made me feel an empty space inside. 'Peggy, I'm going upstairs to do a few things.'

She gave me a long look. 'Okay,' she said with a little smile.

In the dim light of the attic, I adjusted the scarf several times. It looked no different from how it had looked in Heaton's. I went right up to the mirror for a close-up. The figure looking at me went completely still. Two eyes, dark and bottomless, stared back. 'Who are you?' they seemed to demand. 'Who are you?'

Moon over River

1956

There was a night in late summer that I am unlikely to forget. It was about two or three o'clock in the morning and I lay sleepless on my bed, tucked right in under the window in the attic room.

From that height on the hill, four floors up at the back of our house, I stared at the silent moonlit scene spread out below.

If I sat close to the glass, I could see the pale twin steeples of St Peter's away to the right, majestically rising above the shadowed bridge and the faintly glinting water.

I gazed at the scene a long time, like a condemned man. I knew I was being sent away to boarding school in the autumn because they thought there was something wrong with me.

They were right. There *was* something wrong with me. I felt that a whole delicate inner life had been destroyed and that I was a hollow shell, unfeeling, somehow dead.

One for Sorrow, Two for Joy

Had I not been just twelve years old I might have recognised that I had reached a level of meaninglessness that is usually diagnosed as depression. It was the kind of meaninglessness in which suicide is carefully considered, weighed and balanced.

No one seems to have recognised a condition that preceded it, which I learned much later was called agoraphobia. In my case it meant going to extraordinary lengths, in crossing the town from one side to the other, to avoid walking through the main streets.

It was our headmaster, Mr Finneran, who was the first to notice that something was wrong. Towards the end of that last year at school, he noticed that, although it was almost summer, I insisted on keeping my overcoat on at all times.

I was ashamed of the clothes I was made to wear, ashamed of my body, just ashamed to be alive.

It had a lot to do with relations between my parents, which had seriously deteriorated. I felt that I had been born out of hatred or the exigencies of lust and that therefore my existence was a mere accident, meaningless, worthless and unworthy.

It was no longer just a case of separate bedrooms. Because of the violence, my mother lived above her business premises on the Connaught side, and my father stayed in the huge empty house on the Leinster side. It was in this house that the boys at least were expected to live. We had our meals where our mother lived.

There was something in me, I realised, that in spite of everything, made it impossible for me to take my own life. I knew there had to be a meaning. The problem was that it was completely out of my reach.

I watched the sloped ceiling of the attic room become dimly visible. The moon was edging, with velvet tardiness, in over the river. I lay there, completely still, watching for the moment when it would begin to pour a long shimmering bar of light across the water.

The stone walls dividing the gardens far below were whitened bones, stitching a pattern on the hill that swept down to the meadows by the distant river.

The river meadows, or callows, with their waving spears of blue flowers, had become my refuge, a vast open steppe where I could be free, free from people and the ugliness of this world. Here, in this world of wind and waving grass and shining river, was a hint that there was some hidden purpose or meaning to life.

But I was completely unaware at the time that an animal cut out from the herd becomes fair game for predators. The camaraderie, the belonging, the strength in numbers I had known while running with the gang on the Connaught side was gone. I felt unable to make new friends. I became a loner.

The gang of boys who all lived in the cottages down by the river cat-called as they saw me passing by, and their predators' eyes saw that I was always alone.

They blocked my path one day, and as I pushed through, someone delivered a blow to my back. They just laughed when I looked back fiercely. I could not make out who had done it.

What surprised me was that I didn't care. I had never

been a coward and I could look after myself as well as any member of my old gang. But now there was just no fight in me. I just wanted to get away.

One day, they knocked me down, punched and kicked me, and tore my clothes to shreds. I felt nothing, as if I were an inanimate thing or a dumb animal. My only concern was my torn trousers, which I had to hold together all the way home.

Sometime later they stopped me by the river, where boats for hire were drawn up on the grassy bank. This time I got upended into a boat, to howls of laughter. Something snapped in me, and as I sat up gingerly, I was aware of something cold and terrible rising from the depths of my being.

The biggest of these lads, whose name was Mullins, advanced slowly on me, an insolent leer on his face, and I calmly watched him coming. Casually arrogant, he took hold of the collar of my shirt. With what seemed to me to be all the time in the world, I brought up my knee and struck him in the crotch with all the force I could muster. He doubled up with a terrible groan and, as if in slow motion, was sick into one of the boats. His brother was coming right at me. I saw my bunched fist coming up and I clearly heard the crunch of the bones in his nose. Suddenly he was flat on his back, blood all over his face.

I was vaguely aware of the others taking to their heels and of a woman running out of the cottages, shouting something at us and wiping her hands on her apron. I looked around calmly. I saw what I was looking for propped under old Mr McQuillan's boat. It was the stump of an oar, used to make a prop for the upturned boat, which the old man had been painting the day before as I passed by. I had helped him put it in. I yanked it out, and the boat keeled over.

Mullins was still being sick, holding onto his crotch. I advanced with the oar stump. I was going to start by breaking every bone in his body, and then I was going to kill him.

He was on one knee. I brought the oar down with all my force on his leg and he screamed, rolling over on the grass. I advanced again, taking all the time in the world, to carry out my task.

I was grabbed from behind in an iron grip but I shrugged the little man onto the ground. The second man was far bigger and he pinned my arms in an iron lock.

'Go for the guards, Mickey!' he shouted to the little man.

More women were coming out of the cottages. A third man appeared and the two men held me until Sergeant Kelly and another guard arrived.

From my bed, I gazed at the moon and the magical track of silver it cast across the water. The night was so deeply peaceful and beautiful, free from the ugliness and violence of man.

I had never before been forcibly brought to the garda station. The room I was in was not exactly a cell, but there was only one tiny window high on the wall and the door was locked. I had no wish to move. I ached all over. It even hurt to sit on the hard, wooden chair.

I sat, my mind a complete blank, and time stood still. I had no idea how long I had been there, but it seemed a long time.

I heard unhurried footsteps and the door being unlocked. Sergeant Kelly, a huge man, a friend of my father's, stood filling the doorway. In his right hand was a big steaming mug of tea, in the other a plate with something on it. He stared at me a moment, then moved in, and, quietly as a nun, placed the steaming mug and the plate on the bench beside me.

'That'll do you good,' he said quietly.

The second guard stood in the doorway. My only thought was how such a big man could move so quickly and quietly.

I noted with indifference the key turning in the lock again.

The tea was piping hot and poisonous with sugar. I drank it slowly and carefully, feeling the life return to me. Then I started methodically into the bar of chocolate on the plate, eating it just as slowly and carefully, one square at a time. It was as if some outside agency were directing my every movement, deciding what I should think, or whether I should feel anything.

In fact I felt free, as if someone else had taken responsibility for my life.

I sat quietly and peacefully for a long time. It seemed to me that the room had become somewhat darker, and I began to feel cold.

Unhurried footsteps came to the door and I heard the key turn in the lock. It was Sergeant Kelly again, by himself this time. He glanced at me, closed the door quietly, but made no effort to lock it. He stood there, just inside the door, calmly gazing at me. Then he sat down. 'You're a lucky man, John,' he said at last.

I stared at him quizzically, not knowing what to say.

'I've just come back from the hospital,' he said. 'Young Mullins has a broken leg and . . . a badly bruised groin. His brother has a broken nose.'

I stared back and he went on in his quiet, calm way, 'You're just a young lad, I know, so you can't know that it's the easiest thing in the world to kill a man.' He paused, waiting for me to say something.

I felt questions forming on my lips, but no words would come.

'I say you're lucky because two men from the cottages stopped you in time.' He paused to stare at me meaningfully. 'What I mean is, if you had hit that young Mullins lad in the head – the way you broke his leg – it's not on a hospital bed he'd be lying right now. He'd be on a slab.'

The sergeant talked to me for a long time. He told me that the biggest problem would be the mother, a troublemaker if ever there was one. She wanted a court case and swore she would not rest until she saw me put away in a reformatory.

At last, the implications of what had taken place began to get through to me. When he saw that they had, Sergeant Kelly nodded thoughtfully. 'Now, I want you to tell me the whole story,' he announced. He opened the door and called out down the corridor, 'Tom!'

Eventually we heard the other guard coming. He had a notebook and pencil and he wrote down the whole story as related by me. It was getting dark when my father came to the station. He didn't say a word the whole way home.

The Thursday night dance at the Crescent Ballroom was long over. At about one o'clock that morning I had heard the closing signature tune – 'When the saints . . .' – belted out with a big band sound, several streets away. It carried across the rooftops, waxing and waning with the summer breeze.

The last stragglers had long gone down our street, their muffled talk and muted laughter hollow in the echoing canyons of the silent, empty streets.

Across the street from our house, the red and yellow neon sign of the Royal Hotel would blink on and off all night. It was an old hotel, built in the 1700s, with three steps leading up to double doors below a battered fanlight. The old coach light above the doorway had been electrified but seemed at odds with the brash, garish neon fixed to the wall above.

By day, the hotel facade assumed once again its former dignity. Tommy 'The Boots' Carney appeared as regular as clockwork every morning at 8 a.m., winter or summer, with bucket and mop to wash down the doors and three steps, sleeves rolled up, whistling cheerfully and in his uniform waistcoat.

But after dark, the neon lights lent a lurid, seamy atmosphere, and they blinked on and off all night on the walls of the front bedrooms in the attic.

My father slept in the one on the left, my two brothers in the one on the right.

I could hear my older brother snoring in the front room. Because of the terrible fight we had had the summer before I had been moved into the back bedroom, previously my sisters' room. They were now living across the town with my mother.

At the station, the sergeant quizzed me about an incident in Broderick's yard from the previous summer that had resulted in the worst thrashing my father had ever given me.

The sergeant asked me several times if Mullins' cousin Farrell had been there and what damage he had done. The reason for the question turned out to be more complex than I thought.

Mullins and Farrell had vehemently denied being anywhere near the yard and their families had provided alibis. However, the week before I was questioned at the station, Farrell had been caught in possession of a quantity of stolen goods and a considerable sum in cash, which he maintained he was holding for Mullins.

Two days after my interview, Farrell was brought in for questioning and, faced with the prospect of reformatory, he gave evidence against Mullins.

I don't know what deal was done between Mrs Mullins and Sergeant Kelly, but one day he called into my mother's shop and told her that she need worry no more about the Mullinses bringing me to court.

I heard a sort of thump and a loud groan from my father's room. I knew he was an insomniac, but I had never heard him groan like that before.

I listened intently, but there was no further sound. Suddenly, on an impulse, I threw back the bedclothes and crept across the landing. I quietly pushed the door open.

He sat still as stone on the edge of the bed, staring out the window. The lurid red and yellow lights illuminated his profile, blinking on and off.

It reminded me of a similar scene in a film, in which the main character sits in his dark, impersonal motel room, waiting for something sinister to happen. My father at that moment looked like the loneliest figure on earth.

'Dad,' I called softly.

He whirled round, startled. 'What? What are you . . .'

'Are you all right?'

He didn't seem to understand the question. 'I'm all right, I'm all right!' he said testily, but not quite in his usual, intolerant fashion.

I stood looking at him, and he stared back in the semi-darkness. The neon flashed on and off on the back wall of the room.

'Listen,' my father said in a hesitant tone, 'come over and sit here a minute.'

I hesitated, but went and sat beside him.

He gazed at me as if not knowing what to say. 'So, you'll be going away to school in September,' he said, as though somehow I had decided this myself.

I nodded.

Suddenly his arm was across my shoulder and he pulled me a bit closer. It was an awkward moment.

'You'll be all right,' he said hoarsely.

'I will.'

'You go on back to bed now.'

I nodded and, without another word, got up and left. In spite of everything, he was still my father.

The thing I remember most about the journey to boarding school was walking down to the railway station with my father. Nobody had told me anything and everything seemed unreal. I have no recall, for example, of carrying my great heavy suitcase. My father must have carried it, as he would, as if it weighed nothing.

All I know is that the walk, from our house all the way down Mardyke Street, Church Street, Fry Place, across the bridge and the whole way down under the shadow of the military barracks wall, seemed to go on forever, especially as my father didn't say a single word.

Two cannon, relics of the Siege of Athlone, stood as always either side of the main entrance to the barracks. The military policeman behind the barrier looked back impassively as always. Everything seemed unchanged, yet everything had changed.

The sun shone on the river to the right; the beech trees and the sycamores along the bank sighed gently in the autumn breezes. Sid Shine's barge, *The Fox*, was moored as always alongside Watergate Pier, part of a peaceful, well-established world. Yet I felt like a man walking along a dead straight road towards the gallows, in my unfamiliar, uncomfortable, brand-new suit. Worst of all was the collar and tie, something I had never worn. My feet were blocks of wood in my new shoes. I looked down every so often, as if to check that these were really my feet inside those unfamiliar, black shining shoes. The cuffs of my new white shirt came halfway down my hands and – I could still hardly believe it – were fastened with cuff-links! I felt like someone poorly disguised, yet passers-by I knew well would glance at me knowingly, as if they recognised me in any case.

At last, we turned the corner under the bridge and there was the railway station before us. There was also a dusty, green CIE bus, with a few people standing around chatting, holding cases and coats, looking as if they had all the time in the world. The engine was already running.

A large cheerful man in uniform climbed down from the bus, jingling coins in a leather satchel and came straight up to us. Ticket-machine and satchel belts crisscrossed his torso like bandoliers.

'So, this is the man that's going away to school!' he exclaimed, beaming down on me.

'This is the man,' my father replied drily.

'Well,' said the man, 'we'll put your case up first and then find you a place.'

My father handed him the suitcase.

The big man had spoken directly to me, as if I were the important one, thereby marginalising my father. It was subtly done, a cool rebuff, but my father got the message, all right. I knew it was the secret language that goes on between people. It clearly said: *I don't care much for your father, but I'm going to look after you.*

The big man headed for the bus with the case, and I followed.

'John,' my father called. He had stood his ground and I had to walk back.

'You'll need some money' he said, and, extracting two half-crowns from his pocket, dropped them into my extended hand.

Five shillings! I could hardly believe it. I hadn't thought about money.

'Thanks!' I said and turned towards the bus again.

'Wait a minute.' He was reaching inside his jacket pocket.

It was difficult to read the expression on his face. Some kind of struggle was going on there. This time, more deliberately, he extracted a wallet and took out a ten-shilling note. He extended it, and I took it slowly. I didn't know what to say. Fifteen shillings!

'That'll keep you for a while,' he said. 'Better get on the bus!'

I turned and walked towards the uniformed man, who stood waiting on the bottom step of the bus, smiling reassuringly at me. I knew his name was Martin Hoctor, because my mother had told me he would look out for me.

I don't know if my father waited or not because, immediately I was seated, the bus moved off and there was no one there when I looked back.

At the edge of town, the road forked. The bus was already bearing right, bound for Sligo, eighty miles away. Up left was everything I was leaving behind: the road out to Boganfin, Cornafulla and Gallows Hill, place names steeped in the bloody history of the town I loved. Suddenly I realised that a part of my life was over. Something new was beginning and it surged like hope in my chest.

Acknowledgements

This memoir started out as a couple of stories that would never have become a book had it not been for Robert Doran, a truly professional editor who has a sure instinct for what sounds right and for what does not. There were times when it seemed to me that he had a better feel for a particular story than I had. His suggestions on these occasions made all the difference, bringing out, as it were, their essential flavour.

My thanks also to production director Chenile Keogh, whose infectious enthusiasm for the book and for all stages of its production are much appreciated, as are her patience and efficiency in getting it over the finishing line.

I would like to mention in addition proofreader Natasha Mac a'Bháird's appreciation of the story and her enquiry about the possibility of a second book. It made me think! Thank you, Natasha! I would also like to thank designer Andrew Brown for the wonderful cover. Even though I had not explained clearly what I had in mind, I got exactly what I wanted.

Lastly, my thanks to Ferdia Mac Anna and Anna Fox of the Dalkey writing group, where some of the chapters were first read out.